Air War D-Day

Volume 4

Bloody Beaches

Other volumes in this series

Bloody Beaches

Air War D-Day

Volume 4

Bloody Beaches

Martin W. Bowman

Pen & Sword
AVIATION

First Published in Great Britain in 2013 by
Pen & Sword Aviation
an imprint of
Pen & Sword Books Ltd
47 Church Street, Barnsley, South Yorkshire S70 2AS

Copyright © Martin W Bowman, 2013
ISBN 978-1-78159-178-9

Typeset in 10/12pt Palatino
by GMS Enterprises

Printed and bound in England by
CPI Group (UK) Ltd, Croydon, CR0 4YY

Pen & Sword Books Ltd incorporates the Imprints of Pen & Sword
Aviation, Pen & Sword Family History, Pen & Sword Maritime, Pen & Sword
Military, Pen & Sword Discovery, Wharncliffe Local History, Wharncliffe
True Crime, Wharncliffe Transport, Pen & Sword Select, Pen & Sword
Military Classics, Leo Cooper, The Praetorian Press, Remember When,
Seaforth Publishing and Frontline Publishing.

For a complete list of Pen & Sword titles please contact
PEN & SWORD BOOKS LIMITED

47 Church Street, Barnsley, South Yorkshire, S70 2AS, England
E-mail: enquiries@pen-and-sword.co.uk
Website: www.pen-and-sword.co.uk

Contents

Acknowledgements

I am enormously grateful to the following people for their time and effort and kind loan of photos etc, not least to my fellow author and friend Graham Simons, for getting this to press-ready standard and for his detailed work on maps and photographs: My thanks to Ray Alm; Ed 'Cotton' Appleman; James Roland Argo; Peter Arnold; John Avis; Les Barber; Harry Barker; Mike Bailey; Carter Barber; Neil Barber, author of *The Day The Devils Dropped In*; E. W. D. Beeton; Franklin L. Betz; Bill Bidmead; Rusty Bloxom, Historian, Battleship Texas; Lucille Hoback Boggess; Prudent Boiux; August C. Bolino; Dennis Bowen; Tom Bradley; Eric Broadhead; Stan Bruce; K. D. Budgen; Kazik Budzik KW VM; Les Bulmer; Reginald 'Punch' Burge; Donald Burgett; Chaplain Burkhalter; Lol Buxton; Jan Caesar; R. H. 'Chad' Chadwick; Noel Chaffey; Mrs J. Charlesworth; Chris Clancy; Roy Clark RNVR; Ian 'Nobby' Clark; P. Clough; Johnny Cook DFM; Malcolm Cook; Flight Lieutenant Tony Cooper; Lieutenant-Colonel Eric A. Cooper-Key MC; Cyril Crain; Mike Crooks; Jack Culshaw, Editor, *The Kedge Hook*; Bill Davey; S. Davies; Brenda French, Dawlish Museum Society; John de S. Winser; Abel L. Dolim; Geoffrey Duncan; Sam Earl; *Eighth Air Force News*; *Eastern Daily Press*; Chris Ellis; Les 'Tubby' Edwards; W. Evans; Frank R. Feduik; Ron Field; Wolfgang Fischer; Robert Fitzgerald; Eugene Fletcher; Captain Dan Flunder; John Foreman; Wilf Fortune; H. Foster; Lieutenant-Commander R. D. Franks DSO; Jim Gadd; Leo Gariepy; Patricia Gent; Lieutenant Commander Joseph H. Gibbons USNR; Larry Goldstein; Bill Goodwin; Franz Goekel; Lieutenant Denis J. M. Glover DSC RNZNVR; John Gough; Peter H. Gould; George 'Jimmy' Green RNVR; Albert Gregory; Nevil Griffin; Edgar Gurney BEM; R. S. Haig-Brown; Leo Hall, Parachute Regt Assoc.; Günter Halm; Roland 'Ginger' A. Hammersley DFM; Madelaine Hardy; Allan Healy; Andre Heintz; Basil Heaton; Mike Henry DFC, author of *Air Gunner*; Vic Hester; Reverend R. M. Hickey MC; Lenny Hickman; Elizabeth Hillmann; Bill Holden; Mary Hoskins; Ena Howes; Pierre Huet; J. A. C. Hugill; Antonia Hunt; Ben C. Isgrig; Jean Irvine; Orv Iverson; George Jackson; Major R. J. L. Jackson; Robert A. Jacobs; G. E. Jacques; Marjorie Jefferson; Bernard M. Job RAFVR; Wing Commander 'Johnnie' Johnson DSO* DFC*; Percy 'Shock' Kendrick MM; the late Jack Krause; Cyril Larkin; Reg Lilley; John Lincoln, author of *Thank God and the Infantry*; Lieutenant Brian Lingwood RNVR; Wing Commander A. H. D. Livock; Leonard Lomell; P. McElhinney; Ken McFarlane; Don McKeage; Hugh R. McLaren; John McLaughlin; Nigel McTeer: Ron Mailey; Sara Marcum; Ronald Major; Walt Marshall; Rudolph May; Ken Mayo; Alban Meccia; Claude V. Meconis; Leon E. Mendel; Harold Merritt; Bill Millin for kindly allowing me to quote from his book, *Invasion*; Bill Mills; John Milton; Alan Mower; Captain Douglas Munroe; *A Corpsman Remembers D-Day Navy Medicine 85*, No.3 (May-June 1994); Major Tom Normanton; General Gordon E. Ockenden; Raymond Paris; Bill Parker, National Newsletter Editor, Normandy Veterans; Simon Parry; Albert Pattison; Helen Pavlovsky; Charles Pearson; Eric 'Phil' Phillips DFC MiD; T. Platt; Franz Rachmann; Robert J. Rankin; Lee Ratel; Percy Reeve; Jean Lancaster-Rennie; Wilbur Richardson; Helmut Romer; George Rosie; The Royal Norfolk Regiment; Ken Russell; A. W. Sadler; Charles Santarsiero; Erwin Sauer; Frank Scott; Ronald Scott; Jerry Scutts; Major Peter Selerie; Alfred Sewell; Bob Shaffer; Reg Shickle; John R. Slaughter; Ben Smith Jr.; *SOLDIER Magazine*; *Southampton Southern Evening Echo*; Southwick House, HMS *Dryad*, Southwick, Portsmouth; Bill Stafford; Allen W. Stephens; Roy Stevens; Mrs E. Stewart; Henry Tarcza; Henry 'Buck' Taylor; June Telford; E. J. Thompson; Charles Thornton; Robert P. Tibor; Dennis Till; Edward J. Toth; Walt Truax; Jim Tuffell; Russ Tyson; US Combat Art Collection, Navy Yard, Washington DC; Thomas Valence; John Walker; Herbert Walther; Ed Wanner; R. H. G. Weighill; Andrew Whitmarsh, Portsmouth Museum Service; 'Slim' Wileman; Jim Wilkins; E. G. G. Williams; Deryk Wills, author of *Put On Your Boots and Parachutes! The US 82nd Airborne Division*; Jack Woods; Len Woods; Waverly Woodson.

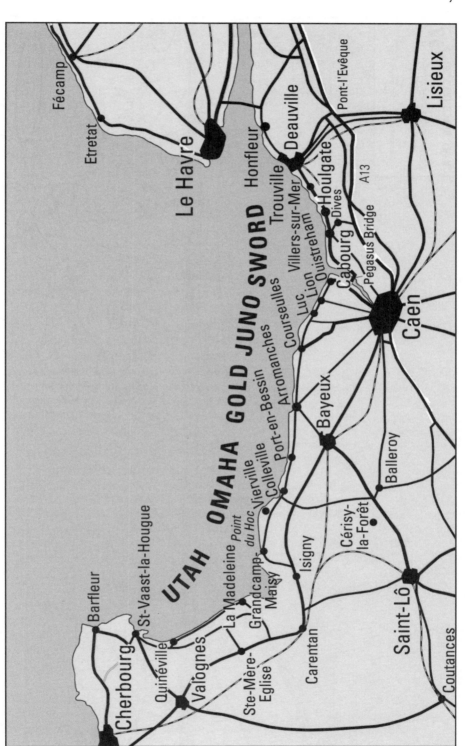

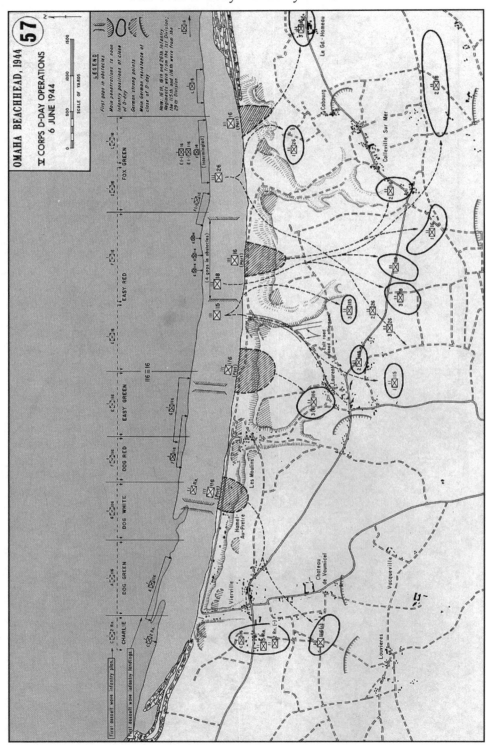

Chapter 1

'Omaha'

Major Werner Pluskat was feeling cold, tired and exasperated. Hours earlier he had been woken by the sound of aircraft and gunfire. Two years of bitter experience on the Russian Front told him that that this was much more than just a routine raid. He telephoned his regimental commander Oberstleutnant Ocker, who was greatly displeased at being woken. 'My dear Pluskat' he snapped 'we don't know yet what's going on. We'll let you know when we find out. Now don't bother me again - and get some sleep.'

The telephone went dead. But Pluskat was not convinced and he decided to go over Ocker's head and contact Major Block the intelligence officer at divisional headquarters. Block was an old friend and merely laughed off Pluskat's nervous enquiries. Pluskat sat on the edge of his bed wondering whether to rush to Wiederstandnest 60 on the coast or wait for further orders. Suddenly the telephone rang. It was Ocker on the line. He sounded nervous, even shaken. 'Paratroopers have been reported on the peninsula. Alert your men and get down to the coast. Now!

For a reason he could not quite pinpoint a great uneasiness kept gnawing at Pluskat as he peered through his 'Donkey's Ears' [high powered artillery binoculars] into pre-dawn darkness of the Channel. Even his friendly Alsatian dog Harras sensed this edginess and stood close to his master, watching his every move. Pluskat swung his binoculars slowly round to the left, pausing over the darkness of the Cherbourg Peninsula. There was a low mist everywhere and the sea seemed peaceful. He sighed and turned to two other men in the bunker, Kapitän Ludz Wilkening and Leutnant Fritz Theen. 'There's nothing out there' he told them - and turned back for a final look.

'I stepped back with amazement when I saw that the horizon was literally filling with ships of all kinds. It seemed impossible to me that this vast fleet could have gathered without anyone being the wiser. I passed the binoculars to the man alongside me and said, 'Take a look' He said, 'My God it's the invasion'. I knew then that this was the end for Germany. I felt strangely detached and turned to Wilkening and Theen and told them 'It's the invasion; see for yourselves.'

Then, with a studied calmness, Pluskat telephoned Major Block. 'There must be 10,000 ships out there' he said.

But Block just exploded. 'Get hold of your-self Pluskat' he shouted. 'The Americans and the British don't have that many. Nobody has that many.' Block paused and then asked 'Where are these ships headed?'

Pluskat replied: 'Straight for me.'

Pluskat and his men were covered with dirt, dust and concrete splinters when the shelling began. The telephone rang again and someone at headquarters demanded: 'What is the exact location of the shellings?' Pluskat snapped: 'For God's sake, they're falling all over the bloody place. What do you expect me to do? Go out *and measure the holes with a ruler? And then he slammed the phone down. There was a lull in the shelling and Pluskat took advantage of it to inspect the damage. To his astonishment, not one of his 20 guns (new Krupps of different calibres) had been hit. Nor were there any casualties. Pluskat telephoned the now shaken Ocker and made his report.*

Pluskat turned to his men, 'Remember no gun must fire until the enemy reaches the water's edge.'

Major Werner Pluskat, commanding I. Abteilung of Artillerie Regiment 352, watching from Wiederstandnest (WN) 60 at the eastern end of 'Omaha' Beach overlooking Fox Green and Fox Red at dawn on 6 June. Like 'Utah', Wiederstandnesten were sited along the 10km (6 mile) shore but the fourteen 'resistance nests' were concentrated around the five small wooded valleys, or 'draws' as the Americans called them, that cut through the bluffs overlooking the beach. Various other bunkers were also built on the sites. To give the defenders clear fire zones, any houses that obstructed them had been demolished.[1]

'This is different from any other exercise that you've had so far. The little discrepancies that we tried to correct on Slapton Sands are going to be magnified and are going to give way to incidents that you at first may view as chaotic. The air and naval bombardments are reassuring. But you're going to find confusion. The landing craft aren't going in on schedule and people are going to be landed in the wrong place. Some won't be landed at all. The enemy will try and he will have some success, in preventing our

---

1   At Colleville, where the beach exit was nothing more than a path, protection was afforded by three Wiederstandnesten. WN60 had two 75mm guns, a bunker with a Renault R35 tank turret, four 50mm mortars and a 20mm flak gun. WN61 just east of Exit 3, overlooking Fox Green, was armed with an 88mm gun, one 50mm and Renault tank turret bunkers and a 50mm mortar. There was an anti-tank ditch in front of WN62, the command post of Leutnant Frerking, the forward observer, sited near Exit 3 (to Colleville-sur-Mer) and was armed with two 75mm guns in casemates, two 50mm Pak guns in casemates to enfilade the beach and four machine-gun positions, two tobruks with mortars and one twin AA machine gun in a concrete emplacement. There were at least five machine-gun tobruks and an 88 mm gun in a casemate to enfilade the beach, one emplaced 50mm gun and a tank turret plus one 50mm mortar in a tobruk in addition to several machine-gun tobruks. WN61 was knocked out at about 0710 hours by a Sherman DD commanded by Staff Sergeant Sheppard of the 741st Tank Battalion. At 07:35 the third battalion 726th Grenadier Regiment, defending Draw F-1 on Fox Green beach was reporting that 100–200 American troops had penetrated the front, with troops inside the wire at WN62 and WN61 attacking the Germans from the rear. The dirt track up Exit 1 (to Ste-Laurent-sur-Mer) was protected by four Wiederstandnesten. WN64 had two 75mm guns, five mortars and a 20mm flak gun. WN65 opposite Exit 1 had one 88mm gun and a 50mm mortar in a casemate. WN68 around Exit D-3 (Les Moulins) had only infantry weapons, but WN66, protected by an anti-tank ditch, had two 75mm guns, three Renault R35 tank turrets concreted into tobruks and six 50mm mortars. WN63 on the Vers Grand Camp Road at Colleville-sur-Mer was armed with a 75mm gun. Deep behind the bluffs near Ste-Laurent were WN67 and WN69; the latter with a battery of rockets. At the western end four Wiederstandnesten protected the exit from the beach at Vierville, which had been blocked with an anti-tank wall or Panzermauer. WN70 on the bluff, was armed with infantry weapons; WN71, with two 75mm guns, one in an open pit and one in a casemate, two mortars and one 20mm flak gun; WN72 at the entrance to the gully with two 88mm guns that covered the shore, one 50mm gun and five 50mm mortars. WN71, and WN73 (the other 'resistance nest' at the furthest point of the western end), were under-strength and men from construction pioneer were added to their compliment.

gaining lodgement. But we must improvise, carry on, not lose our heads. Nor must we add to the confusion.'

Brigadier-General Norman D. Cota, 51-year old deputy commander 29th Division speaking to the advanced HQ group in the aft wardroom of the USS *Carroll*. Cota, who had seen action in North Africa, would land shortly after 0730 on Dog White with the main command group of the 116th Regimental Combat Team.

'We foregathered at Belfast and immediately were put under complete security. No one was allowed ashore - no one was allowed on board. Then, for the first time, the operation orders were opened. These were very extensive and consisted of several sacks of orders. They also included a sort of rubber model of the whole of the 'Omaha' Beach, which we were going to attack. It had been made in sections about a foot square. I understand that each section was made in a different part of the United States, so that they were never put together until they finally arrived in this country for D-Day. We assembled all of this in our hangar and we were able then to sit down and look at the beach from a suitable distance. You saw the exact beach, including the background - as we would see it on the day. The security was intense and even if a man went sick, he was sent to one special hospital in Belfast - which was under guard - and was not allowed to be removed.'

Major Cromwell Lloyd-Davies aboard HMS *Glasgow*.

'The LST-505 loaded up several days before the invasion at Plymouth, Devon... We took about 445 officers and men and spent a number of days in this crowded condition... Living conditions aboard ship were not at all happy. Our tank deck and main deck were both filled with various trucks and motor vehicles but did not include any tanks. Finally on June 4 we set out for the landing in France. The weather was heavily overcast and the seas rather rough and we had not proceeded far before we received orders to return to port at Plymouth. There we waited until the next day, when we again set out on the same course to the east. During the night we turned south toward the French coast and I can remember making out the Cotentin Peninsula in the dim light, off to our starboard. On D-Day morning we left the Cotentin to starboard and turned east toward 'Omaha' Beach and we anchored about two and a half or three miles offshore. We located our position as off Colleville-sur-Mer [behind the eastern end of the beach] by being able to see the steeple of the village church there. We could tell that a lot was going on ashore... We were at General Quarters when we arrived... I remember looking over the side of the ship and seeing several bodies pass by close to the ship. One was a young sailor whose hair was long enough to be streaming back in the water. The whole thing took on an air of grim reality... We could see explosions on the beach and we could see smoke rising from various sites... We could see many small ships and craft in the water just offshore, some under way and others obviously wrecked.'

Lieutenant James West Thompson, USN, Stores Officer aboard LST-505. An LST was nicknamed 'Large Sitting Target'.

'It was in the night and I was sleeping and my sergeant came running and said, 'There are a thousand different ships coming in the English Channel. We could see landing boats of American troops. Then came thousands of men at one time coming on land and running over the beach. This is the first time I shoot on living men and I go to the machine gun and I shoot, I shoot I shoot! For each American I see fall, there came ten hundred other ones!'
German soldaten, Franz Rachmann.

'The invasion alarm of the previous day and last night has been lifted. The storm has abated and it has stopped raining. The sun is even shining today, as if it wants to compensate us for the unbearable tension of the last 24 hours. The rumour is going round that the Allies have ordered their invasion fleet to turn back because of the poor weather. This can only help us - a stay of execution. Today no Rommelspargeln are planted, instead of this we have machine-gun exercises in the field. We march out to the surrounding meadows and move into cover positions. Unteroffizier Geiss, our platoon commander, allows us to catch up on the sleep we missed last night. As well as we can, we all seek out a place with good cover in the hedges, or sunbathe.

'At high altitude above us one enemy bomber squadron after another flies into the hinterland and from there we can hear a terrible thundering. The daily reconnaissance plane does his rounds and now and then a few fighter-bombers buzz by like hornets. Our morale is good, but the old front veterans have 'something in their water'. They don't trust the overall aura of peace.

'Arthur Volker, my bunker comrade, has indigestion. He says he always feels like this when something's afoot. Even I can't conceal a sense of unease. After the relative calm of the last few weeks I turn my thoughts to the massive bombardments of the hinterland. Something is going to come down on us.

'The food today was wretched once again - a lot of groats and no meat - a lot of jam and no sausage. Hopefully it will remain quiet tonight and we're all hoping that there won't be another 'false alarm'.

'Arthur and I are assigned the task of 'high-chair watch'. This is a very exposed and windy job. There's a stiff breeze coming in from the sea, the moon shines brightly now and again through the gaps in the clouds. It is not cold - just chilly - and up on the high-chair in the poplars you get a real shaking.

'At midnight I have to take over from Arthur and until then I try to get a few winks of sleep. No chance. I just can't get to sleep. I'm getting more restless with every hour that passes. I try to read with only the Hindenburg light, but I can't concentrate. What the devil is going on? The night is so quiet, no sound of engines. Only the wind rustling through the poplars. I have to take over from Arthur soon. Since I can't get any sleep anyway, I take over from him earlier. I get dressed, fasten my belt, check my machine pistol and magazine and crawl out of the bunker. The fresh air suddenly makes me shudder and I look around in the darkness. Strange - this peace is just not normal. I have the feeling that there's something lying in wait for us.

'I go up to the high-chair tree and call out, 'Arthur, come down. I can't sleep, I'm going to take over now'. Arthur climbs down the ladder and says, 'Bloody wind. It's damned cold and there's absolutely nothing to report' and he disappears into the night.

'I climb up to the high chair and look at my watch. Still ten minutes before midnight. I hang my binoculars round my neck, load my machine pistol and put the catch on and then I sit down and make myself comfortable. A few minutes later I can hear the familiar but distant sound of aircraft engines. 'Bloody hell',' I think to myself, 'there's more than a few - I hope they're not going to drop their bombs on us.' I look at my watch again and take a look through the binoculars.

'It was seven minutes after midnight when I saw masses of red and bright white lights in a north-westerly direction. To every soldier with any experience at all this could mean only one thing - ENEMY ATTACK!!!

'My common sense told me 'this is the invasion'. After the first shock I grabbed the telephone connecting the high-chair position with the regimental command post and turned the handle like a madman. At the regimental command post: 'Duty clerk here, Obergefreiter?' I told him what I had seen. In the meantime the sound of the engines could be heard over our position.

'One moment, I'll get the adjutant'.

'Regimental command post: 'Leutnant Peiser! What's going on? Report!'

'I give the report: 'Obergefreiter Thiel here, platoon, direction north-west, Cherbourg, red and white lights sighted, loud aircraft noise. The enemy is attacking!' As the receiver was not put down at the command post I could hear Peiser give the duty clerk the order to fetch the Major straight away. Then I could hear the major rushing up and could pick out a few scraps of the conversation - 'this afternoon' - 'Frenchmen' - 'damn' - 'why no alarm?'

'Major: 'Platoon, report!'

'Obergefreiter Thiel here. Mass of lights direction of the coast and Cherbourg. Enemy attacking. This is the invasion, Herr Major, should I sound the alarm?' I look at my watch - it's 11 minutes after midnight.

'Major: 'Sound the alarm! Unteroffizier Geiss to me immediately.' The receiver is put down.

'I put down the receiver and shout out as loud as I can: 'Alarm, alarm!' Again and again I shout 'Invasion! Invasion!' and fire off two machine-pistol magazines...'

Obergefreiter (Corporal) Hans-Rudolf Thiel, Regimental platoon of the 6th Paratroop Regiment.

'The view will remain in my memory forever; the sea was like a picture of the Kiel review of the fleet. Ships of all sorts stood close together on the beach and in the water, broadly echeloned in depth. And the entire conglomeration remained there intact without any real interference from the German side! I clearly understood the mood of the German soldier, who missed the Luftwaffe. It is a wonder that German soldiers fought hard and stubbornly here.'

Oberstleutnant Fritz Ziegelman, Chief of Staff, 352nd Infantrie-Division who went forward to the Wiederstandnest 76 command post

near Pointe et Raz de la Percée during the early morning. A journey of 30 minutes had taken 5 hours because of enemy fighter patrols overhead.

'Beach bombardment was already underway. We were in the vicinity of battleships and heavy cruisers, which were firing continuously towards the beach. You could see the shells from each ship, two glowing red projectiles, sailing off from their twin big guns, into the lightening but still misty skies. We continued on our way and passed the troop transport area, which was about seven miles off shore. Combat infantry were loading into LCVPs. We were passed by LCIs also headed for the shore, which was still invisible to us. We continued in good order with around ten LCTs in our group and we arrived at our point of departure marked by an LCI acting as a control vessel, fitted for communications and control. Nervously we joked about the shells whistling overhead from the battle wagons and cruisers and from destroyers who were closer to the shore. Other LCTs fitted with rocket launchers were carrying out saturation rocketing firing of the beach. Finally, we got a go-ahead signal and in an approximate line of attack, we headed in for our last few miles to the beach.

'We knew from reconnaissance photos and briefings that the last thousand yards or so would be sowed with obstacles, designed to impede landing craft approach. Generally, they were of two types: hedgehogs, consisting of three steel bars welded in a triangle shape and the other, merely telephone poles sunk into the sand. Tidal rise and fall in that area of the English Channel was around 20 feet and with a gently sloping beach, the difference between the low and high water line was quite a long distance. The landings were on a rising tide and the troops that landed first had a long way to go with no cover before reaching sand and shell dunes. The obstacles were also outfitted with mines on their face electrically connected, so the setting off of one would set off others close by. It was the job of the Navy underwater demolition teams to go in first and clear and make paths through the obstacles for the landing craft to follow. We saw two of these UDT men in a rubber boat close by and we offered to pick them up, but they profanely refused.

'It was bright now, but visibility on the beach and the hills beyond was poor because of smoke from burning brush. We were opposite our designated beach, but there were a number of LCVPs, LCIs and LCTs milling around about a mile off shore. Bill Lynn, who was still up in the bridge looking through the binoculars, shouted, 'For Christ's sakes, they're pinned down!' The landing operation which had looked so good just a short while ago had the prospects of a complete disaster. The obstacles were still largely in place and no markers could be found. The landing craft were under considerable enemy gunfire. Some craft had made it in but not out. Two LCIs were broached and lifeless. Three or four tanks were sitting disabled with sea water from the advancing tide covering their tracks. Some of the Navy beachmaster party had gotten in. I could tell by the special identification markers that had been set up there.

'We cautiously moved in to try and find a way through the obstacles and get to the beach. I noticed a beach party member, half-crouching, waving his semaphore flags furiously at us. Without much thought, I grabbed the pair of flags and scrambled to the top of the wheel house and gave him a 'king' which meant go ahead. His message was 'stay low, keep your head down.' Our chances of reaching the beach were very poor, but the chances of being slaughtered by machine gun and mortar fire were very high. I was on my stomach, keeping my head down and looking up at the skipper, who was still on the step halfway through the top. I was really excited and I said, 'What the hell are you doing here? You'll get us all killed! There's more of a chance to get in to our right.' Some LCTs and LCVPs were moving in a section where the obstacles had been blown. The skipper bought that suggestion and we turned to starboard and moved to what appeared to be a better location.

'We were on the beach for some time. Finally one of the beach masters told the skipper that the tide would start receding very shortly and it was then time to go. Our gunners had stopped firing because there was now some movement by the troops over the sand dunes and up beyond and we didn't want to take any chances of hitting our own people. As we pulled off, 'Curly' who was down in the engine room, reported a hole in our port side, which was just at the water line and we believe it was caused by hitting one of the teller mines. He was down there by himself and had just calmly shut down the port side generator, closed the water-tight door and started the pumps. With our cargo off, we were considerably lighter and riding quite high in the water, with little threat from the obstacles now covered by the sea except for those in close to the shore.

'We ran full speed towards the transport section, having reported our situation by radio to our control vessel, who had alerted the transport commander. As we neared the transports we were asked for identification and then advised by blinker as to which transport to go to. They were ready for us and had booms rigged to load litters. We tied up. Some hospital corpsmen came aboard the LCT with medical supplies and they helped considerably in comforting the wounded as they awaited their turn to be put on the ship. A jerk of an officer on the transport was trying to chew out our skipper for leaving the wounded on the deck instead of moving inside. He was ignored and I hope he was suitably chastised when we started to bring them out from the deck houses. Among them was the beach engineer who had been stricken with appendicitis the day before. We had just forgotten all about him during the invasion. We finished unloading the wounded and called our flotilla commander for orders. He told us that we had enough for the day and to anchor, clean up and be ready for a big D+1 work schedule.

'The LCT was a mess: decks littered with debris, bunks, mattresses and blankets blood soaked, galley littered with bandages, the hole in the engine room and we were peppered by the machine gun fire on the starboard side. We did a cursory clean up and set just a one-man watch and a very tired crew did their best to catch up on sleep. Rather than make the trip to the LCT sector, we anchored close to the transport area. All appeared to be calm, but just before daylight, probably around 03:00 or 04:00, we were awakened and went to general quarters pending an air attack. Some German planes did come over and dropped flares and as we found out later, dropped some mines. We did not even fire our guns, but we must have been hit by a spent explosive anti-aircraft shell, probably from one of the transports. Shrapnel chewed up the side of the relief skipper's left leg and the side and arm of one of the seamen. These wounds weren't serious and with our replenished medical supplies, the cook fixed them up. It was our intention to find a doctor for them later in the day. The raid didn't last long, so I didn't bother to try to go back to sleep as I had the next watch. Instead I just had a couple of cups of coffee then relieved the fellow that was on watch.

William Thomas O'Neill, LCT 6-544.

'We loaded on an LCI which held one Company of Infantry (180 men and 6 Officers) in broad day light at Plymouth Hoe on a nice sunny day. The men were not laughing. They used to say we were in England to take the place of the 'Home Guard'. They now knew that the jig was up. They had been briefed on what our job would be. We were just thankful that we were not the first wave. As we loaded on our craft you called out your name, rank and serial number. There was a fellow recording this information. We started out the night of June 4th; the landing was to be on the 5th. As we sailed out the weather got stormy and the seas rougher and rougher. Finally we put into Weymouth and the men thought it had been called off. We sailed again during the night. During the crossing we heard speeches by President Roosevelt and General Eisenhower. It was in this speech that Eisenhower coined the phrase 'a great crusade' and said that God was with us. The crossing was not too bad, but the seas were still quite rough. Luckily most of the men were fishermen from the Eastern Shore of Maryland. We were to land at the Les Moulin draw. Primarily our job was to move through the 116th Regiment, who would have assaulted and cleared the beach. We would advance and secure the towns of Ste-Laurent and Vierville and move on to a line which would run from Trevieres through LaCambe. This was not to be too difficult a job 'as there were only labour troops in the area.' Famous last words. They weren't throwing shovels at us when we landed. Intelligence said the nearest German fighting troops were at St. Lô about 60 miles back from the landing area. This proved to be wrong as later we found out that the German 352nd Division had moved up from St. Lô to practice counter invasion tactics. They knew we were coming but not exactly when. I think they were a little surprised. In hind sight, if we had landed at night, we might not have had as many casualties. They would have had a harder time seeing us, but that would also apply to us seeing them.

'We had one man who stabbed himself in the foot with his bayonet during the crossing. There was no going back. The Navy would not keep him on board and take him back after unloading us. He landed with a bandaged foot. On our way toward the landing beach we passed across the bow of the Augusta. It looked huge from our perspective which was close to the water. The Augusta ended up later on as our artillery support since the 110th Field Artillery, which was our regimental artillery support, had lost their guns in the channel. The Texas was a little further beyond the

Augusta and was firing its big guns. There were big halos of flame around the muzzle of their guns when they fired. It made you feel good to see this as it was kind of reassuring. 'How could they take this pounding by the Navy.' Sad part was they did and were waiting for us. I felt sorry for some fellows in the crossing. They were riding on huge flat barges loaded with fuel and ammunition. These barges rode only a foot or two out of the water. As we went quite closely by one of them, I waved and wished them good luck. The weather was cold, gray and forbidding.

'As we approached our designated landing sector, we knew the jig was up as there was so much noise, smoke and firing of big guns. It was difficult to see the beach through all the smoke and haze. We didn't land at our selected area but about 1500 yards to the North or left. We were to land on Dog Red at the Les Moulin draw. Instead we landed in the 1st Division sector on one of the Green beach sites. This resulted in my platoon being mixed in with the 18th Regiment of the 1st Division. At this spot the fire was not too intense but there was enough artillery and mortar fire to make you move. The LCI had a disembarking ramp on each side of its bow. There was no loitering. I led my platoon off the right side without too much difficulty. The water was cold and rough and in my case chest deep. I was about six feet tall. (Many days later I found out that the Navy changed our original landing site because the original landing site was covered with corpses, under heavy fire and littered with disabled equipment and the naval officer in charge 'didn't want to waste the men'. He said our craft had been hit and sunk and did I know how many men were lost. I replied that I wasn't aware of this and that I must have been off the craft and also my men when it was hit). My platoon was the first off the craft. I surmised the craft was hit and sunk after we had departed it as the Company was pretty much intact.

'As we were approaching the beach in the landing craft, I saw a little dip, or niche, in the skyline of the bluff. Below that niche, there was a small shelf-like piece of land. I made this my first objective and had as many men as were about me to go with me. Forget about the original plans, try to stay alive. We were under artillery and mortar fire. When wading in through chest deep water, some shells exploded nearby. I thought 'good thing we're in the water' but realized that shrapnel travels through water as well as through the air. An LCT was backing off the beach and he offered to take us in to the beach. I declined the offer thinking it would take too long for us to scramble up into that craft and when doing so we would be a good target, standing still in the water. Some of the men near me didn't like my decision and the craft moved on. There were runnels under the water and when you stepped in one you could be in water over your head. That is why men wearing their life belt too low would up-end and drown. When finally got to the beach there were some men with me. The beach was flat and it looked like a mile to the base of the bluff. I remember saying, 'follow me' and thought at the time 'how corny'; I sound like John Wayne'. I never looked back to see what the rest of the company was doing or where they were. It would be certain death to stand or wait on that beach. The beach was wide and flat and there were no craters for us to take cover, so we made for the bluff and that little 'shelf'. The artillery and mortars were giving us a fit. On the way to the bluff we went by a little marshy area with cat-tails in it and a sign saying 'Minen' which told us the area was mined.

'By the time we got to the 'shelf' we were tired and we sat there to rest. It was discouraging to make our way up the bluff (about 200 feet) and not be able to see who was firing at you and you had no target to fire back at, just take it and keep going. I had looked at my watch as our craft touched down and it was around 09:30. As we rested, we could see that was an enemy artillery emplacement to our left and they could see us. I think they had communication with the people on top of the bluff as every time we moved a little it would bring fire from above. This wasn't too effective so they began to drop hand grenades at us. As I sat there and looked down on the beach, I was shocked to see the number of bodies and the amount of material that was littering the beach. At this point, I didn't think I would ever see England again, let alone the United States. I thought my number was up.

'We watched as suddenly one of our destroyers come straight toward the beach. I thought it was going to run aground. It suddenly turned broadside to the beach and began pumping rounds into that artillery emplacement. After about five rounds the artillery piece ceased to function and we resumed our ascent of the rest of the bluff. We were ascending the bluff along a trail of dead men, who had given their lives to make it safer for us. I speculated that they had set off personnel mines as their bodies were quite mutilated and mangled and reminded one to be cautious. Walking, in a crouch position, along their bodies it was safe, but the goriness was very sobering to say the least. I passed one fellow who had been blown in half. You could see the organs hanging out of the upper half of his body. Moving up the bluff, the most frustrating thing was not being able to see who or from where you were being fired on. When we got on top of the bluff, we rounded up as many of our men as possible. I had no idea where the company was. By this time it was early evening. It was light until 23:00 at this time of year. I remember lying behind the rear wheels of a truck and being shot at.

'One of the things that made this landing so disastrous was the fact that we had no place to take cover on the beach. The Air Force was to have bombed the beach creating craters for us to use. They missed the beach by three miles. Their explanation being they were afraid they might hit the landing craft, as the water was full of ships. However, this bomb preparation was to take place long before we got on the beach. As a result, that beach was as smooth and flat as a road and looked about two miles deep. The Germans were in a 'shooting gallery' and we were the 'ducks.'

'It was getting dark and I didn't know where the rest of the company were. I had a Sergeant round up what men we had and put them inside a walled courtyard. Then set out to find the company. I found one of my brother officers, but he didn't know anything either. At least we were in an area with some of our company so didn't feel too alone. I remember, when doing this wandering around, a lone German fighter plane came over the road so low, I felt like I could reach up and grab his tail wheel. During this wandering I fell into a ditch with a dead horse. I ran across the road and jumped into the ditch only to land on a dead German. That poor sucker must have been there all day as he was beginning to smell ripe. My introduction to 'war'. The odour was very unpleasant but in the days to come you got used to the stench of dead bodies, human and animal and to eating in such perfumed air. To this day, France has an odour of 'death' for me.

'One of our Officers, a Catholic, just had to go to Confession. He was the first Officer of our company killed on D-Day. Somebody said he had entered a building and was cut in half by a German 'burp' gun; actually it was a Schmeiser machine pistol. We named this weapon a 'burp' gun because it fired so fast that a burst from it sounded like a 'burp'.

'The thing that really struck me was that I had never seen so many dead and dismembered human bodies in my life. For a kid of my upbringing this was a real shocker. However, before I left combat, it was 'old hat'. The amount of abandoned and ruined equipment on the beach was staggering.

'Recalling how we were equipped for this operation, in my opinion we were overloaded. The men had close to 60lbs on their backs. We were loaded with ammunition each man carrying a couple extra bandoleers of ammunition and several grenades. Our clothing, impregnated against gas, was hot and smelly. We wore a Navy type gas mask, almost under our chin, to keep our head above water if wounded while in the water. We had a CO_2 operated life belt around and above the waist. Some fellows wore them too low and when they got in deep water and expanded the belt, they floated upside down and drowned.

2nd Lieutenant Richard J. Ford, Company 'K', 115th Infantry Regiment, 29th Infantry Division.

'It came as quite a shock to many when, just prior to going ashore, the men... heard that they might have to land fighting. Briefing had stressed the fact that the landing itself would be relatively simple; that troops would merely walk ashore, make for the high ground and then walk until the objective was reached.'

Historian of the 115th Infantry Regiment, which were in the second wave. With the initial targets unaccomplished, the second and larger wave of assault landings started bringing in reinforcements, support weapons and headquarter elements at 07:00, only to face nearly the same difficult situation as had the first. The only real relief for the second wave was that there were more of them, so the defender's fire was less concentrated. The survivors of the first wave were mostly unable to provide effective covering fire and, in places, the fresh landing troops suffered casualty rates as high as those of the first wave. Failure to clear sufficient paths through the beach obstacles also added greatly to the difficulties of the second wave; now, the incoming tide was beginning to hide the remaining obstacles from them. There was high attrition among the landing craft as they hit these defences, before they had even reached the shore. As in the initial landings, difficult navigation caused very disruptive miss-landings, scattering the infantry and separating vital headquarters elements from their units. Along with the infantry landing in the second wave, supporting arms began to arrive, meeting the same

chaos and destruction as had the rifle companies. Combat engineers, tasked with clearing the exits and marking beaches, landed off-target and without their equipment. Many half tracks, jeeps and trucks floundered in deep water; those that made it ashore soon became jammed up on the narrowing beach, making easy targets for the German defenders. Most of the radios were lost, making the task of organizing the scattered and dispirited troops even more difficult and those command groups that did make the shore found their effectiveness limited to their immediate vicinity. Except for a few surviving tanks and a heavy weapons squad here or there, the assault troops had only their personal weapons, which, having been dragged through surf and sand, invariably needed cleaning before they could be used. The survivors at the shingle, many facing combat for the first time, found themselves relatively well-protected from small arms fire, but still exposed to artillery and mortars. In front of them lay heavily mined flats exposed to active fire from the bluffs above. Morale naturally became a problem. Many groups were leaderless and witness to the fate of neighbouring troops and landings coming in around them. Wounded men on the beach were drowning in the incoming tide and, out at sea, landing craft were being pounded and set ablaze.

'I was really shocked. The landings were all messed up. As I neared the shoreline I saw men drowned, a beach full of dead and wounded and troops going around obstacles in the water and then crawling along the sand to the cliffs just off the waterline. I directed the coxswain running my LCVP to drop anchor before we touched bottom and the last words I gave him before we dropped the ramp were 'Don't let the boat touch bottom and keep your engine running at a good speed'. This he did and I stepped into about 4 feet of water and moved toward shore. We'd underestimated the number of underwater obstacles planted by the Germans, some with barbed wire and other fence wire around them. Bodies were floating everywhere and men shouting and screaming.

'Every half minute or so a spray of water would kick up and pass down the beach. This, I realized, was machine gun fire from atop the hills, spraying the beachhead. I watched the men ahead of me dive out flat and wait for the spray to pass by.

'Words will never cover the bravery and guts of those men that went ashore at 'Omaha' and cleared the way inland. I know, because I was there with them and I'll never forget.

'Thank God for them.'

Jim Van Orsdel, an officer in the US Navy aboard the *Augusta*. [2]

'All afternoon, Monday, 5 June, the *Augusta* scudded past the 'Utah'-bound convoys, heading for her rendezvous with the 'Omaha' force. High above the cruiser's bridge a radar antenna rotated monotonously under the woolly

2   *Invaders: British and American Experience of Seaborne landings 1939-1945* by Colin John Bruce (Chatham Publishing 1999).

sky. In the plotting room below, an officer bent before the radar screen searching for the tell-tale pips that would signify enemy air. But day passed and evening came without a bogey report. 'Seems hard to believe,' I said to Kirk, 'maybe we're going to have a Sicily all over again.' There, too, we had held our breaths in anticipation of air attack against the convoys. Yet in Sicily the enemy had slumbered on until we piled up on his beaches. But in the narrow English Channel we could scarcely count on slipping through the enemy's alert without sounding an alarm.

'...1,300 RAF bombers swarmed over the French coastline from the Seine to Cherbourg. An enemy AA battery stabbed blindly through the night. A shower of sparks splintered the darkness and a ribbon of fire peeled out of the sky as a stricken bomber plunged towards *Augusta*. It levelled off, banked around our stern and exploded into the Channel. By 5.30 first-light had diluted the darkness and three Spits whistled by overhead, the first sign of our air umbrella. High above the overcast, relays of American fighters formed a second layer of air cover.

Lieutenant-General Omar Bradley on the bridge of the *Augusta*. At 05:50 Bradley stuffed cotton wool in his ears as the *Augusta's* turret guns were trained on the shore 'and the ship shuddered as it opened fire upon its pre-designated targets among the beach defences. The salvo coasted over the armada and we followed the pinpoints of fire as they plunged down towards the shore.

'As the morning lengthened, my worries deepened over the alarming and fragmentary reports we picked up on the Navy net. From these messages we could piece together - only an incoherent account of sinkings, swampings, heavy enemy fire and chaos on the beaches. V Corps had not yet confirmed news of the landing. We fought off our fears, attributing the delay to a jam-up in communications. It was almost 1000 before the first report came in from Gerow. Like the fragments we had already picked up, his message was laconic, neither conclusive nor reassuring. It did nothing more than confirm our worst fears on the DD tanks. 'Obstacles, mines, progress slow... DD tanks for Fox Green swamped.'

Born in Clark, Missouri, General Omar Bradley was the son of a farmer. He joined the US Army in 1911 and after graduating from West Point, opted to join the infantry. He rose slowly through the ranks of the peacetime army and commanded II Corps as part of Patton's Seventh Army in the invasion of Sicily in 1943. Eisenhower then chose Bradley to lead the US landings in Normandy as commander of the US First Army.[3]

By the beginning of June the British knew almost the entire disposition of German forces confronting the Allies in Northern France... 'We didn't get exactly what one panzer division was going to do, which was to attack the left hand section of the British landing[4] and we didn't get the positioning of the

---

3   After the war, Bradley was promoted to five-star general and as chairman of the Joint Chiefs of Staff, developed the Cold War policy of containing the USSR. In the Vietnam War, he was one of the elder statesmen who advised President Lyndon B. Johnson on policy and strategy.
4   The exact dispositions of the 21st Panzer Division were uncertain, but it was believed to be stationed south-east of Caen. *'The Struggle For Europe'* by Chester Wilmot.

352nd Division, which was the one that held 'Omaha' Beach. We didn't get the detail that it was going to be in so close up and if we had we would have warned the American 1st Army…'

Ralph Bennett, one of the Intelligence reporters working on 'Enigma' decrypts in Hut 3 at Bletchley Park. Hut 3 was responsible for analysis and collating the intelligence contained in the decrypts, as well as translating them.[5] According to *D-Day* by Warren Tute, John Costello and Terry Hughes; the 352nd Division who had been moved up from St Lô to exercise in the 'Omaha' sector in the week just before D-Day. But until just after sailing, Allied intelligence did not realize that they were so close to the beaches. Only General Bradley and a handful of commanders were informed - the news had arrived at Plymouth just as the convoy sailed for France. It had been too late to re-brief the men and might have dented their morale on what was already a difficult assault.'

'When the American plan was made it was thought that this four-mile sector was manned by little more than a battalion of the 716th Division,[6] which was then holding 45 miles of coastline from the Orne to the Vire. This was an indifferent formation, containing many foreign conscripts and equipped only for a static role, but a mobile division of good quality, the 352nd, was known to be in close reserve around St. Lô. In May British Intelligence had come to suspect that this division had moved up to strengthen the coastal crust by taking over the western half of the Orne-Vire sector, but the evidence of that move was slender and the Americans were disinclined to accept it. (There it took under command the regiment of the 716th which was holding this extensive front and proceeded to nose in three of its own six battalions to defend 'Omaha' and another likely beach at Arromanches on the British front. This left three battalions of the 352nd in close reserve behind 'Omaha' and by chance one of these was carrying out an exercise on that stretch of coast on June 5th-6th. There were thus eight battalions in the area between Bayeux and Isigny, where the Americans had expected to find four and the defences had some depth, provided moreover by troops of fair quality, equipped for something more than a static role…) When some confirmation was received early in June,

5   *Action This Day: Bletchley Park from the breaking of the Enigma Code to the birth of the modern computer* edited by Michael Smith and Ralph Erskine (Bantam 2001). Though Ultra intercepts indicated troop movements in the area, they did not identify the formation or its size. The Allied planners and intelligence staff believed the positions to be manned by Ist/726th and 3rd/726th Grenadier Regiment, part of the 716th Static Infantrie Division commanded by Generalleutnat Wilhelm Richter. In fact, the division was the 352nd Infantry Division that had been based in the St Lô area. Two of its regiments, the 914th, under Oberstleutnant Heyna and the 916th under Oberst Goth covered the western end of 'Omaha' beach. The 726th were-still in place at the eastern end of the beach and it may have been that the radio traffic of the 914th and 916th was masked by that of the 726th.

6   It was believed that the coastal defences between the Seulles and the Orne were held by two or three battalions of the 716th Division with several other battalions of unknown quality in close support. This sector of the coast was, in fact, held by three battalions of the 716th Division. It was the weakest of the German divisions confronting the Allies on D-Day with only 7,771 men (of whom 6,261 would become casualties by 11 July) or 35 per-cent of the established strength of a division. One of its battalions comprised Osttruppen - Polish, Czech and Russian volunteers. Their officers and NCOs were German but the German troops they commanded were not fully committed to the cause. Its transport consisted of bicycles.

it was too late to pass the warning on to the assault troops who were already embarking. Consequently, they went into action believing that though 'Omaha' was strongly fortified it was not particularly heavily garrisoned.'

'The Struggle For Europe' by Chester Wilmot. Often described as a 'battle-hardened' unit, the 352nd was in fact formed at St Lô in September 1943 from divisions which had been decimated on the Eastern Front. It had some veterans but most of its recruits were aged between 18 and 20 years old. Lack of ammunition meant that few had conducted live firing of their weapons before D-Day and between March and June each soldier had spent two-thirds of his day helping to build the Atlantic Wall rather than training. [7]

'The scene in the Channel was quite amazing. It was almost like Piccadilly Circus - there were so many ships there and it was incredible to us that all this could be going on without the Germans knowing anything about it. But we never saw a German aircraft the whole time. Our air force had kept them completely out of the air. We arrived off the approaches to Normandy and *Glasgow* was then told to take the head of the line of the force going into the 'Omaha' Beach. As we steamed down the line, the padre said to me, 'Shouldn't we say a prayer?' And so I said, 'Why not say Nelson's Prayer?' because it was exactly right for this day. So he started to read Nelson's Prayer and as we passed the *Texas,* all their ships company took off their helmets as they heard us reading the prayer going in.'

Lieutenant-Commander Cromwell Lloyd-Davies aboard HMS *Glasgow.*

'The sea was littered with ships of all descriptions ploughing doggedly towards the enemy's coast, looking very grim and very determined. The bombardment was terrific and one could actually see the shells in the form of red and white lights as they left the ships and flew towards the shore...I stayed at 1,000 feet and watched five of the naval vessels, which were about a mile from the beach and turned broadside on, proceeding to belch flame and destruction. It was a most terrifying sight, for as they fired rockets, a sheet of flame fifty yards long completely enveloped the ship. By this time, the first boat was almost ashore and, as I watched it, the front came down and the men inside jumped into the water and ran towards the beach. It was a wonderful moment when I reported that the first men had actually landed.'

Flight Lieutenant R. H. G. Weighill, 2 Squadron, 35 Wing RAF, flying a Mustang to spot the fall of shot of HMS *Glasgow.* **Weighill was probably the first eyewitness of the landings. An Air Spotting Pool at Lee-on-Solent, Hampshire reported the fall of shot for the naval escorts bombarding the coast defences. This consisted of four Fleet Air Arm squadrons flying Seafire IIIs, two RAF Spitfire squadrons flying Spitfire Vs and VCS-7, the only US Navy squadron to fly Spitfires. The American squadron had been quickly formed from pilots of floatplane and scouting flights using borrowed Spitfires to scout for the Western Naval Task Force. General Bradley, reviewing Allied troops in England had promised the soldiers that the**

7 *Monty And Rommel: Parallel Lives* by Peter Caddick-Adams (Preface Publishing 2011).

have ringside seats for the greatest show on earth (naval gunfire)'. Later analysis of naval support during the pre-landing phase concluded that Force 'O' had provided inadequate bombardment, given the size and extent of the planned assault. The defences were shelled by two battleships, USS *Arkansas* with twelve 12-inch guns and USS *Texas* with ten 14-inch guns, along with three cruisers, HMS *Glasgow*, FFS *Montcalm* and FFS *George Leygues* which between them had thirty 6-inch guns. In addition to these, eleven destroyers added their 4-inch and 5-inch guns to the bombardment, firing 2,000 shells into the resistance nests. Kenneth P. Lord and other US Army planners for the invasion, upon hearing the naval gunfire support plan for 'Omaha' Beach, were reported to be very upset - especially in light of the tremendous naval gunfire support given to landings in the Pacific. Others have said that American casualties would have been greatly reduced if a longer barrage had been implemented.

'At precisely 0600 on June 6 the big guns of the combined fleets, the allied fleets, began a muddy barrage of the invasion coast striking for predetermined coastal defence batteries. Shortly after 6, we began filing topside again for our morning ration of food. We all ate something because none knew how soon we would be lucky enough to eat again. It was still too dark to discern the coast line but the next 40 minutes filled with the deafening roar of the coordinated gunfire from our battle wagons, cruisers and destroyers, blasted and rocked the coast into a smoking and firing line.

'Everything seemed to be going smoothly and very few of us inexperienced men could shake off the feeling that this was just another manoeuvre. At 0640 the allied sea monsters, belching forth their message of death, suddenly ceased firing. Just as abruptly as they had begun and we knew that this very moment, the very first waves of the invasion craft were scraping bottom in an attempt to land their fighting cargo.

'We dipped our mess kits in the cold greasy water with an effort to clean them and took another hasty glance at the smoking and blazing shoreline before ducking through the hatchway leading down to our quarters. At approximately 0740 five of us, Johnakin, Bosun's Mate First Class, tall, gangly, serious-minded and 21; veteran of North Africa and Sicily and leading petty officer of this platoon. Haynes, Bosun's Mate First Class, also a veteran of previous operations, Arts and Beemus and me went topside to move all of our units, medical, hydrographic, communications, ship repair, geared to a prearranged position on the ship, alongside the conning tower, portside, amid ships and on the fantail. We had volunteered because of our swimming ability to cut loose and throw over the side the rubber raft lashed against the conning tower. Loaded with the aforementioned gear and paddle, swim or drag this precious cargo safely ashore somehow while the remainder of our group landed in the usual manner from the two forward landing ramps.

'According to our schedule our craft was to land on Dog White at H hour plus 100 minutes or approximately 0810 through a 50 yard patch cleared by our demolition men and the maze of obstacles and mines prepared by the Germans. Our ship's crew were veterans of North Africa, Sicily and Salerno and promised they would get us ashore somehow.

'At 0755 only 15 minutes left before our scheduled landing. No shots had been fired on us and we were rapidly approaching what seemed and actually proved to be an impassable barrier. Nowhere in sight was the hope for clear passage. Finally with only a few minutes between us and our appointment with fate, our LCI veered sharply to the right and headed straight directly for the right flank of the Dog Green beach. Some few yards to the right of us another LCI was drifting aimlessly and German machine guns were mercilessly cutting to ribbons any floundering troops who had managed to jump clear of the smoking and burning hull. On our left along the obstacles I could see two or three LCMs aft, sunk or overturned by shell fire or mines.

'Only 100 yards from the first row of obstacles it was still quiet. 'Yes', I said to myself, 'it's too damned quiet'. I spoke briefly with my executive officer, Lieutenant Commander Southward who was standing by the number 3 hatchway forward and eased myself back to a position of readiness beside the rubber raft.

'Suddenly, without warning a blast shook our sturdy little craft from stem to stern and a sheet of flame shot up 30 or 40 feet in the air through the number 1 hold directly forward of the conning tower. A fire broke out below and smoke poured out of the gaping hole torn by the flames. As if the explosion were a prearranged signal, the Jerries opened up with everything: 88s, mortars, machine guns and so forth. Terror seized me as I gazed horrified at the burned and bleeding frantically rushing and stumbling past me trying to get away from the blinding fire and smoke. I fought off the weakness in my knees and struggled to keep my mind clear. Then I heard a voice yell 'for blankety blank sake' somebody cut the 'blankety-blank' line and there against the rear of the thickening smoke I could see Johnakin slashing at the lines, holding the rubber raft against the conning tower. Haynes cut the remaining strand and with the appearance of Arts and Beemus we quietly dropped the raft over the side. As Johnakin tied the aft's stern line to the LCI, I climbed over the side and dropped the remaining seven or eight feet and landed on all fours in a pitching and rocking craft. Haynes made fast the bow lines and I braced my knees against the gunnels to prevent my being pitched overboard while catching the radio set and medical packs they began dropping to me. Arts leaped into the other end of the raft and together we managed to catch all the gear safely and stow it as compactly as possible. Next came our personal gear, packs, Tommy guns, ammunition, canteens and finally, Haynes, Johnakins and Beemus dropped into the loaded craft.

'Arts handed me his knife which was to cut loose three paddles, secured forward which we used heading towards shore 150 yards away. Machine gun and rifle bullets whined past our ears, or plunked into the water near our craft. As we pushed our way through the iron and wooden ramps and poles to which were wired telemines. As we reached more shallow water, where three and four foot waves were breaking, I marvelled that there we were not dashed against some mine or reeled to pieces by gunfire as yet.

'We slipped off the ramp into the cold Channel water and keeping the ramp between us and the beach we pushed it into shore where we crawled out along the sides and dragged the equipment to the water's edge. From our position to the three feet seawall was a scant 30 yards of beach littered with dead and dying soldiers, unused weapons. Off to our left 50 or 60 yards away, an amphibious tank with its treads in the water was firing bursts of machine gun bullets at German pillboxes and gun emplacements in the side of the hill while about 300 yards beyond the sea wall. Destruction and chaos engulfed the entire area. Troops were dug in and still fighting from the beach. It was even tougher than we had anticipated. All this took just a matter of seconds to observe. I did not know just what to do next. As we dragged the last bit of gear out of the ramp, Johnakin yelled, 'Hey Bacon do you think that we can make it out to the ship again. Some of these wounded guys will never make it ashore.'

'I'll give it a try if you will Johnny,' I replied. So while Haynes, Beemus and Arts pulled the units gear away from the water's edge to the shelter of the seawall, Johnakin and I quickly tossed our packs, Tommy guns and helmets on the beach and crawled around behind the raft to catch our breath before starting out around the raft.

'Wow,' Johnakin cried as a bullet ripped into the water where he had just been. 'Those SOBs mean business.'

'A couple of more bullets plunked into the water harmlessly nearby and we began crawling backward out into deeper water, keeping the ramp between us and the beach. Bullets continued to whiz near us and our gas impregnated clothes were trying to pull us under as we struggled into deeper water.

'We finally managed to fight our way out through the barriers and obstacles to the side of the ship. In a matter of a few minutes 15 or 20 wounded or non-swimmers were crammed into it or hanging on the outside of the raft and with the help of free hands and feet flailing the water we all managed to reach shore once more where several able-bodied men helped to take the wounded to the protection of the seawall and administer first aid wherever possible.

'Safe for the moment, I shouted to Haynes, 'Where's my gear?'

'Here's your helmet and a pack but someone grabbed your gun and ammunition,' he answered. I muttered something unprintable out of my breath and crawled out of my foxhole long enough to pick up an unfired carbine lying useless beside one of the countless bloody uniforms littering the beach.

'The rapidly rising tide and stiff breeze had by now swung our LCI around broad sides of the beach and was slowly drifting to the obstacles toward shore. There were still some survivors struggling in the water trying to reach shore. Wading through the choppy sea in my direction I could see two soldiers about 10 feet apart.

'Just as it appeared that they would make it to the beach, I heard that already familiar but clear whooshing sound that an 88 shell makes, zipping through the air overhead and wham, it burst so class that the concussion blew them sideways in the water. One staggered drunkenly to his feet with a stunned expression and then gave a hysterical scream, grabbed frantically at his face as blood spurted and poured down his face and the front of his jacket from a head wound. The complexity of mingled expressions of surprise, pain, fear and bewilderment he showed were indescribable. His buddy came up unhurt and yelled, 'For God's sakes take hold of your-self.' That seemed to snap him out of it momentarily and together they stumbled past the breakers to the beach. The amphibious tanks were holding their own with small arms fire but the deadly accuracy of the 88's fire forced them to change their positions on the beach occasionally to prevent them from being blown apart.

'Every time they changed position compelled those of us dug in close to that particular tank to move and dig in again out of immediate danger such as this target presented. Since most of our group were 1,200 yards to the right of our assigned beach we took advantage of a lull in artillery fire to gather all the radio and medical gear we could carry and began to trek along the beach. This trek lasted ten hours instead of it taking 30 minutes. We were crawling under coils of barbed wire, swishing our way through wooden ramps and barriers washed ashore, ducking behind burned out tanks and digging foxholes. When the enemy opened up with the artillery and small arms fire at one protected point, Lieutenant Carpenter in charge of Dog Red beach requested that a message be sent to the flag ship asking for supplies and men on our beaches as the situation was quite desperate. This was one of our beach battalion jobs. Our radiomen and I put the waterproof radio set 609 together which we had been lugging along with us and after trying unsuccessfully for about an hour we finally got a call through. All of us were beginning to shiver as the cold wind whipped through the water so close. The allied planes flying overhead with their wings and fuselages plainly bearing five newly painted black and white stripes were very reassuring as we were quite vulnerable to the attack. Occasionally, broadsides from those close lying cruisers and destroyers gave strength to the fainthearted.

'Since my assignment was to locate my commanding officer to help set up a command post, I asked permission from Lieutenant Carpenter to go further down the beach and search for him. Leaving my packs in the foxhole, I picked up an abandoned M-1 rifle and set off down the beach. The seawall at this point was about three feet high so I crouched low, ran about ten yards and hit the dirt for a few seconds. In this fashion I covered 200-300 yards without mishap. The army ships I requested had not seen any of my battalion as yet. I got up again for the umpteenth time and dashed another few yards.

'Suddenly I found myself in the midst of 50-75 men all prostrate on the sand or rocks. Thinking they were lying there held down by gunfire, I threw myself down between two soldiers and buried my face. Suddenly I realized there was no rat-a-tat-tat of a machine gun or rifle bullets whining overhead so I lifted my head cautiously and looked around. The sickening sight that met my eyes froze me on the spot. One of the men I had dropped between was headless; the other was blown half apart. Every last one of them was dead and apparently blasted and battered by 88 or machine gun fire during the first assault wave. Directly in front of me there was an opening in the seawall through which this murderous gunfire would probably come. Although the Jerries were responsible and undoubtedly met their just fate, I did not wait around to find out. In no second flat I leaped up and put considerable distance between me and the squad. I continued my search for another hundred yards of beach without success, so I holed up behind a protecting bank for a few minutes to decide my next move. I concluded that my commanding officer had either hit the wrong beach or was among the missing so I turned back and retraced my steps to Lieutenant Carpenter's small group without mishap from the harassing small arms fire.

'It was noon now and we could see that the outgoing tide had left our LCI lying broadside to the beach in about two feet of water. Several men volunteered to go back along the beach and get aboard the craft for whatever food or other useful supplies they could find. Johnakin led a small group toward her and threw down a few cartons of self-heating soup and some blankets to a couple of us. We broke open a carton of soup for noon chow and used the blankets to keep some of the wounded men warm. I was one of the lucky people that had saved his D-rations, that's chocolate bars, so we divided the three bars equally among six of us to ease our hunger a little later in the afternoon.

'Although our four beaches were closed for landing men or supplies until the tide had receded, beyond the obstacles about 1500 hours there was a gradually increasing stream of trucks, jeeps, tanks, men and supplies landing further down to our left. Taking advantage of the receding tide, about eight or ten of our demolition squad began securing among the obstacles hastily stringing wire in preparation for blasting open a passage through which landing craft might pass undamaged when the tide rose again later in the day. Just as they seemed to be finished and were grouped together fixing the fuse a detonator, a small shell came hurtling out of nowhere with precision-like accuracy and landed plump in their midst sending their mingled bodies flying in all directions. Three or four did not get up and there were a couple of them who could do nothing but hobble with the aid of their luckier shipmates out of sight behind a wrecked and overturned LCM. In the same murderous manner, the Jerries would wait until a small craft beached, dropped its ramp and as the troops were bunched forward ready to leap onto the beach, a shell would explode among the unsuspecting men, killing or maiming a greater portion of them.

'By 1800 the entire beach 300 yards wide at high tide was a mass of men, supplies and equipment waiting for the moment when the two roads leading off our beaches to Le Milan and Vierville-sur-Mer would be cleared of mines. According to the invasion plan these particular roads were to have been cleared of mines for traffic by HR+12 hours; approximately 1830.

'The Germans opened up again in a terrific barrage on the vulnerable troops and supplies sitting helplessly on the narrow beach. It was no wonder that many of us were speculating just how prepared we were going to be for a German counterattack. In our briefings we were informed that mobile Panzer units were only eight to nine hours away from our strategic strip of beach. To make matters worse the tide was already on its way again and within an hour or two we'd covered most of the area occupied by the mounting mass of vehicles and supplies. During this heavy bombardment in our section directed at the equipment lying on the beach we sought cover in the only direction possible, good old Mother Earth. We used our hands and feet to push the stones away from our bodies and dug ourselves down into a hastily formed foxholes as far as possible. During this a wounded soldier and I shared a foxhole. Closer and closer the shells kept dropping methodically, blasting the cluttered beach every few yards. The last couple I remember hearing shirred us with loose stones and metal and debris. Then 'blam'; something exploded in my head making crazy patterns of dancing lights. My head swam and my entire body seemed to be vibrating. Everything continued to whirl and with a fading of the flashes of blinding lights and tremors through the body I opened my eyes to find everything black. From far away I could hear my foxhole buddy asking, 'Mate are you hit?' 'My limbs seemed paralyzed and it was all I could do to slowly mumble, 'I don't know. I think so. Maybe it's a concussion.'

'Now I began to feel a heavy pounding in my head and my neck hurt too. With extreme effort I raised my hand to my neck, the back of my head and felt a warm stickiness that could only mean one thing. I had been hit but how badly I could not know. I was blind and that was plenty for me. Fortunately, I still had a dry handkerchief in my pants pocket and the soldier kindly tied it over about my head to keep out the dirt.

'Throughout the remainder of the bombardment lasting about an hour, I prayed silently and fervently that God would spare me my eyes, man's most precious gift. Little did I know that a few days hence my prayers would be answered and my eyesight restored.

'At approximately 20:00 hours the barrage lifted and the roads to Le Milan and Vierville-sur-Mer were opened to traffic. At long last, I was piled onto a truck with 12 or 15 other wounded men and taken inland. We were laid in a row in a small sheltered area on the seaward side of a ridge which began its rise 300 yards beyond the beach. The army men, whoever they were gave each one of us a blanket to help protect us from the cold of the night and the intermittent showers. As I was starting to climb into the truck I got a cramp in my leg and yelled and someone said, 'Oh, he's dying,' and it gave me a laugh then and I said, 'No, it's just a hamstring.'

'While we were being settled as comfortable as possible on the rocky ground I heard a sharp command to move an anti-aircraft battery being set up nearby to a safer position. In as much as they were exposed to the enemy snipers still active in the area. As they disassembled the unit I asked softly, 'Are you leaving a guard with us?'

'Sorry, we need every man we have here, but you'll be okay buddy until medical men get to you in the morning.'

'Quietly they slipped away and I resigned myself to sweating out a long and eventful night turning my intermittent attention to wrapping my single blanket closely around my weary body to ward off the cold, damp night. Sometime during the night some enemy bombers came over and bombed the ships in the harbour and the still of the night was often broken by sporadic bursts, machine gun fire or the clang-clang of a tank's treads as it changed position to cover some new sector with its guns. Not being able to see I could only surmise and imagine what was transpiring. The boy on the left of me was very restless and in pain and his body kept jerking spasmodically. I did not know what his injury was but the lad on my right was moaning softly. He could not stand the pain in his right arm much longer. The cold ground and sharp stones we lay on caused us to shift our close-huddled bodies often during the night. It was a weird feeling lying there blind, listening to the jerky movements of the chap on my left and the heavy breathing of the soldier on my right breathlessly listening trying to identify any unusual sounds such as might be caused by German snipers prowling about. I dozed off to sleep many times for short intervals and it seemed that the night would never pass. Guns began firing more regularly so I turned to the soldier on my left and whispered, 'Hey Joe is it daybreak yet?'

'After receiving no answer or movement from him I rolled over and nudged the boy on my right. He too was unresponsive. Thinking out loud I mumbled, what's wrong with these guys anyway?

'They're dead, buddy, lost too much blood...' was the unexpected answer from further down the row.

'Oh, sorry' I said, wondering just how many more of our little group would follow that example before medical help could reach us.

'Just before midday, June 7 an army medic managed to get to us uninjured, gave us each some sulpha pills and a sip of water from his canteen. He explained to us that the stretcher bearers could not come up to move us until all the remaining snipers holed up in the side of the hill were wiped out. It gave us hope. Sometime in the afternoon they could get to us and we were rushed to an evacuation centre. Late morning and the early afternoon the naval gun firing increased in intensity as observers sought out the positions of the murderous 88s. The noise was so deafening, it was necessary to open our mouths to prevent our eardrums from shattering from the concussion of nearby bursting shells. Four of our group died during the day from lack of blood. Just before dusk we were carried down the ridge to the beach and after examination to an evacuation centre.

'Those of us considered critical were placed on a jeep and were taken to the waiting LCM around midnight. About 20 of us were loaded on the small craft. After getting stuck by the outgoing tide and pushed off by a group of men, we bounced our way out to an LST. A crane was rigged to swing us aboard, being lashed to the stretcher. About one third of the way up one side slipped off and I was raised the rest of the way hanging head down lowered into a hold where several naval corpsmen kept constant watch to care for the needs and desires of the wounded. We had no sooner loaded aboard and we experienced another brief but distasteful air attack through which we lay unscathed. We had our damp heavy clothing cut away from our dirty bodies and were given sulphur pills periodically. The pills stayed down but the water didn't. I couldn't hold the pill in my stomach until about June 13. We lay overnight in Normandy to await the formation of a convoy and late on the night of June 8th we pulled out and headed for the subsequently proved to be Portsmouth.'

Chief Yeoman William Garwood Bacon, USNR, naval engineer, 7th Naval Beach Battalion. On 10 June X-rays were taken and pieces of 88-shell fragments were removed from his skull. Later Dr. William R. Lipscomb of Denver, Colorado operated removing bone and shell fragments and inserted

a large titanium plate during a 5 to 6 hour operation with local anaesthesia. In September 1944 Bacon underwent a third operation.

'About 01:00 we were awakened, those who could sleep that is and had chow consisting of toast and G.I. coffee. At 01:30 the order came through to board the smaller Landing Craft, 'LCM's' as they were called and at a given signal were to rendezvous for the frontal assault on Normandy Beach. These boats were large enough to accommodate a full platoon, 41 men, combat gear and all and had a ramp in front which the operator could lower to allow fast exit. Ours was the 2nd Platoon, Company 'B', 121st Engineer Combat Battalion and was scheduled to be the lead of spearhead because of the nature of our mission. We were to demolish a masonry wall about four feet high and four feet thick that ran parallel to the water's edge so that the tank forces could get in. Every man carried 40lb satchel charges of TNT for this purpose plus one 7 foot Bangalore torpedo and full field pack, rifle, etc. A few yards from the beach was a barbed wire entanglement that we would encounter before getting to the wall. The Bangalore torpedoes were for the purpose of cutting huge holes through those obstacles.

'I had been on the English Channel at least four times before and had never seen the water so rough. It was vicious. Waves would throw the LCM up out of the water and it would slam down with a bone-breaking jar. Every man jack of us was so seasick we had regurgitated on ourselves and everyone around us by 05:00. 'H-Hour' or landing time was originally set for 06:00. This was changed, moved to 06:20 because of high tide and rough water. Our radio operator was so sick he missed the message so our 'H-Hour' was still 06:00 sharp. As we neared the beach we began to look about us. Never did I think there were so many boats and ships in the world. They were everywhere!

'The Air Force had taken the paratroops in earlier in what appeared an endless stream of planes. Then about 06:00 they started bombing and strafing the beach to try and soften up the defences. The large battlewagons behind us opened up with their big guns lobbing shells over our heads to the beach. It would seem that nothing could have withstood such a bombardment of shells and blockbusters but somehow the German personnel escaped serious injury. At least they were still very much alive and alert at 06:00.

'About 200 yards out our LCM floundered, nosed up on a hidden sandbar and stuck fast. The operator seesawed back and forth but she wouldn't give. The machine gun fire rattling off the sides set up such a din of noise you could hardly think. The operator threw the ramp down and yelled, 'Hit it!' I was the 3rd man out. We three wheeled left and jumped off the side of the ramp. Machine gun fire was now raking the inside of the LCM and a high percentage of our men were killed before they could get out.

'When the first three of us jumped we landed in a shell hole and what with all the luggage we had plummeted to the bottom like a rock. We walked along the bottom until we climbed out of the hole. It seemed an eternity before we reached the surface. We were then on the barren sand but there was another stretch of water between us and the beach. This stretch contained a maze of tank traps, mines and every object the Krauts could plant to thwart a landing attempt.

'It all seemed unreal, a sort of dreaming while awake, men were screaming and dying all around me. I've often wondered if all the men prayed as fervently as I did. I remember going past one of the log type tank obstacles with 'legs' attached to the back end. I ran up beside it and got down as low as I could to rest a moment and find as much shelter from the hail of machine gun fire as possible. Looking over the log I discovered about half way up was a large Teller Mine with 'trip' wires running in every direction. Since some of this type detonators are tension devices I knew that if a bullet cut one of those wires it would blow me to bits. But the question was how to get past? I knew I had to make it, so without hesitation I angled off to the left and by the divine help of God I made it through the maze of wires with all my gear.

'I suddenly found myself confronted with what seemed a mountain of rusty barbed wire. I slid the Bangalore as far under as I could, cut as short a fuse as I dared, lit it and ran back about ten paces and flattened myself out on the ground. It blew a gap about twenty feet wide in the wire. This section was under intense fire from the pillboxes that we could see on the hill. Every fifth bullet used in machine guns is a tracer, which you can see in the form of a glow. These looked so dense and crisscrossed that it is hard to believe anything could get by unscathed.

'With heartbreaking slowness I arrived at the wall behind which several of our men were already waiting for us. I threw my satchel charges onto the wall and attached the lead fuse to the primacord they had already stretched and started crawling down the beach for safety from the coming explosion. When the explosion occurred, the first wave of infantry was about a hundred yards out. At this time our initial mission was completed so we huddled behind the ragged remnants of the wall we had just blown. I turned my gaze toward the coming infantry and saw my Sergeant, Steve Kleman, not forty yards from me. He was sitting down, had been hit through both hips. I tried four times to get out to him to drag him in. Each time I left cover a hail of machine gun fire would drive me back. By this time he had been hit so many times it was hopeless.

'Company 'B' sustained 73% casualties on this landing, but lying behind the cover of the wall we could not tear our eyes off the infantry. They ran through and up the hill in a never-ending stream, the dead and dying piling up behind them. I honestly could have walked the full length of the beach without touching the ground; they were that thickly strewn about. Stark raw death in every imaginable form lay all around us. I remember a corporal, still walking, looking for a medic, with his whole chin and nose shot away, cut cleanly and evenly.

'I wonder if I shall ever be able to forget all this.'

Melvin B. Farrell, 2nd Platoon, Company 'B', 121st Engineer Combat Battalion.

'About two or three o'clock in the morning we were woken up to transfer onto our landing barge. I was already sea sick, not much sleep, hungry, cold, but the boats began taking their places heading for Normandy. Airplanes started bombing the gun nests on the hillside, explosion after explosion ahead of us. The big ships started shooting their rockets into the beach, lighting up the whole area. This was between 0500 and 05:30; just at daybreak. I was in the first wave. It was foggy. I thought if I live through this it would have been the biggest Fourth of July I have ever seen in my whole life. The tide was coming in about four or five feet at a time. Instead of being on the beach, I was under my arms in water and I knew next time it would be over my head. (I am 6′ 5′). Some of the shorter guys, it was over their heads. I had to move forward. Every fifth round was a tracer. I watched the high and low places on the ground as a guide where to go. I walked out on the beach for about fifty feet. I thought this wasn't going to take long. I had my full field pack, satchel charges and Bangalore torpedo for the barbed wire entanglement, my rifle and a cartridge belt on; a pretty good load in itself. I had been told to take the mess kit spoon with me that morning. I had wondered why. Now it came in handy. I started a hole in the pebbles with my spoon and used my feet to push out a furrow to get a little lower in the ground.

'All of a sudden all hell broke loose. Machine gun fire criss-crossed over my head and I was shot on my right lower buttock. My buddy, Anthony Lala from Louisiana had been shot in the hip. The bullet made a hole in canteen and a stream of water the size of a lead pencil was coming out. It was not life threatening but he died from shock. How I got through was a miracle.

'At the barbed wire I tied on my torpedo and tied on my satchel charges on a hedgehog like the ones we practiced on, four foot tall with a 1 inch I-beam, 8 feet by 7 or 8 feet tall. When I saw violet smoke I knew it was fixing to go off. It was a ticklish situation. I could not get up and run on account of bullets over my head. I said a prayer or two and thought about what the fortune teller had told me. I thought if it gets any worse, I may not live through it. When I was tying on my satchel charges, a bullet hit the other side of it and I could smell the heat. I wanted that bullet for a souvenir but it was too far away for me to reach for it. I moved to the right far enough for the falling debris to miss me. It sounded like fence posts falling around me. I was lucky, some small pieces hit me but no damage.

'There is no way I can use words to explain all that was going on. Hollering, shouting, blowing up, seeing men shot; trying to survive. I finally got across the beach, I think about 11:00. This is what was in my mind: they had given us a K-ration. I wanted to wait until 12:00 to eat. I had a pretty good spot under the embankment. I could see fire trucks being blown up, men trying to come in and getting shot like fish in a barrel. I was doing pretty good until a half-track parked beside me. After his first shot I could not hear anything. It was still a comfort. I'd rather hear that than dodge bullets.

'That evening we assembled on the hillside, which seemed like about 300 yards' high. I went nearly to the top to dig a foxhole. I thought if a German threw a hand grenade, it would go over my foxhole. We were lucky no one came, thank the Lord. My good buddy, James W. Krahl, from Oklahoma, boat crew 7, was just to my left and rear. I had him look at my buttocks to see how bad I was hit. The bullet had gone in and come out about two inches where it went in, a flesh wound and left holes in my pants and underclothes. I had Max

S. Norris my medic look at my wound. He made a field dressing on it for me. (Norris got hit also and went to a hospital in England).

'I worked on the beach the next day, clearing the debris so trucks, half tracks, tanks could drive through from their boats. This was our mission and it was dangerous. Some dud rounds and ammunition hadn't been fired. One bulldozer operator got blown off his dozer from the like. I found a blown up half-track on the beach. I think the driver had been blown to pieces. Anyhow, I saw a pair of nice leather gloves. I always wanted a pair. I put my left hand in the left glove and it fit fine. I was having trouble putting my hand in the right one and discovered it still had three fingers in it. I pulled off the left one and laid them both down. This poor guy had a better safety razor than I did, so I traded razors with him and went on with my business. There were pieces of barbed wire entanglements, pieces of steel and blown up equipment all over the place.

'I saw medics and men taking care of the poor fellows that had been killed on the beach the day before, carrying them, moving them to another location. I had seen the wounds being treated best as could be. Some were blown up too bad to save. The next day, D+2; was still dangerous. The Germans had zeroed their 88s in on us. We didn't know whether we were going to be killed or not. This lasted for the next two or three days. Their airplanes would come over and fire at us also.'

William D. Townsley. He fought in five different battles, made T-5 corporal and was discharged on 6 December 1945 at Camp Fannon, Texas. The Department of the Army finally awarded his Purple Heart, on 15 May 1997.

'When we arrived on the beach at about 06:30 the pillboxes had not been knocked out so we sailed back and forth parallel along the beach. We saw destroyers go in very close to fire on the big guns but they could not silence them. Light and heavy cruisers took turns and the box on the west was knocked out. Then a battlewagon came up and fired 16' guns over us. We could see the projectiles going on and the concussion caused the LCI to keel over to a steep angle before righting herself. She finished the last box. Somewhere around 08:00 to 09:00 we turned for the beach and we must have hit the beach at flank speed. My battle station was the stern winch and I let the anchor go when told. We unloaded the 29th Engineers without a hitch and the order was given to retrieve the stern anchor but it never grabbed a hold and I retrieved it and secured it. Then LCI 555 came in and shot a line in three times but the wind was so strong the line did not reach us. Milliken, the Executive Ensign dove into the water and retrieved the line but LCI 555 could not shake us and since the German 88 had gotten our range, the captain cut the LCI 555 loose to get them out of danger. Captain Don DuBrul saw to it that Ensign Milliken was awarded the Bronze Star.

'I was sent to the engine room to secure the generators and engines and watch for fire. 'Scottie' (Roland Scott) the QM had gone to the engine room with me. Everyone abandoned ship and took cover on the beach. A few minutes after they left we came up from the engine room and we went on the beach.

He went one way and I went the other. I crawled under a half track and coxswain Stephens was there. Shortly after one the 29th Engineers told us to move out because it was loaded with ammo. I seemed to be in a spot I was not trained for; we agreed to leave the beach which was 100-150 yards to the water as the tide had been going out ever since we had landed. Again a 29th Engineer told us to avoid the little puddles of water because they were mines. As we ran toward the water I could see spurts of sand at regular intervals as the sniper sprayed the beach. We stopped about 50 yards from the LCVP boat to help a wounded GI to the boat. We helped him aboard and we scrambled on but we were broached so Stephens and I jumped out and pushed the VP off the sand. When the boat coxswain was free he gunned it and we grabbed a handhold to hang on; others helped us aboard as we headed out to LCI 94.

'They took us out further to LST 316. I was given pants and shirt and told to take a shower. Since we were in the salt water and were wearing gas proof clothing, the green dye bled onto our skin. No amount of salt water soap and salt water shower would remove the dye; we looked like frogs. We were given chow which was the first since 4 am. Then I went up on deck. It was dusk and looking toward the beach we could see the flashes and hear the big guns.'

Robert M. Leach, Motor Machinist Mate 3rd class, LCI(L) 553. LCI(L) 553 was commissioned in Perth Amboy, New Jersey and had left Norfolk, Virginia on 24 March. Leach did not know then that he had chronic seasickness. After 13 days, on 5 April the ship docked in the Azores and he had lost 35 pounds. They left the Azores on 7 April and landed at Falmouth on 12 April. Then on 17 April they engaged in T-6 Exercise Tiger at Slapton Sands and he never knew about the loss of life that night. He boarded the *Queen Elizabeth* on 24 October and started on 33 days survivors' leave on 4 November.

'We were fed a meal about two o'clock on the morning of June 6th and very shortly thereafter went over the side into our LCVPs. This little vessel circled for a considerable length of time until we were ready to make the run into the beach. A firing of the large sixteen inch guns from the American warships standing off shore in the Channel was horrendous. As we made our run to the beach we passed several life rafts filled with airmen who had been shot down. As we went by they gave us the thumbs up gesture indicating that everything was alright. Looking towards the beach we couldn't believe that anybody was left alive after the tremendous bombardment that they received both from the battleships, the rocket launching ships and the air force pounding. Once we hit the beach we found out how wrong we were. The British coxswain of our boat got us right up onto the beach and we only got off into water perhaps knee high. Our training stood us in a good stead because we did not run straight up the beach but zig-zagged back and forth trying to make ourselves more difficult targets to hit.

'As I moved up the beach I got behind the bluff perhaps ten feet high and sought shelter there. We were moving laterally on the beach looking for an area that could afford us cover so that we could move off the beach. At that time, shells landed about ten yards away and the concussion just flipped me over on my back. A man immediately to my right was killed and I had a numb feeling in my right leg. I thought that it was just from the concussion but when I tried to stand I kept falling down. We had been issued uniforms that had a chemical added to the material that was supposed to repel gas in case the Germans had used it. We had also treated our canvas leggings and shoes. After falling down twice, I looked at my leg and saw that there was blood coming through the legging. I pulled the legging off and pulled up my trousers to see that I had been hit halfway between the knee and the ankle. I crawled against the bluff and tried to put a bandage on to cover the wound. Our lieutenant came along and said we were moving off the beach and he was upset that I had been laying back. When I stood up and fell down he realized I was wounded and said to stay where I was and that they would try to get me some help.

'Succeeding waves of ships came in and a great many of the men were cut down coming across the beach. The fire from the 88s and machine guns took their toll. I later found out that of 180 men in our assault group only 79 of us came across the beach alive.

'Those that could moved off the beach because it was better going inland getting away from the terrible artillery fire we were exposed to. I handed over my rifle and my grenades to some of the men who struggled across the beach. Some of the coxswains of the LCVPs approached the beach and let the ramps down so that the men that got off into the water waist deep and in some cases higher. They struggled ashore and many lost their packs, their helmets and their rifles. As a result when they got up to the beach they had nothing to use and that is why I gave them my weapons. A fellow that was lying next to me on the beach had been wounded in the leg. I was talking to him when a very concentrated bombardment came very close to where we were located. We hid our heads and when the shelling stopped I looked up to talk to him and found out that he had been hit again and he was dead.

'I lay on the beach for about twelve hours and once during that time a medic just gave a cursory examination of my leg and told me to keep my bandage covering the wound. At approximately six pm that evening, a team of medics came along and started evacuating the wounded from my area. Some of the men had to be carried out to the water's edge on stretchers. When they had one of the landing craft loaded with wounded, they headed out towards the Channel to put them aboard hospital ships. The medic that came to help me put me on his back and was carrying me down to the water's edge. The Germans started heavy bombardment with their 88mm cannons. When we were halfway down the beach to the landing craft, the medic who was carrying me suddenly dropped to the ground. I was concerned that he had been wounded, but found to my great relief that he had just fallen flat so that neither one of us would be struck with the shrapnel that was flying all around us. At the time the shelling stopped, he scrambled to his feet, put me on his back and took me down to one of the landing craft that had just come into the beach. I was placed on a stretcher and we took off immediately for a ship.

'We came along the LST (Landing Ship Tank) and they lowered four ropes that were put around the handles of the stretcher and started pulling me up the side of the ship. At one time, the men that were pulling the ropes at the head of the stretcher pulled too quickly and I was dangerously tilted towards the bottom end and almost slipped off into the water. They finally got me on board and took me down to the operating room. A doctor was there and they cut my clothing off me and cleaned me up the best they could. The doctor immediately went to work on the shrapnel wound in my leg and after about an hour's work I was taken below and put into a sailor's bunk.

'After dozing off for a couple of hours, I was awakened by some noise in the area and found a seaman had come down and was looking after the other men who had been brought on board for medical treatment. He came over to me and asked if I would like something to eat. As I had not eaten in almost 24 hours, I said yes. He came back very soon with a bowl that had cold peas. I ordinarily do not like peas, but it didn't make any difference. I ate them as quickly as I could and I felt much better for it. After eating he brought me a basin of water so that I could wash my face and refresh myself. He noticed I hadn't shaved in over a day and asked if I'd like to be shaved. I told him that I didn't think that I could do it myself and he said, 'Don't worry about it; I'll take care of it for you.' He then proceeded to lather me up, shave me and I felt much better. I complemented him on his professional way he had shaved me and asked if in civilian life he had been a barber. His answer was no but he had experience shaving people as he had worked for his uncle who was an undertaker and he would prepare the bodies for viewing before burial period. This was a rather ironic note to this whole episode and I laughed about it when he told it to me. I also inquired as to whether or not the boat was headed back to England, only to find out that the ship was fully loaded with tanks and personnel who were going into the beach. We laid off 'Omaha' for another day until we made the run into the beach so that the tanks and personnel could be unloaded. We then took on more wounded and headed back for England.

'By this time, the crews' quarters were pretty crowded, so those of us who had already received medical attention were taken down to the tank deck. It had metal arms that were folded flat against the bulkheads when the tanks were on board ship. When the tanks were unloaded, these metal arms were unfolded. Our stretchers were put on the arms, supporting us at the head and the foot. We were stacked three high on the tank deck. We then made the run back to Weymouth and were carried off the LSTs and onto trucks or ambulances that took us to the train station. From there, we were put on hospital trains that loaded up quickly and took off for hospitals in the Salisbury area.

'Upon arrival at the hospital, we were cleaned up and put in regular beds. Doctors came around for examination of our wounds and further treatment. I spent one month in the hospital before being shipped back to my unit, which by that time had moved inland.

'General impressions that remain with me of that momentous day in history was the courage and determination of the men who were responsible for leading the troops. Almost all of us were very frightened by the noise and the action going on around us. The difference between the men was that some of us could act, despite the fears and carry out our duties. Others just cringed in fear and were no help to anybody. The training that we had gone through for those many months in England where we learned dependence on one another paid dividends during those first crucial hours of the landing. We had trained long and hard and knew that the efficiency of the team was dependent on everybody doing their job at the time that was necessary.'

Steve Kellerman, Company 'L', 3rd Battalion, 16th Infantry Regiment of the 1st Infantry Division.

'We arrived at the rendezvous area about fifteen miles off the coast of Normandy at about 3 am on the morning of June 6. There were four or five big battleships lined up about a mile apart. It was very dark but each time one of the battleships fired a salvo, the sky would light up everything as far as the eye could see. We managed to 'marry' our Rhino to the LST and began unloading by about 5 o'clock. It was just getting light. After three or four hours, we cast off and headed toward the shore. I was a signalman and deckhand on the tug. Because of the intense enemy gunfire throughout most of the day, our Rhino was not able to beach until late in the evening when it was just getting dark. As we arrived on the beach, we could see bodies floating around in the shallow water like logs. It was very disgusting. While we were unloading, a small plane flew across the beach dropping bombs. I don't think it caused any great damage, but it did cause some excitement. Finally, around 10 o'clock, we pulled the Rhino off the beach and headed out to sea. After we got about a mile out, we dropped anchor and crawled into the pontoon because we were exhausted. We would be on duty for 24 hours unloading ships and then off for 24 hours.

'Around 7 o'clock the following morning, our chief woke us up chanting 'they are shooting at us!' Sure enough, you could see little 'plinks' in the water nearby. Instead of pulling up the anchor by hand, someone got an axe and chopped the chain in two and let it go to the bottom. We promptly got further out to sea. We spent the rest of the day tied up to a liberty ship that was unloading military vehicles and supplies by crane with large cargo nets and ferrying them to shore.

'For the first three or four days, we slept on a troop ship and if it was near meal time when we were unloading a cargo ship, we ate with them. They always had excellent food, as did the troop ship. Anything was better than the K-rations we survived at first. The whole invasion process was so stressful; I doubt that any of us ate anything on the first day. After the bluff above the beach had been secured, a camp area was established and a mess tent set up which served hot C-rations. Heat didn't improve the flavour but the hot food was much appreciated. Each of us had been given a half of a pup tent back at boot camp and a fellow by the name of Howard Larsen from Oregon became my roommate. He was about five and a half feet tall and I am six foot four so we were referred to as 'Mutt and Jeff.' We discovered a barge with canned goods in cases - six gallons each. I stole a case of fruit cocktail and Howard got a case of peaches. And we supplemented our hot C-rations with delicious canned fruit and shared them with a number of our neighbours and we were very popular for a couple of weeks afterwards. We dug a 'foxhole' about six and a half feet long and four feet wide and about 18 inches deep. Then we pulled all the grass we could find for a mattress and it became very comfortable

for sleeping and shelter when the wind blew.'
   Roy Aron Ford.

'During our stay on LSTs during the night there were many men that were so nervous it was hard to believe that they were the same men that we had known for months and some for years. Some were quiet, others were more talkative. I was concerned with the men in my platoon as they were the ones that I'd be close to in combat. I'd talk to the men that wanted to talk and pray with those who wanted to pray. It was hard to not show too much worry of what we had to do. I tried to give courage to all, especially the men who had not seen combat. It was still dark the morning of June 6. The advance forces had landed, bright searchlights lit up the whole shore and the beach, but our men knocked them out in a short time. All along the water front there were vehicles and equipment that had been knocked out by enemy fire. On the beach wounded men and a group of prisoners were being guarded by US troops. The LSTs carried 33 tanks. I was in the third tank off the ship as we mounted up preparation to move off the ship. Sergeant Martin, my platoon sergeant, yelled to me, 'Let's go ashore and keep them running.' I yelled, 'I'll be waiting for you in Berlin.'

'We often joked about who would be the first one in Berlin. Our division was the first occupation troops in the American sector, but we never decided which one of us was there first. When we got on land we went directly to a wooded area, not far from the beach and waited for our company to assemble. It gave us a little cleared space in the landing area. It took more time than planned. We didn't engage the enemy because the beachhead was only three miles deep and we had fewer men from other units than expected. The original plan was to be in 12 miles.

'There was unusual rough water and it delayed our unloading for several days so we couldn't push on for lack of supplies and equipment.'
   Sherman Baxter, born 6 September 1919 at Dover, New Hampshire. He entered the service 22 January 1942 and was assigned to D company, 66th Armoured Regiment, 2nd Army division. 'I was wounded in August by a bazooka. It hit my tank at night while we were pushing on. I returned to my outfit two months' later to find I had been promoted to sergeant. Only a short time later I was promoted to staff sergeant which rank I held until I was mustered out. I lost three tanks during the whole time, but only one man was killed. I'm proud to say that I'll always be proud of my division. We saw lots of combat and made a good name for itself. Much credit should go to General Patton, who made the 2nd Armoured an unbeatable force. He was a division commander when I joined them.'

'It was 7.30am when we neared the marker for our entrance. At this time we got hit and quite a few men were burnt. We got hit again by 88mm shells. By this time the Engineers came on deck to disembark but we were nowhere near the beach. We all crawled to the back of the craft and men were already jumping overboard. The water was cold and the second thing I realized was that my equipment was too heavy. I took off my pack and medical pouches and struggled to get off my gas mask. I came across Captain Albert and Smitty. All this time 88s were aiming at us in the water and there was machine gun fire from the hill off the beach. Men who couldn't swim or were afraid of the water managed to hold onto obstacles which were mined. Some went off either by pressure of the man or from machine gun fire, I don't know which.

'The water was rough and only with the help of the waves could we get near the shore. It was still over our heads when I felt a hard blow and heard a loud noise. Captain Albert just disappeared. I didn't notice Smitty until after I got up for I'd been knocked out and didn't know if I was hit or not. Smitty was holding my hand, asking me to take him in and then I noticed that he was hit for he had shrapnel wounds all over his face. Every time the waves went out I saw blood coming up the water from Smitty's lower body. He started to cry that he didn't want to drown. I cannot express my feelings but I'm sure I cried too, for here was my first taste of war. Smitty said: 'Take me in, Sol. I'm losing a lot of blood'. Honest, I must have swallowed a quart of his blood. His voice got weaker all the time. Finally I touched bottom and we walked very slowly. Smitty was getting weaker and I had to half carry him. The stones went up the beach for about 10 feet and there was a wooden structure on the side of a little incline. That's where all the men were. As we got out of the water my feet wouldn't hold me. The further I got on the beach, the heavier Smitty was getting. He passed out and finally a Ranger Lieutenant ran down, exposing himself to fire and helped me drag him up to the stones. I started shivering and nothing could stop me. I sat up and Smitty's head was in my lap when he died.

Sergeant 'Sol' Evnetzky, 147th Combat Engineer Battalion.

"Omaha' was indescribable... there were dead people everywhere, there were people floating in the water, there were wrecked tanks, there were wrecked jeeps, there were tanks that were supposed to be floating in water that were dead on land and some of them had been knocked out by the .88 guns which were firing straight down the beach... we'd been told it would be a walk-over, we'd just walk on to the beach and the Germans would have been obliterated, the air force and the guns and the combat engineers, they'd make it so that the infantry could just walk ashore... but it wasn't like that. Not at all.'

Colonel Edwin Woolf, an engineer in the 6th Special Brigade.

'We were instructed to blow up obstacles and as soon as the beach was cleared and the small arms enemy fire was eliminated initiate the landing of cargo and the evacuation of the wounded. Most of the men had sloughed off their packs. The .50 calibre and the .30 calibre machine-guns were left on the boat along with the bazookas and flamethrowers, there wasn't any question of getting them ashore - although they had been packed as floatable with extra life-jackets and large waterproof bags - we called them 'elephant's condoms'. You could put a whole gun in them and tie the end up and keep it secure both from the water and the sand. Most of the chaps just got ashore with their pistol and cartridge belt and canteen and their rifle and perhaps their gas mask which was a helluva good piece of equipment to keep your head up.'

George Itzen, a platoon leader in the US 147 Engineer Combat Battalion.

'When I came to the surface all I could see was just a blur in front of me and I could see guys trying to swim that way. So I went that way too. The next thing I knew I was touching bottom, standing maybe armpit deep in water and the little waves were shoving me back as I walked in. Then I saw what chaos was going on up on the beach and I could hear mortar rounds, possibly artillery shells, hitting up there. I could also hear rifle and machine gun fire. They had some big steel cross things sticking up out of the water and I remember going under one of them and trying to stay behind that steel. There were so many guys around there that I felt kind of guilty trying to stay behind something. So I thought. Well, I could see the beach and a number of fellows lying on the beach and about 35 yards across the beach there were cliffs. And I knew that if I could get under that cliff, at least I'd be safe from small arms fire coming down and possibly from mortar fire. So I finally inched my way up out of the water and all of a sudden I realized how cold I was. Anyway, I jumped up and started running. As I ran along the beach I picked up a rifle. There was a guy lying on the beach with two bandoliers of ammunition in his hand and I took them.

'...As we were sitting there, either too scared to get up or not wanting to, a lieutenant colonel came down the beach and nonchalantly walked in and said, 'Who's the non-commissioned officer around here?' I didn't say a word. I didn't see any other NCOs making any move to get up. And this fellow in my gun crew - if I ever wanted to strangle anyone, it was him - said, 'Here's my sergeant'. This lieutenant colonel turned to me and said, 'Are you a non-commissioned officer?'

'Yes, I'm a sergeant in the artillery - a chief of section'.

'Well, you start gathering these men up, since you are the only sergeant here'. Then he pointed to a place down the beach and added, 'Go down there and see the Lieutenant'.

'But I'm not an infantryman, I'm an artilleryman'.

'I don't care what you are. Have you ever had any infantry training?'

'Well, no, but I was in the cavalry once'.

'That's good enough. You're in the infantry now'.
Jerry W. Eades, 62nd Armoured field Artillery, US Army.

'We stood looking over the side at the beach we were to go in at soon. We were all happy and smiling, telling jokes and yelling. Six o'clock came and we went in... There hadn't been a shot fired from the enemy yet. But soon as we dropped our ramp, an 88mm came tearing in, killing almost half our men right there, the officer being the first one. We all thought him the best officer the navy ever had... From then on things got hazy to me. I remember the Chief starting to take over, but then another one hit and that did it. I thought my body tom apart. When I woke I saw a big hole in the bulkhead between the sergeant and me. He was dead, it must have been instant. I was blood from head to foot but didn't know it at the time. Later I found the shrapnel had got me in the left leg and arm. I looked round and seen no one else alive. The explosive was on fire and was burning fast, so I went overboard and headed for the beach. The surf was filled with soldiers trying to get ashore. But the bullets in the surf from the enemy were thick. They were getting killed fast. I reached the obstacles and got behind one to shelter. Just then the landing craft blew up, that got me, not caring whether I lived or not I started to run, through the fire up the beach, which was plenty far to run; it probably seemed longer at that time. That's when I found my leg and arm stiff. After a while the soldiers were pouring in thick. I did a little rifle firing with them...'

A demolition man on 'Omaha' Beach. **The six weeks of training of the demolition force near Barnstaple in Devon, had been hurried and incomplete. It was hurried because obstacles on 'Omaha' Beach had only been seen in reconnaissance photographs for the first time in April and then, under Rommel's pressure, had multiplied very quickly. It was incomplete because nobody knew exactly what the obstacles were like... Even the organization of their teams was rather an improvisation. They had started as a naval force divided into teams of one officer and seven enlisted men: 16 teams, to blow 16 gaps in the defences. But whenever new photographs were taken, the belt of obstacles was seen to have grown more complex; and the naval command concluded that a team of eight men was too small to blow a gap during the half-hour which the plan allowed them. The navy had no more explosives men to spare, so the army lent them some. Five army men were added to each of the naval teams. The commander of this peculiar composite force was Joseph H. Gibbons, a naval reserve officer. He had probably been chosen more for his character than for his knowledge of demolition, which was small. He was a powerfully built man of moderate height with a bulldog's tenacity and a habit of saying exactly what he thought no matter who was listening: strict, outspoken, fair, a man to whom right was right and wrong was wrong and no shades of rightness existed in between. He was very much aware of his responsibility to the navy and especially to his men, whom he treated like a very stern, old-fashioned and yet affectionate father. These qualities probably dated back to his upbringing in the woods and the blue grass country of Kentucky and perhaps they owed something to his training at the Naval Academy at Annapolis; for he had graduated there in the twenties but then had left the service, which seemed a dead end to him and taken a job in a telephone company. [8]**

'The Naval Combat Demolition Units were charged with the responsibility of clearing sixteen 50-yard gaps on the beaches assigned to that force. They worked in conjunction with the Army engineers who were charged with the responsibility of clearing the shoreward obstacles...The plan called for the NCDU to land at H-hour plus three minutes. Unfortunately, gunfire was not neutralized and as we approached the beaches we were subjected to heavy enemy gunfire of 88 mm, 75s, .50 machine-gun and rifle fire. In the engagement we suffered 41% casualties, 20% killed, 21% wounded. This excluded those who were wounded but were not evacuated from the beaches. The gunfire was intense, but we were successful in clearing initially six gaps [of] 50 yards each and three semi-partially cleared gaps. By the end of D-Day we had been

8   *Dawn Of D-Day* by David Howarth (The Companion Book Club 1959).

successful in clearing ten gaps completely. By D+2, 85% of the enemy obstacles on the beaches had been cleared and by D+4 the beaches on 'Omaha' were cleared of all enemy obstacles dangerous to invasion craft.

'Some of the unusual events which occurred were first the complete decimation of one crew, which was killed by a direct hit of an 88mm gun. The boys went into the beaches carrying 40lbs of specially prepared explosives. We carried in rubber boats 300lbs of additional explosives. This particular unit had place their charges on the obstacles and in placing these charges, they were all hand placed. They were prepared to pull the fuse detonating the charges, when an 88 shell made a direct hit on one of the rubber boats exploding the auxiliary ammunition. The concussion set off the explosives on the obstacles, which in turn killed all members of that crew with the exception of one man who had gone up the beach to place markers to guide in subsequent craft.

'Another crew received a direct hit by an 88 in the boat and all except two men were killed. In another case an officer was standing by to pull the fuses after the charges had been placed when rifle fire cut his fingers off and the fuse assemblies. In still another instance enemy rifle fire set off the charges which had been placed on the obstacles which cleared the gap but unfortunately also caused casualties. One unit was decimated with the exception of three men by enemy sniper fire. Throughout the entire operation the loyalty and bravery and devotion to duty of the men were most outstanding. All of those who were killed died with their faces toward the enemy and as they moved forward to accomplish their objectives.

'Three of my officers were walking down the beaches, which were strewn with mines. They were walking in the wheel ruts of a truck. Twenty paces behind a soldier came by, stepping in the footprints made by the last naval officer. He set off the mine and was blown to pieces. One officer had a sniper shooting at him for five minutes, without success but unfortunately he did hit the man adjacent to this officer, shooting him between the eyes.

'On the enemy placed obstacles on the beaches they had also placed Teller mines. These were placed on approximately 75% on top of stakes, at the apex of ramps and at the top of the elements 'C' and in some cases in the center of hedgehogs [beach obstacles constructed of clusters of wooden or metal stakes sticking into the air at different angles]. In order to detonate those mines, it was decided that they should be detonated at the time the obstacle was destroyed in order to avoid having those mines blown into the beach unexploded to be a hazard later.

'To accomplish that, it was necessary to place a charge alongside the mine to assure it being detonated when the obstacle was demolished. To accomplish this men shinnied up the stakes and stood on each other's shoulders all in the face of heavy enemy gunfire.'

Lieutenant Commander Joseph H. Gibbons USNR, CO, US Navy Combat Demolitions Units in Force 'O', which were awarded a Presidential Unit Citation. Of 272 engineers, 111 were killed or wounded, almost all in the first half-hour. Yet their gallantry was largely wasted, by hastiness in planning. The fault lay with the markers they had been given. Some of the buoys and posts they had brought to mark the gaps were lost or broken in the landing.

The posts which they set up at the top of the beach were easily knocked down and were not conspicuous enough to be seen through the smoke from seaward. The buoys, which they laid on each side of each gap, were ordinary metal dan buoys with a spar and a flag on top; but they could be punctured and sunk by a single rifle bullet and instead of being port and starboard buoys they were all the same colour, so that when one was sunk, nobody could tell which side of the gap was marked by the one which remained. So when the tide had risen and covered the obstacles, the gaps which had been made by such sacrifice were practically impossible to find. All the morning, landing craft skippers milled around off-shore looking for buoys and posts and most of them, knowing that gaps had been planned, hesitated to trust to luck and charge the obstacles. [9]

'In the initial plan the NCDUs (Naval Combat Demolition Units) were to destroy a path through the beach obstacles while they were protected by being partially under water; but that plan was scrapped when more and more obstacles began appearing in the spring of 1944. It was then that the US Army Gap Assault Teams were formed and were trained by the NCDUs. Gap Assault Team 8 included 25 army engineers, two medics and the Officer in Charge, plus NCDU 137 which included Ensign Harold P. Blean, six seamen and five army engineers. 'After spending a miserably cold and seasick night in the English Channel on 4 June, the invasion fleet reversed course about midnight and we returned to Portland. We left Portland again on the evening of the 5th. Rough seas kept us wet and cold, as well as seasick, although the Sherman tanks did afford some protection from the waves and spray. Sergeant Bill Grosvenor slept with the navy crew and gave his dry bed to me; a lifesaver, as mine was soaked! Around midnight, Grosvenor persuaded the navy cooks to provide us with a hot meal. Except for a D-Ration chocolate bar which was upchucked 22 hours later, it would be my only food for that entire period.

'The four support Gap Assault Teams crossed the channel on the Princess Maude. Sergeant Paul Gray said that the food was less than appetizing - 'slop' he called it. At the appointed time, sometime after 0400, the support teams also crawled down rope ladders and jumped into their bobbing LCM. One man failed to follow directions and had his legs crushed when he crawled down too far and was caught between the bobbing landing craft and the Princess Maude. In the dark at about 03:30 and carrying all of our gear, we scrambled down the heavy rope landing nets into our wildly bobbing LCM and then left for our assembly area. There we circled around for over an hour, waiting for the signal to head on in. Most of us were so miserably seasick by then that we almost welcomed the chance to debark on any old beach. We saw a number of our bombers overhead. Later, as we circled around marking time, we heard but didn't see the planes through the heavy mist; and we saw no bombs saturating the beach as promised. The only bomb crater seen by me that entire day was the one that was fortuitously placed right where needed - almost dead centre in the obstacle demolition area for Gap Assault Team 8 - a twenty foot diameter

9   *Dawn Of D-Day* by David Howarth (The Companion Book Club 1959).

'Super Foxhole' with its surrounding sand parapet!

'Suddenly we straightened out and headed for the beach - partially hidden by the fog and mist. Just as we passed close by west of her bow, I looked up at the name 'Texas' on a huge battleship. Moments later she fired a broadside from her 14 inch guns. The flame and dark brown smoke was a quite a spectacle in itself, but the blast was almost unbelievable and would have blown off my helmet had my chinstrap not been fastened. However, it did cure my seven-barf bag case of seasickness, demonstrating that seasickness is mostly mental! As we moved shoreward we could hear the distinctive 'whhuutuu-whhuutuu-whhuutuu' of those 14 inch shells as they passed overhead on their way to soften up the German gun emplacements.

'A few hundred yards off to our right at about 06:10, LCTRs (LCTs modified to fire high explosive rockets) cut loose with a number of volleys of several hundred rounds each. The boat's long axis was aligned toward the targets and the rockets were fired when at the proper distance from shore. We watched the winkling on the hill above the beach as hundreds of rockets gave the Germans their early morning 'wake up call'. Near the middle of 'Omaha', where we were heading, the rockets appeared to be hitting the hill beyond the beach and therefore were quite effective! As we approached the beach, I began seeing splashes in the water from the mortar, artillery and small arms fire, so I quickly lost interest in being an observer and ducked down behind the steel ramp and sidewalls. This was really fingernail-biting time, as detonation of our explosives by mortar or artillery fire would have been devastating. This unfortunate scenario was visited upon two Gap Assault Teams when their explosives were detonated prematurely. Two army teams must also have suffered similarly.

'As we came close in, our navy gunner began 'hosing down' the beach ahead with his twin .50 calibre machine guns, mounted near the stern of our LCM. This certainly was a morale booster, because as we approached the beach we saw several dead GIs face-down, bobbing and rolling in the surf. This was was just a few minutes after our infantry covering force had been programmed to be the first foot-soldiers ashore. These men may have been tankers in the DD tanks that sank in the heavy surf. Had they been in our initial infantry cover force, their under-the-chin assault gas masks should have kept them face-up in the water even though they drowned.

'There were no visible tankdozers or infantrymen near our landing area when we scurried from our LCM, five minutes' late from our planned landing time of 06:33. This had an adverse affect on our mission, as will be seen. Our tankdozer was late and I had thought that our infantry covering force was also late. (We had landed on Easy Green, approximately 200 yards west of our assigned spot and the infantry may have landed properly.) The fortified house near the mouth of Les Moulins Draw (D-3) was a short distance east. All eight primary Gap Assault Teams landed reasonably near their designated areas. Gap Assault Team 8 landed on Easy Green, a few hundred yards west of plan. Team 7, which was also scheduled for Easy Green, landed about 200 yards west of Team 8. Due to a strong eastward current and possibly because they were 'following the leader', all four support teams landed much later than scheduled. Team C landed on Fox Red at the extreme eastern end of 'Omaha'

Beach where the obstacles ended and the bluffs began. They were off target by about 4,500 yards. We began suffering casualties soon after landing, mostly from small arms fire, but our medics began taking care of the casualties where they lay. Many of the less seriously wounded didn't even bother calling for help. Minden Ivey, a rugged little Texan, took a bullet through the wrist, resulting in a compound fracture; but he kept right on shooting, refusing medical aid in favour of the more seriously wounded, although he did accept some assistance in reloading his M-1. Lieutenant Donald Latendresse, OIC of that Boat Team was hit in his lower legs by machine gun fire soon after the ramp came down. John Heenan and Albert Tucker left their protected location in defilade below the bluff and went back into the machine gun-swept surf to drag their boat team leader to safety. Both received the Distinguished Service Cross and both ended up in my 3rd platoon two months later. Great guys!

'As for Gap Assault Team 8, its members hurried inland 150 yards near our 'foxhole' and began placing the C-2 charges. Bill Garland, Earl Holbert, Bill Townsley, several NCDU members and I slid the rubber raft out of the LCM, containing the backup explosives and Bangalore torpedoes. It took some real tugging to skid out the raft, all the while sweating it out while presenting a stationary target with our backs to the enemy. Earl then pulled the raft eastward beyond the edge of our gap and tied the long small-diameter rope to one of the wooden obstacles. Running a zigzag path up to our Super Foxhole located midway between the wooden obstacles and the steel hedgehogs, I found Sergeant W. Grosvenor firing his M-1 at the fortified house near the mouth of D-3 Draw, attempting to suppress the machine gun fire coming from there. After a short discussion, I grabbed his big Signal Corps wire-reel containing the primacord ring main (two strands of primacord friction taped at two foot intervals to a small rope) and took off in high gear. Running in multiple short dashes and hitting the ground often, denied the enemy gunners an easy target. Bullets knocked splinters from the wooden obstacles overhead after I hit the ground - or so I heard later! I ran the ring main clockwise around the wooden obstacles and Garland ran his ring main around counter-clockwise. We square knotted the ring mains together where we met. We then joined the team, who had almost finished tying on the C-2 charges. Grosvenor apologized for not performing per plan. My response - 'we got the job done - end of conversation'. It was never mentioned again.

'While proceeding with the placement of the charges, I just happened to be looking eastward into the pre-sunrise sky, when an artillery round hit the sand sixty feet away. It ricocheted twenty feet into the air and its pointed nose was clearly visible against the morning sky before exploding. It split along its length and sent a two foot long 'V-shaped' chunk of steel flopping over and over toward the northeast! High explosive artillery rounds are designed to produce multiple high velocity fragments, so this was a faulty round; the result of slave labour sabotage? If so, it was much appreciated! We were under heavy small arms fire almost immediately and machine guns were tracking our movement. Three riflemen slinking to my left, in defilade behind the natural sandbank seawall above the high water line headed east toward the fortified house near the mouth of les Moulins Draw and may have been attempting to silence the enemy machine gun fire. Without warning and from ten yards behind, our tankdozer fired an HE round into the left jamb of the right window in the fortified house 200 yards to our left front; and me without earplugs! That silenced the machine gunners who had been giving us so much trouble. Until that blast I was unaware that Tankdozer 8 had finally landed - about 15 minutes late.

'Less than twenty minutes after landing, Gap Assault Team 8 had the fifty yard section of the wooden obstacles, consisting of posts and ramps, ready to blow. Garland and I tied 45-second detonators to opposite ends of the ring main, tossed out the purple smoke canisters as warning signals to the infantry and moved a short distance inland. The blast made quite a bunch of kindling and poles, but several of the obstacles were not destroyed in this initial effort. I suspect that the primacord ring main had been cut by the artillery, mortar, or small arms fire - or possibly by our tankdozer. We then tied 22 second detonators to opposite ends of the remaining ring main and tried again. Two posts survived that blast, so I ran back and attached an eight second detonator to the short fragment of ring-main, pulled the igniter and splashed shoreward in water up to mid-calf. Successful blast; our 50 yard gap was now clear through the wooden obstacles. Only the steel hedgehogs remained to be blown! Ensign Blean then asked what his NCDU team should do. Since the NCDUs had Hagensen packs and no 15 pound Tetrytol satchel-charges destined for use on the heavy steel hedgehogs, I released him and his 11-men navy/army NCDU team to take cover behind the sand bank sea wall. I noticed a soldier sitting upright on the sand fifty feet to the west, facing seaward at the water's edge. Small arms fire was kicking up the sand around him and I yelled for him to take cover behind one of the steel obstacles. Soon after, he slumped over on the sand and the water sloshing around him slowly turned a delicate pink.

'Heading for the seawall Tom Wilkins yelled for Jessie Cleveland to take cover from the heavy enemy fire. Jessie airily replied 'I'll still be going when you're dead and gone'! Soon after Tom was shot through the hip while attempting to rescue a wounded infantryman, for which he was awarded the Silver Star. Jessie was decapitated by a direct hit from a mortar round. His body was picked up the next day.

'By the time Garland and I moved shoreward to the hedgehogs, our demolition team had positioned the tetrytol satchel charges and tied them to the ring main and we were ready to watch them disappear as if being swept away by an oversized broom! Just as we were attaching the 45 second detonators to opposite ends of the ring main, an infantry LCVP landed 150 yards seaward near the east border of our gap. From a past experience I knew how deadly explosive-driven steel fragments could be; and in the 45 seconds until detonation, those men would be nestled in and around the hedgehogs about to be blown. So even though I agonized about a delay, I could not bring myself to shred our own infantry so the demolition was delayed and eventually postponed when the incoming tide inundated the hedgehogs before our infantry had cleared that area. My decision was a mistake. I could have reinforced the demolition warning to the infantry by tossing out an additional canister of purple smoke and/or sent a runner down to guide them further east on their way up to the sea wall. Flying steel may still have killed some of these men, but this might have reduced the overall death toll by allowing a succession of landing craft to quickly disgorge their men through our blown gap.

'As the water was lapping at our feet, we began gathering our wounded and transferring them past the three foot deep runnel to an area in defilade below the natural sand sea wall. Sergeant Roy Arnn (in charge of a mine detector crew) was lying on the sand. He had severe wounds from an artillery round which had landed so close by that his uniform was grey from the explosive residue. A chunk of meat had been gouged from the rear of his right thigh; and another artillery fragment had torn open and broken his right shoulder and clavicle, causing a bubbling puncture wound. He was also bleeding heavily from his forehead where the edge of his helmet had been driven down by the blast. Arnn's right arm and leg were useless, so he held on as we began hunching forward like wiggle worms on the sand. As we neared the runnel a machine gun burst splattered sand in our faces, so we slithered behind a nearby hedgehog with the Tetrytol still attached. The machine gunner found other targets of opportunity and we were then able to slip unnoticed into the runnel, now about four feet deep and 30 feet wide and cross with our noses just above the water. Arnn was carried up the bank and given further attention by our medics.

'Meanwhile, Boat Team 8 members had congregated near Tank dozer 8, just above the high water line near the natural sand sea wall. It must have gone back on to the beach and been disabled. Only one M-4 tank dozer, out of the sixteen, survived D-Day. Lademan had difficulty in getting his weasel started. Only after the others had departed was he finally able to drive it off. When he stopped and attempted to move aside a dead body that was floating in his path, Captain Doyle yelled 'run over him and get the hell out of here before you get us both killed'!

'After a quick check on my men I hurried eastward along the beach to find Lieutenant Colonel Isley for further orders. I had gone about 75 yards and as I stopped and twisted to my right to check again on my crew, a mortar round hit the shingle eight feet to my front. Had I not stopped, the mortar crew would have dropped that round on my helmet! There were small fragments in my right great toe, foot, instep, calf, both knees; and a slug of fragments in left mid-thigh. Being sideways to the blast reduced my exposure area and surely saved me from being further spiculed. The thigh wound was quite painful; possibly because the fragments were red hot and were travelling at fairly low velocities. Once an experienced mortar crew registers on a target, they normally fire several more rounds in rapid succession. Knowing that, I quickly hopped inland above the shingle, just as two more rounds dropped into the area just vacated. I had been scared spitless while in the LCM, but once we landed I was too busy to bother being terrified. Now finding I was not indestructible, I again became concerned about my welfare. I began digging a foxhole in the sand with my hands and then with my helmet - after slicing my hands on buried barbed wire - thus gaining protection from the fierce enemy fire. Max Norris found me sometime later and we enlarged the foxhole to a two man job. He then poured sulphanilamide powder into the thigh wound hole, bandaged it and gave me a morphine injection. Max then brought me up to date on our casualties. About 60% of our army team had been wounded; most not seriously. Arnn, Grosvenor and Lala were my major concerns. Two of our Charlie Company soldiers and Lieutenant Joe Gregory were killed on 'Omaha' that morning.

'Sometime after 0800 a landing craft unloaded a group of 1st Division men near Les Moulins draw in the 29th Division sector approximately 400 yards west of the 1st Division border. Once in defilade, they took a short time to organize and then began infiltrating up the hill. I'm not sure if they were the catalyst, but soon thereafter more and more infantrymen began to appear on the hill west of Les Moulins draw and were working their way inland.

'By 0900 the enemy fire had quieted somewhat, probably because the smoke from the brush fires, started by rockets on the hillside above, had reduced their visibility. This must have led some of our commanders to believe that this was now a safe beach! About 0945 an LCT landed and medics with Red Cross armbands clearly showing came ashore looking as if they were on their way to a Sunday school picnic! They were bunched together and talking and seemed in no hurry to get off of the beach. The Germans had the area well zeroed and several large calibre mortar or artillery rounds landed in rapid succession in their midst. Some, who did not get back on their feet, were probably killed.

'A while later I noticed a beached LCT, a short distance west, sending up a large column of black smoke. Soon after, an explosion below deck lofted a 2½-ton truck twenty feet into the air before it crashed almost upright back on the deck. The destroyers and other ships continued to furnish fire support against the pillboxes and other designated targets. I could not assess the effectiveness of their gunfire, but I'm sure that the Germans in those target locations were impressed! Since the navy gunners were firing over our heads, we were glad that they had good zeros.

'In late morning Colonel Isley found my foxhole as he was checking on his boat teams. Earlier as he was reconnoitring the beach with Joe Manning on his left and Sergeant Robert Campbell to his right, an artillery shell landed in their midst and Campbell was killed instantly. Joe Manning was unhurt, but an artillery shell-fragment ripped through the top of Colonel Isley's helmet, peeling back the steel as if it were a soup can. A large section was ripped out of the top of his helmet liner and the wool stocking cap beneath was frayed. However, except for a massive headache, he was unhurt. Good reason not to stand too tall!

'Until late afternoon, before being moved to an aid station in defilade on the west side of les Moulins Draw, I was a scared but wide-eyed spectator with a front row seat as the battle unfolded. I heard an occasional fighter plane overhead, but did not see them. At dusk a small boat rigged to carry stretchers laid across the gunwales, ferried the wounded out to the LST hospital ship anchored near Colleville Draw a mile to the east. The Channel was still rough so I was miserably seasick again and upchucked the chocolate D-Bar; my only nourishment since midnight. I was transferred by a derrick and sling on a wild ride up to the ship's deck and was soon settled in a comfortable bunk. A nurse pulled off the thigh bandage and a thin bloody fluid messed up the clean white sheets. I then discovered the small mortar fragments in my feet and legs - probably unnoticed until then due to the anaesthetizing effect of the cold water.

The navy doctors and nurses were superb and although we made snide remarks about their soft life on board ship with good food and comfortable beds - we appreciated them beyond mere words!

'Captain John K. Howard the Company 'B' commander and Sergeant Roy Arnn were nearby. I was happy to see Arnn, as I had been concerned that he might have been our first fatality. Howard had taken a bullet through his shoulder and he walked over and filled me in on the operation as he knew it. It was feared that a determined German counterattack might shove our forces back into the Channel. That this did not happen was due to some very brave infantrymen who overcame monstrous odds in attacking up the hill with little more than their M-1 rifles, grenades and a large supply of guts; to our outstanding naval gunfire support that decimated the defenders at the strongpoints; and to our superb fighter pilots who gave us such great overhead cover.'

2nd Lieutenant Wesley Ross, Company 'B', 146th Engineer Combat Battalion, Officer In Charge Gap Assault Team 8. [10]

'Somewhere in the English Channel we had to transfer from the LCT to our assault boat (LCM) which we had towed behind us. We each had a pack of plastic explosives (about 5lbs each) that we carried on our chests and backs. These could be used to blow up the obstacles on the beach. I also had a mine detector, my rifle, a coil of rope with a triple hook on it and a couple of rolls of tape that would be used to mark the gap or lane from the obstacles inland. The rope was to be used by throwing it ahead of me and then dragging it back to trip any booby trap wires, etc.

'We were all pretty sea-sick after getting into the assault boat because of the rough water and we were using the puke bags that we had around our necks. As the assault boat neared the beach, machine gun fire hit around the front of the boat and some of the sea-sickness left. When the ramp went down we started for the obstacles. I was one of the last ones off of the boat as we had to put a rubber raft, filled with plastic explosives, into the water so it could be taken to the beach. We waded in about two feet of the water to reach the beach. As I went through the obstacles I disposed of the plastic explosives that were on my back and chest and then hit the ground as a machine gun in a house to our left pinned us down. I was trying to get the mine detector out of the box but couldn't as the lid was jammed. There was no place to hide in the open and people in the house kept firing. As I got my rifle up to my shoulder to shoot, a tank came up out of the water. The gunner put a shell into the house. About the same time, a sniper shot at me. The bullet kicked sand in my face and passed under my left armpit, which caused me to flatten out. At the same time a shell from a German 88 artillery piece exploded near my feet. Had I not been flattened out, the shrapnel from the artillery shell would have probably killed me. Instead the shrapnel hit my right shoulder and leg. The explosion and concussion seemed to push me into the ground and knocked the breath out of me. The force of the explosion blew my helmet off and cut the corner of my left

10   '146 Engineer Combat Battalion – Essayons' by Wesley Ross.

eye. I soon lost sight in my eye because blood was running into it. I turned to look back of me and tried to yell to Corporal Lee to get a medic. He looked at me with astonishment and started screaming for the medic as though he were hit. Max Norris was the medic and as he tried to get the rifle from my shoulder; it hurt something awful. I found out later that the scapula and clavicle were broken besides the deep wounds in my shoulder and leg. He took my first aid kit and gave me a shot of morphine; also some sulpha drugs then bandaged my shoulder and leg. I must have been one of the first ones hit as calls for medics started coming from all over. As I lay there wondering just how badly I had been hit, the tide water started to go around me from the incoming tide. I tried to get up and run or crawl to the high water mark, but I couldn't get my leg to work. I fell back down a couple of times.

'The Germans were firing everything they could and Lieutenant Wesley Ross told me to stay down and he would come out to get me. He crawled out to me and I put my head on his butt and grabbed his leg. He crawled and dragged me to the high water mark where I stayed for most of the morning. As he left he was wounded in the leg. Later, some of the fellows in my unit got me on a stretcher and took me to the water's edge to put me on one of the small assault boats returning to one of the larger ships at anchor. About that time the Germans started hitting the beach with artillery so we started back to the high water mark. As the shells come near they dropped me to hit the ground and one of the shells hit so close that it blew me out of the stretcher and a small piece of shrapnel hit me in the little finger on my left hand. They loaded me back on the stretcher and left me at the high water mark as they had other work to do. I had prayed to God before we hit the beach that morning. Also, after I was hit and a few times more while lying in the sand and rocks unable to move about. Things on the beach did not look good. One soldier near me was crying and asking for his parents. Other wounded soldiers were nearby and also a couple of dead bodies that the tide had washed in.

'Some time that afternoon some fellows picked me up and moved me to an aid station. I guess I went into shock and started to shake. One fellow sat on me to keep me from bouncing off the stretcher. Soon after that Max Norris got me on an assault boat back to a LST. Many years later, Max (who became a doctor) told me that every time I breathed, bubbles would come from the wound in my shoulder as if my lung might be punctured, but it wasn't. I felt safer on the LST. The doctors cut my clothes off and I found out then how big the holes were in my shoulder and leg. The clothing consisted of two sets of pants with one treated in case of contact with some sort of gas and the other with a map made of a very thin material sown into the seat of the pants in case we were captured. These helped stop the bleeding in my thigh because a piece of my pants, about 6 inches square, had been jammed into the wound. The LST I was on had not unloaded and it made a run for the beach that evening with more shelling before we started back to England. Most of the wounded were on stretchers on the side of the tank deck. While I was about half asleep, Captain Howard, with his arm in a sling stopped to ask me how I was doing. He pointed out Lieutenant Ross sitting on a stretcher across the tank deck. The captain never said anything about a court martial.

'We arrived back in Southern England on the afternoon of the 7th or 8th. Evidently the doctors on the ship had tagged us in some manner, to identify us as critical, because as soon as we were unloaded three of us were rushed directly to an ambulance for delivery to a tent hospital. The driver drove so fast that one of the fellows told him to slow down because it hurt so much and the driver said, 'I don't want any of you fellows to die in my wagon.' I won't say what the fellow told him in response. We were in the tent hospital for a few more days before they put us on a train for a general hospital near Coventry. I was a bed patient for three months with soldiers from the 101st and 82nd airborne. My left eye was swollen and closed with a big black and blue mark covering the side of my head, where the helmet hit me as it was blown off. It was about a month before I could see from my left eye. My thigh was bandaged and my right arm was strapped to my chest so the bones would heal. Since my left hand was bandaged, someone had to feed me for about two weeks. The beard that I had grown was longer so one of the nurses was going to shave me. Instead of clipping the hair first, she took a safety razor and tried to shave me. She delicately put the shaver between two fingers and made one stroke, as the razor skipped it took hair and hide. A few days later a soldier came by with a straight edge and shaved me. After about two months my wounds had healed so that they could sew up my leg and shoulder; although I still had to remain in bed for another month. After three months they transferred me to a convalescent hospital for three months of rehan. When we had been told that we were all scheduled to go home, Eisenhower put out an order that anyone who could do any kind of work for two hours a day had to go back because of the Battle of the Bulge.'

Sergeant Roy Arnn, Boat Crew 8, 146th Combat Engineering Battalion. Roy was discharged from the Army and arrived home in Ruth on 15 December. He had planned to take the Dodge sedan he had bought on the day Pearl Harbor was bombed to drive to California to pick up his fiancée Oma, a Lieutenant in the Air Corps, so that they could get married but Oma quit her teaching job and came to Ruth on the bus. After Roy borrowed $100 from her, they were married New Years Eve.

'I was with the first wave at zero hour and one of the lone survivors of that day. I could not swim when we jumped off the LCI. I was tied to my platoon sergeant with a nylon rope. Imagine being sent on this type of mission when I couldn't swim. I also had a life preserver on. It was not so humorous then because I was too scared to even know my name. A lot of the guys were hit below the waist and lost the use of their arms or legs and the tide came in and got them before the medics got them. Another tragic thing I saw when I went back to the beachhead after it was secured - they had bodies stacked in rows like one would stack cordwood.'

Dale L. Shrop, part of a demolition squad of the 1st Engineer Combat Battalion attached to the 1st Division.

'At the water's edge the enemy is in search of cover behind the coastal zone obstacles. A great many motor vehicles - among these ten tanks - stand burning on the beach. The obstacle demolition squads have given up their activities. Disembarkation from the landing boats has ceased, the boats keep further seawards. The fire of our strong-points and artillery is well placed and has inflicted considerable casualties among the enemy. A great many wounded and dead lie on the beach.'

Oberst Ernest Goth of Wiederstandnest (WN) 76 at Vierville commanding 916th Regiment, to Generalleutnant Dietrich Kraiss at 352nd Divisional Headquarters near Littry. Kraiss was a veteran of WWI and in WWII had already fought in Poland and France and in the invasion of Russia. He was so convinced that the American attack on 'Omaha' had failed that he redirected his reserves to the 'Gold' Beach area. Following D-Day the Americans believed that they had eliminated the 352nd Infantrie Division but Kraiss had retreated to a new line 12 miles from the beaches and his division held its new position until reinforcements reached them in the line at St. Lô. By 25 July the 352nd would suffer 8,583 casualties, or 66 per cent of its D-Day strength. Kraiss died of his wounds on 6 August. He was awarded posthumous Oak Leaves to his Knight's Cross.

'Men they lay there motionless and staring into space. They were so thoroughly shocked that they had no consciousness of what went on. Many had forgotten they had firearms to use. Others who had lost their arms didn't seem to see that there were weapons lying all around them. Some could not hold a weapon after it was forced into their hands. Others, when told to start cleaning a rifle, simply stared as if they had never heard such an order before. Their nerves were spent and nothing could be done about them. The fire continued to search for them and if they were hit, they slumped lower into the sands and did not even call out for an aid man.'

Captain Richard F. Bush, 16th Infantry Regiment. The 16th Infantry had fought at Gettysburg, the Argonne, in North Africa, Sicily and Salerno. At the Battle of Gettysburg in July 1863 three Virginia Brigades took part in Pickett's Charge, which ended in slaughter and has been called the 'high water mark' of the Confederacy because it represented the supreme bravery and daring of its troops and its commanders, but no army could withstand such a shock as this…' The writer might just as easily have been referring to 'Omaha' Beach.

'At approximately 0345 hours the 2nd Battalion and the 3rd Battalion debarked from the USS *Henrico* and HMS *Empire Anvil* respectively to assault beach 'Omaha', north of Colleville-sur-Mer, Normandy, France at 0630 hours. Heavy seas, numerous underwater obstacles and intense enemy fire destroyed many craft and caused high casualties before the assault battalions reached shore. Most supporting weapons, including DD tanks, were swamped. The 2nd Battalion landed 100 yards to 1,000 yards from its scheduled points, was pinned down on the beach by extremely heavy fire from concrete fortifications, machine-gun emplacements and sniper nests which remained intact through severe naval and air bombardment. Casualties were extremely high.'

Part of the US 16th Infantry Regiment's Report.

'At about 04:00 we began boarding the LCA that would take us to the shore in the first wave of the assault. Each had thirty men on board. Once on board, our LCA was lowered into the water, which was very rough. One of the LCAs from our ship capsized just after it entered the water and six of the men were drowned. Once our boat was in the water, we proceeded to the staging area where we circled for about an hour or more, until all of the landing craft were ready for the assault. I carried 30 pounds of TNT, twenty clips of ammunition, a combat vest, pills, K-rations, special clothing in case of a gas attack, a shovel and a lot of other equipment. In all, the gear weighed about 75 pounds while I weighed 170. We were told we would have to run across 300 yards of open beach while under machine gun and artillery fire and we knew that casualties would be high. I was a member of a demolitions squad consisting of five soldiers and our assignment was to destroy the concrete bunkers built into the beach from which German machine guns fired.

'Once all landing crafts were on line we headed for the beach. To both my right and left and as far as I could see, landing crafts were headed at full speed to the coastline. With the sun rising, it was a remarkable sight. Almost immediately, we came under fire. Within minutes, for some reason, our boat started to take on water and we began to lag behind the other landing crafts. About seventy-five yards from the shore, with our boat sinking, our platoon commander, Lieutenant Kenneth Klink, gave the order to abandon ship. Just as he gave the order, we took a direct hit by an artillery shell to the middle of the craft, killing a number of men instantly. The ramp was dropped and those who were able began to get out. Several more men were killed or drowned as they exited the front of the boat. Some men climbed over the side. I had been seated in the back and attempted to the exit ramp at the front. I had to step over the bodies of my fellow soldiers and friends who were now lying dead on the floor of the boat. As I got close to the ramp I was hit by a large wave that knocked me all the way to the back of the boat. Again, I made my way to the front and managed to leave the boat just as it was sinking behind me. I was the last man off. As I stepped off, another large wave hit me and I went completely under the water. With the weight of all the gear on my back, I began to sink fast and knew that I was about to drown. Fortunately, I was able to get my pack off and reach the surface of the water. I then swam to shore.

'As badly as things had begun for me, once I made it to the beach, it got worse. The entire beach was a killing field. Artillery and machine gun fire were exploding all around me. Men were lying dead and wounded on the beach. Since I had lost my rifle along with my gear, I picked up a rifle lying on the beach and began running forward with the aim of reaching a three to four foot high sea wall about 200 yards inland. Because I no longer had the heavy pack on my back, I was able to cover a lot of ground fast. As I was running across the beach, machine gun bullets began whizzing past me and hitting the ground just inches from my feet. Thinking that a German machine gunner had me as a target, I hit the ground. I laid there motionless, hoping that he would think he had killed me and stop firing in my direction. It must have worked because the bullets that had been landing right next to me stopped. After a few seconds, I got up and continued running. Just as I got to within about twenty feet of the sea wall, I heard an artillery shell pass over my head and I immediately hit the ground again. It landed about fifteen feet behind me and exploded. Shrapnel passed over me but hit five men who had just reached the sea wall in front of me. Two of the men were killed instantly and three were wounded, including our company commander, Captain John Armellino, who subsequently lost his leg as a result of the explosion. I got up again and ran the remaining distance to the sea wall and the minimal shelter that it offered. Somehow I had made it across the beach. Of the thirty men from my landing craft, only twelve were now left. The invasion had been underway for about an hour.

'I then discovered the rifle I had picked up from the beach wouldn't fire, probably due to being clogged with sand. I picked up a second rifle that was on the beach close to the sea wall. This one wouldn't fire, either. After the third rifle I found wouldn't fire, I realized I would have to clean it in order to have a functioning weapon. So, while still behind the sea wall, I stripped down the M-1 and cleaned the trigger housing with a toothbrush that I still had from one of my pockets. That one worked. Lieutenant Klink, who had also successfully crossed the beach, took charge of what was left of our platoon and we began climbing a hillside in an attempt to accomplish the mission. After proceeding a short distance, we had to retreat back to the beach because the hillside was on fire and there was no way forward. As we were returning, I pointed out an area to Lieutenant Klink where I had seen Lieutenant Montieth's 2nd Platoon, also of Company 'L', go to get off the beach.[11] Lieutenant Klink decided that we would proceed in the same direction.

'As we started to climb the hillside, we were blocked from advancing by a heavy mass of barbed wire. I went back down to the beach where I was able to find a bandoleer torpedo and returned with it to our position. We then used the torpedo to detonate the obstacle and, with our path cleared, continued our advancement. Soon after we began to move forward again we became engaged in a hand grenade battle with the Germans at the top of the ridge. Because of the steepness of the hill, most of the grenades the Germans were throwing rolled down the hill past me before exploding. Unfortunately, one grenade rolled to within less than ten feet of me and the explosion blew me off my feet. I was thrown about five feet in the air and landed hard on my back. As I was getting up, I heard Lieutenant Klink give the order to fix bayonets. We then continued up the hillside and a short time later knocked the Germans out and secured the area. It wasn't until then that I realized I had been wounded by shrapnel in my left leg from the grenade. A medic treated my wounds and that night I was evacuated to a hospital ship.

'At the start of the day, my company consisted of 187 men. By nightfall, only 79 were left. For me, the day had been frightening, exhausting and painful in many ways. Yet, I was more fortunate than many others - I had survived.'

22-year-old Pfc James H. Jordan, 1st Platoon, Company 'L', 3rd Battalion, 16th Infantry Regiment, 1st Division. For his actions on 6 June he was awarded the Silver Star, Bronze Star and Purple Heart. In July, after

---

11   1st Lieutenant Jimmie W. Montieth was killed a few hours later. He was posthumously awarded the Medal of Honor for his heroism that day.

recovering from his wounds, he rejoined his unit at St. Lô, where he was again wounded, this time severely. He was evacuated to England and eventually back to the United States where he spent approximately one year recovering in a hospital in Richmond, Virginia.

'I had 20lb of explosives strapped to my back. I was supposed to blow up a block-house and what with the TNT and everything else that was strapped to me, when I stepped off the LCT I went up to my neck in water. There were bullets pinging into the water all around me... and then I got on to the beach and I lay there right next to my company commander. He looked at me and he said, 'What are you doing?' and I said, 'Same thing as you, sir.'

Pfc John Dandker, who was trapped for five and a half hours on the beach before he got the order to go across the open beach. 'They were shooting but we got the order, we just had to go; that's what we were trained to do. You are ordered to advance and so that's what you do.'

'On D-Day our target was Coutances, a small town in the Cherbourg area that held a communications centre. The area was covered with an overcast to about 13,000 feet. We did not want to drop the bombs because we were afraid of hitting our own troops who had advanced in from the beachhead which was well established.'

28-year old Harry Reynolds from New York, bombardier/navigator on B-24 Liberator The Hot Rock in the 491st Bomb Group. Out of the 446 Liberators sent to bomb 13 targets on or about 'Omaha' Beach 329 dropped more than 1,000 tons of bombs. None hit the beach or German positions guarding the beach exits.

'The Air Corps might just as well have stayed home in bed for all the good that their bombing concentration did.'

An officer in the 1st Bomb Division, 8th Air Force.

'That's a fat lot of use. All it's done is wake them up.'

Captain Logan Scott-Bowden, Royal Engineers, who with Sergeant Bruce Ogden-Smith of the Special Boat Section, just before D-Day, had swum ashore from the midget submarine X-20 to make sure that the sand on 'Omaha' Beach was firm enough for tanks. The equipment they took was simple and included a reel of fine sand-coloured fishing line with a bead on it at every ten yards. The fishing line and the reel had been made in Ogden-Smith's father's workshops in the neighbourhood of St. James Palace where the family had made fishing tackle for nearly 200 years. Scott-Bowden had reported back to General Bradley at Norfolk House in St. James Square, 'Sir, I hope you don't mind my saying it, but the beach is a very formidable proposition indeed and there are bound to be tremendous casualties. Bradley replied, 'I know my boy, I know.' Scott-Bowden's work resulted in the award of an immediate DSO.

'Our LCI and five other LCIs among LSTs and LCMs pulled up to the beach just at daybreak. We hit an obstacle in the water and were not able to get right up on the beach. I was on the bridge/conning tower with Lieutenant H. H.

Montgomery USNR, Neikerk, helmsman and W. R. Wilson, signalman. Wilson was a real clown. He kept us laughing. Our ship's complement included four officers and between 25-28 enlisted men. I was one of the senior men on board and these 18 year old fellows seemed terribly young to be fighting. My heart really went out to them. Mike Yakimo was the cook. John S. Spampinato, the bosun was from New York. Robert Clyde Hart, coxswain was from Tennessee. He had a coffee cup in his hand day and night. I teased him that it was permanently attached to his hand. Another coxswain, Frances Paul Scavetta was a jockey from New York. His mother used to send us salami. Willie Lee Edwards Jr was a black man from the south. Black people weren't allowed to have many high positions or ranks in the Navy. Willie served as steward for the officers. He was well received and popular among the crew. Willie was a boxer, not professional. He would box anyone willing just for fun. Joe Louis was his hero.

Suddenly all hell broke out. Montgomery yelled, 'Get off the bridge' and we abandoned the bridge immediately. The German bunkers that were supposed to have been blasted out in an air raid weren't. Fire started coming from everywhere. To make things worse, the water was very rough. We carried men from the 1st Division (the Big Red One) to 'Omaha' Beach. Wood timbers/cross ties and barbed wire were attached to mines. I saw a couple of dead men draped over these obstacles in the shallow water. Later I learned that these men were sent in to clear and mark channels for other landing craft and us.

'The fighting on the beach seemed to be the most horrendous for the first 5-6 hours. It eased up a little around what I thought seemed like lunchtime, but the shelling continued for two days. You should have seen my helmet. I wish I had saved it for my kids to see. I was told that the Germans wouldn't aim fire directly at men in the Red Cross helmets. A few hours into battle, I took my helmet off because I was certain they were aiming right at that Red Cross. I guess the German's figured for every hospital corpsman they took out, the more overall casualties there would be. Dead corpsmen can't save lives.'

'It seems a miracle that we did not lose one crewmember on our LCI on D-day. Sometimes the air was so full of fire that is seemed impossible that any of us survived. The mess hall and deck were filled with men from the Big Red One and soldiers on other landing craft alongside us. Travis Wilton 'Al' Allen, who was from Florida brought wounded men to me all day on the 6th and 7th of June. He never stopped even though he took a surface shot across the knee. He was a good young man. He probably saved more lives than we can count in those two days; literally hundreds and hundreds. I don't know how he maintained the stamina to keep bringing the injured from the beach onto the LCI. I patched these men up the best I could and got the really injured ones transferred to hospital ships. When Allen couldn't get the injured to me, I went to them on the beach. It was so loud with strafing, shelling and mortar fire. I'd yell, 'Look out behind you Allen!' Allen would yell, 'Hit the deck, Doc!' We looked out for each other.'

James Roland Argo, born and reared in Gadsden, Alabama, Pharmacist Mate 1st class, LCI 489. He turned 23 on 7 June. LCI (L) 489 was decommissioned in November 1944 in Edinburgh, Scotland.

'As we neared the shore we could hear the sound of the German artillery - not a very inviting sound. But since I was unaccustomed to anything like this I still didn't have enough experience to be scared.

'As we got nearer the shore I heard the shouts of personnel in the sea shouting 'help, help, help.' I thought to myself 'what can I do? When I jumped from the landing craft I too sank deep underwater. I walked along the sea bed, occasionally jumping up to the surface for air. After about 10 minutes of this I heard a huge blast. I turned around and the landing craft from which I had just disembarked went up in flames with about half my outfit still on board. I finally hit the beach and saw machine gun bullets kicking sand up in a trail which was racing toward me. I thought 'what can I do?' Answer: nothing, just stand there and wait for the inevitable, for that bullet to hit. I waited and waited. The bullets missed and I carried on into battle.'

'Dusty' Rhoads, a 22-year-old with the 6th Engineering Special Brigade.

'What we could see was mostly lots of dead and wounded soldiers. It was horrible to see them run into such a rampage of fire that they couldn't resist. My landing craft, with 50 men under my command on board, landed further to the left of where the 116th regiment had been butchered. The Australian skipper of the landing craft had made some more landings in the Pacific and he told us 'If I can't get you in dry, I'm not taking you in' and by golly he got right into the beach. He lowered the ramp and we stepped one foot in the water and the next on dry land. We got in with no opposition and got up on the high ground. Our landing, 15 metres to the left, really saved the day in terms of taking the beach.'

23-year old Lieutenant (later Brigadier General) Alvin Ungerleider, 115th regiment in the second wave to arrive at 'Omaha'.

'The beach was dotted by crawling bodies - the rest of our 100 men each running his own grim race with death. Sometimes they would stand up and run, falling instantly when a shell came near them. Sometimes they did not rise again. The beach was strewn with abandoned equipment. Almost instantly men had thrown away packs, which averaged little less than 100 pounds each. It was sheer idiocy to think of running such a gantlet with such an enormous burden. The ridge [shingle strip] seemed miles away, a hopeless beautiful paradise I could never possibly reach.'

Gordon Gaskill, a war correspondent who landed at 'Omaha' Beach in the first hours of the assault.

'A destroyer reported receiving word that the Germans were using a church tower at Vierville as an observation post. The Admiral ordered the ship to open fire. And the first salvo scored a direct hit, knocking off the upper part of the steeple. Another salvo and that observation post was eliminated.

'Nick Carbone, from Brooklyn, watched a great German shell skip in the water just between the *Texas* and a British cruiser. Imitating a famous American voice, Nick said, 'I hate war, Eleanor hates war.'

'Now, in rapid succession, our targets were: a mobile battery near Maisy, which we blew into limbo; German troop concentrations in the town of Formigny, which we scattered killing many; truck convoys centering on Trevieres, which we smashed completely; and tanks converging on woods near Surrain. In all of these, our RAF spotter, the daring and excitable Englishman, commended our shooting in rapturous tones.

'Finally, he said, 'Now I'll try to get you in a new target. I'm diving down to see if these tanks are friendly.'

'A few moments later: 'They definitely were not friendly. I'm baling out, good-bye!'

'So we sent for a new spotter and kept firing on targets of opportunity from Ste-Laurent-sur-Mer to Pointe-du-Hoc.'
Saturday Evening Post report from USS *Texas*.

'The warships were 600 yards offshore and firing flat trajectory at the German gun emplacements above us with eight to 12-inch shells. The emplacements were being completely destroyed and chunks of cement as big as a foot square were falling all around us and on us. The shells were coming in no higher than 100 feet over our heads. They hit and blew that cliff right out.

'I remember distinctly taking my trench knife and pressing it into people's backs to see if they were alive. If they were alive I'd kick them and say, 'Let's go!' Later it dawned on me, after I'd checked a few, that some of them were alive, but they couldn't turn around - just absolute terror!'
Lieutenant John Carroll, 16th Infantry.

US Assault Divisions 'Omaha' Beach
V Corps
Major-General Leonard T. Gerow
29th US Division

115th Infantry Regiment	116th Infantry Regiment

1st US Division
Major-General Clarence R. Huebner

16th Infantry Regiment	18th Infantry Regiment
116th Regimental Combat Team (Attached)	

111th Field Artillery Battalion	81st Chemical Battalion
741st Tank Battalion	7th Field Artillery Battalion

Beach Timetable
Objective: The only breaks in the 100-foot high cliffs running between 'Utah' and 'Gold' Beaches were at 'Omaha' Beach. The landings at 'Omaha' are therefore vital to connect the US troops at 'Utah' Beach with the British and Canadian beaches to the east. Allied planners proposed an intense pre-landing bombardment. Before dawn at 05:55 hours, 329 B-24 Liberators would hit the beaches and this would be followed by a naval bombardment by the battleships USS *Texas* (flagship) and *Arkansas*, the French cruisers FFS *Montcalm* and FFS *Georges Leygues* and HMS *Glasgow*. In addition, 11 destroyers would provide close range support. The command ship, the USS *Ancon*,

would be in position about 13 miles offshore at 02:50 hours.

0220 Fire support ships led by the battleships *Texas* (flagship), *Arkansas*, two French cruisers, FFS *Montcalm* and FFS *Georges Leygues* and HMS *Glasgow* arrive.

0250 USS *Ancon* takes up position about 13 miles offshore. Assault elements of 1st and 29th Divisions in 16 large transports, 205 beaching craft and numerous small craft arrive.

0355 Minesweeping by British and Canadian minecraft, which began before midnight, ends.

0430 Naval Force 'O' (Rear Admiral John L. Hall Jr.) concerned about fire from coastal batteries, begin lowering assault craft 12 miles off shore (the British are lowered less than 8 miles from shore). Leading assault craft have to start their run in while it is still dark. The heaviest landings are to be made directly in front of the enemy strong-points covering the natural exits off the 4-mile long beach instead of between them. Bradley and his staff will rely on a heavy aerial and sea bombardment followed by a direct assault by troops to swamp the fortifications, which are believed to be under-manned.

0520 First landing craft carrying the 116th Infantry Regiment of the 29th Division and the 16th Infantry of the 1st Division set off.

0535 Two companies of the 741st Tank Battalion destined for the eastern half of 'Omaha' were to begin launching their 32 DD Shermans 6,000 yards out from the shore. The DD tanks should have been launched from about 2 miles off shore so that faster LCIs and LCAs would not reach the shore before them and be deprived of immediate armoured support. 27 are lost when they are broached and they sink in 100 feet of water. 33 men drown. Three tanks are spared the ordeal by the jamming of the ramp of the landing craft and were carried in. Two make the shore. The 32 DD tanks of the 743rd Tank Battalion are not launched because of the rough sea and in their eight landing craft are taken all the way to the beach. At least ten LCVPs (Higgins Boats') that are top-heavy with guns, ammunition, sandbags and men on board are lost when they are swamped or roll over in the sea during the run in. Waves swamp eleven of the thirteen DUKW amphibious trucks carrying the 105mm howitzers of the 111th Field Artillery Battalion of the 116th RCT, most of them when still circling in the rendezvous area. Of the 13 DUKWs being used to carry this unit in, five were swamped soon after disembarking from the LCT, four were lost as they circled in the rendezvous area waiting to land and one capsized as they turned for the beach. Two were destroyed by enemy fire as they approached the beach and the lone survivor managed to offload its howitzer to a passing craft before it also succumbed to the sea. This one gun eventually landed in the afternoon. The commanding officer of the 111th Field Artillery, who had landed ahead of his unit, was killed as he tried to direct the fire of one tank. The 1st Division's Cannon Company of the 16th Infantry lose all six of its 105mm howitzers in DUKWs. The 7th Field Artillery Battalion is unable to land any guns, most of them also sinking in DUKWs.

0550-0625 USS *Texas* and other gunfire support ships pound the beach exit leading to Vierville amid low cloud and bad visibility and smoke and dust makes further identification of targets difficult. Rocket ships open fire at extreme range and most fall short among the landing craft. USS *Arkansas* and HMS *Glasgow* pound the Les Moulins area; French cruiser *Georges Leygues* and other ships hit Ste-Laurent plateau. The weather and smoke and dust also hamper aerial bombardment and bomb release is delayed to avoid hitting US troops. Most tonnage dropped by 484 B-24 Liberators lands 3 miles inland.

0630. First Allied troops to land are 16th Regimental Combat Team (1st Division) and 116th Regimental Combat Team (29th Division), 2nd and 5th Ranger Battalions. Less than half the companies in assault battalions are landed within 800 yards of their sectors. In the first wave eight companies (1,450 men of the 1st Infantry Division in 36 landing craft) head for the beaches in heavy seas. Infantry storm ashore without sufficient armour and suffer terrible losses as they are pinned down on the beach by the 352nd Field Regiment. It takes some companies' survivors 45 minutes to reach the cover of the sea wall.

0700 Chaotic situation on the beach, as troops are pinned down and take cover behind mined beach defences. Engineers are unable to clear obstacles. 40 per cent of the 270 specially trained demolition men are killed or wounded. Only six of the 16 armoured bulldozers reach shore and three are immediately destroyed. One is unable to manoeuvre because of the infantrymen who cling to its shelter. 25-year-old Private Carlton Barrett of the reconnaissance platoon of HQ Company 18th/1st Infantry wades ashore in neck-deep waves and then returns under fire to rescue floundering comrades who are close to drowning. Ashore during the day, he works as a guide, a runner and assists the wounded and those unable to care for themselves. For his actions and inspiration he is one of three men on the 'Omaha' landings who are awarded the Medal of Honor.

0730 The second wave of troops adds to the confusion and over-crowding on 'Omaha' Beach. Two companies of 2nd Rangers, in the first wave, coming in on the edge of Dog Green around 06:45, did manage to reach the seawall, but at the cost of half their strength. Survivors of Charlie Company 2nd Rangers have, by 07:30, scaled the cliffs near Dog White and the Vierville draw. They are joined later by a miss-landed section from B/116 and this group spends the better part of the day tying up and eventually taking WN73 defending draw D-1 at Vierville. The 1st Battalion's B/116, C/116 and D/116 were due to land in support of A/116 at Dog Green. Three boats, including their HQ and beach-master groups, landed too far west, under the cliffs. Exact casualties in getting across the beach are unknown, but one-third to half that make it spend the rest of the day pinned down by snipers. Not all sections of the badly scattered B/116 land there, but those that do are quickly forced to join those survivors of A/116 fighting for survival at the water's edge. To the left of Dog Green sits the Dog White sector, between the Vierville and Les Moulins strongpoints (defending draws D-1 and D-3). C/116 find themselves alone at Dog White with only a handful of tanks from the first wave in sight. Smoke from grass fires cover their advance up the beach. They gain the seawall with few casualties. Although the 1st battalion is effectively disarmed of its heavy weapons when D/116 suffers a disastrous landing, the build up at Dog White continues. C/116 are joined by the 5th Ranger battalion almost in its entirety. The Ranger commander, recognizing the situation at Dog Green on the run-in, orders the assault craft to divert into Dog White. Smoke covers their advance too, although the 2nd Rangers are caught out on the right flank of the Ranger's landing. The 116th RCT regimental command group, including the 29th Division assistant commander Brigadier General Norman Cota, is able to land relatively unscathed.

0740 5th Ranger Battalion lands on beach.

07:50 C/116 leads the charge off of Dog White between WN68 and WN70 by forcing gaps in the wire with a Bangalore torpedo and wire cutters. 20 minutes later, the 5th Rangers join the advance and blow more openings. The command party establishes themselves at the top of the bluff and elements of G/116 and H/116 join them, having earlier moved laterally along the beach and now the narrow front has widened to the east.

Between 07:30 and 08:30 Elements of G/16, E/16 and E/116 come together and climb the bluffs at Easy Red between WN64 (defending Exit-1) and WN62 (Exit-3). On the eastern-most beach, Fox Green, elements of five different companies become entangled and the situation is little improved by the equally disorganized landings of the second wave. Two more companies of the 3rd battalion join the melee and having drifted east in the first wave, I/16 finally make their traumatic landing on Fox Green, at 08:00. Two of their six boats are swamped on their detour to the east and as they came in under fire, three of the four remaining boats are damaged by artillery or mines and the fourth is hung up on an obstacle. A captain from this company finds himself senior officer and in charge of the badly out of shape 3rd Battalion.

From 0810 hours The destroyers of DESRON 18 begin to break the cease fire order that suspend naval gunfire support at 0630 hours. The attack up the cliffs begins, assisted by tanks and destroyers firing from close inshore.

0830 Rangers and 116th Infantry reach top of the cliffs at Les Moulins. Movement inland halted in the western sector and little movement in the east. Congestion on the beach becomes so great that the head beachmaster orders no more boats to land until it is cleared. 'Omaha' is on the point of catastrophe. The absence of special tanks offered by the British to demolish fortifications and obstacles and lack of sufficient DD tanks and heavy bulldozing equipment means lightly armed troops have to make frontal assaults on pillboxes and strong-points without armour. US casualties are heavy but the Germans cannot halt the attack and on the second tide of the day 25,000 more men and 4,000 vehicles are ashore. 5th Rangers blast a hole in the sea wall and 35 men get behind the defenders.

Before 09:00 Small parties from F/116 and B/116 reach the crests just east of Dog White. The right flank of this penetration is covered by the survivors of the 2nd Rangers' A and B companies, who have independently fought their way to the top between 08:00 and 08:30. They take WN70 (already heavily damaged by naval shells) and join the 5th Rangers for the move inland. (The 5th Ranger battalion is halted in its advance inland by a single machine gun position hidden in a hedgerow. One platoon attempts to outflank the position, only to run into another machine gun position to the left of the first. A second platoon dispatched to take this new position runs into a third and attempts to deal with this met with fire from a fourth position. The success of the MLR in blocking the movement of heavy weapons off the beach means that, after four hours, the Rangers are forced to give up on attempts to move them any further inland). The 3rd battalion 116th RCT forces its way across the flats and up the bluff between WN66 at Les Moulins and WN65 (defending Exit-1). They advance in small groups, supported by the heavy weapons of M/116, who are held at the base of the bluff. Progress is slowed by mines on the slopes of the bluff, but elements of all three rifle companies, as well as a stray section of G/116, gain the top by 09:00, causing the defenders at WN62 to mistakenly report that both WN65 and WN66 have been taken. More than 600 American troops, in groups ranging from company sized to just a few men, have reached the top of the bluff opposite Dog White and are advancing inland. On Fox Green at the eastern end of 'Omaha', four sections of L/16 have survived their landing intact and are now leading elements of I/16, K/16 and E/116 up the slopes. With supporting fire from the heavy weapons of M/16, tanks and destroyers, this force eliminates WN60 defending F-1; by 09:00, the 3rd battalion 16th RCT is moving inland.

0900 Captain Sanders, commander of DESRON 18 in USS *Frankford* orders his destroyers to close on the beach and support the assault troops.

09:05 German observers report that WN61 is lost and that only one machine gun was still firing from WN62. 150 men, mostly from G/16, having reached the top hampered more by minefields than by enemy fire, continue south to attack the WN63 command post on the edge of Colleville. Meanwhile E/16 led by Second Lieutenant John M. Spalding, turn westward along the top of the bluffs, engaging in a two hour battle for WN64. His small group of just three men effectively neutralizes this point by mid-morning, taking 21 prisoners, just in time to prevent them from attacking freshly landing troops.

0925 General der Artillerie Erich Marcks's HQ reports, 'The forward positions in the area of 352nd Division have been penetrated but the situation is not so critical as in the area of 716th Division,' i.e. between Bayeux and Caen. It is for this sector that Marcks requests immediate counter-action by Panzer divisions. By 09:30 the 16th regimental command post is established just below the bluff crest and the 1st and 2nd battalions of the 16th RCT are being sent inland as they reach the crest.

0930 A signal from the troops ashore to Major-General Huebner says: 'There are too many vehicles on the beach; send combat troops. 30 LCTs waiting off-shore; cannot come in because of shelling. Troops dug in on beaches, still under heavy fire.'

0948 USS *McCook* destroys a 75 mm gun position in WN74.

0950 Rear-Admiral Carleton F. Bryant, Naval Gunfire Support Group 'O', orders his 17 US, British and French ships in closer to provide artillery support for the beleaguered troops on 'Omaha'. 'Get on them men, get on them. We must knock out those guns. They are raising hell with the men on the beach and we can't have any more of that. We must stop it.' Employing pairs of Spitfires to air spot because of the absence of any surviving fire control officers, at least eight destroyers - *Baldwin, Carmick, Emmons, Frankford, Doyle, Harding, Thompson* and *McCook* - some as close as 800 yards from the beach, open up on inland strong-points and batteries. *Texas* (Bryant's flagship) and *Arkansas* between them fire 771 rounds of 14-inch shells (1,400lbs each). (Part of the naval effort, especially the *Arkansas,* had been directed against heavy German batteries far out on the flanks which threatened the sea approaches but did not affect the beach). (An engineer, who had landed in the first wave at Fox Red, watching the *Frankford* steaming in towards shore, thought she had been badly hit and was being beached. Instead, she turned parallel to the beach and cruised westwards, guns blazing at targets of opportunity. Thinking she would turn back out to sea, she had instead begun backing up, guns still firing. At one point, gunners aboard the *Frankford* saw an immobilized tank at the water's edge, still firing. Watching the fall of its shot, they followed up with a salvo of their own. In this manner, the tank acted as the ship's fire control party for several minutes).

1000 elements of the 16th Infantry reach the top of the bluff overlooking 'Omaha' and then move laterally to attack enemy fortifications but in the absence of clear reports Lieutenant General Omar Bradley, 1st Army, on the USS *Augusta* orders Major Chester 'Chet' Hansen to the beach 11 miles distant in a landing craft to gain first hand situation report. Another staff officer reports landing craft milling around 'like a stampeded herd of cattle'.

1000-1100 The advance on Vierville-sur-Mer and Ste-Laurent gradually begins. The beach is very congested. Reinforcement regiments are due to land by battalion, beginning with the 18th RCT at 09:30 on Easy Red. The first battalion to land, 2/18, arrives at E-1 30 minutes late after a difficult passage through the congestion off shore. Casualties though, are light. Despite the existence of a narrow channel through the beach obstacles, the ramps and mines there account for the loss 22 LCVPs, 2 LCI(L)s and 4 LCTs. Supported by tank and subsequent naval fire, the newly arrived troops take the surrender at 11:30 of the last strong-point defending the entrance to E-1. Although a usable exit is finally opened, congestion prevents an early exploitation inland. The three battalions of the 115th RCT, scheduled to land from 10:30 on Dog Red and Easy Green, come in together and on top of the 18th RCT landings at Easy Red. The confusion prevents the remaining two battalions of the 18th RCT from landing until 13:00 and delays the move off the beach of all but 2/18, which had exited the beach further east before noon, until 14:00. Even then, this movement is hampered by mines and enemy positions still in action further up the draw. On the Dog Red/Easy Green boundary the defences around the Les Moulins strongpoint take a heavy toll on the remaining 2nd battalion, H/116 and HQ elements struggling ashore there. The survivors join the remnants of F/116 behind the

American troops on board LCIs (Landing Craft, Infantry) .

Mrs Ehlers flanked by her sons Staff Sergeant Walter Ehlers (left) and Staff Sergeant Rolland Ehlers (right) at home on leave in Manhattan, Kansas. It was five weeks before Walter found out what had happened to his older brother on D-Day. It gave him nightmares for fifty years.

General Eisenhower is all smiles for the camera but the devastating losses on Omaha prompted him to issue an order for B-26 Marauders of the Ninth Air Force to pound the beaches in an effort to stem what was considered impending defeat. Thankfully, the order could not be carried out and the Americans pinned down on the beach were not blasted to oblivion by their own air forces' bombs.

Train loads of anti-tank guns and howitzer mountings at a rail head in southern England.

Exercise 'Tiger' on Slapton Sands went almost to plan but it was no indication of the disaster to come on Omaha on D-Day.

Infantry landing craft pass the cruiser USS *Augusta* in the rough sea off Omaha.

Men, who had not had much sleep, were hungry and cold and unable to overcome sea-sickness on the two hour crossing to Normandy which in rough seas was misery for many.

Omaha beach at dawn on D-Day; the fire-swept beach ahead.

A famous image of GIs wading ashore on Omaha Beach with the bluffs behind the beach obstacles.

Waves of landing craft going ashore on Omaha Beach while others are pinned down at the water's edge and in the sand in front of the bluffs.

Robert Capa (born Endre Ernő Friedmann) was a Jewish-Hungarian combat photographer and photojournalist who covered five different wars: the Spanish Civil War, the Second Sino-Japanese War, World War II across Europe, the 1948 Arab-Israeli War, and the First Indochina War. He documented the course of World War II in London, North Africa, Italy, the Battle of Normandy on Omaha Beach and the liberation of Paris.

His images of Omaha Beach shot using a small, hand-held Contax camera during the landing on Easy Red by the first wave are among the most significant photographs ever taken under fire.

Only eight of Capa's images survived when the other 98 shots melted during processing by a young and inexperienced lab technician in London.

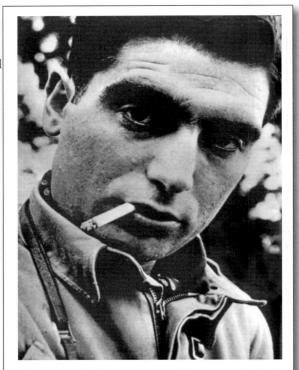

The one of the lone GI struggling in the water is Ed Regan, who recalled: 'Everything came apart. All that we trained for just seemed to go by the boards. And I was so exhausted physically and mentally that I just collapsed. It was a struggle not against the Germans; it was a struggle to survive, to save your life. And fortunately, I was able to do that.' .

Tracked vehicles going ashore after a toe-hold was finally established on Omaha Beach.

GIs look towards the approaching Omaha Beach after it had been taken at great cost on 6 June.

A German gun emplacement just prior to the landings.

Right: The beach secure, a GI looks down at a dead German defender outside one of the enemy resistance nests.

Below: : GIs bring one of their exhausted buddies ashore.

The exposed sweep of the beach at Omaha at low tide littered with a number of tanks and armoured vehicles.

A column of GIs in southern England on the march. Note the car driver who is indicating V-for Victory to the photographer.

The Enemy: Top: General der Artillerie
Erich Marcks. Middle: Freidrich
August Freiherr von der Heydte and
Left: Franz Gockel.

shingle and here the battalion commander is able to organize 50 men for an improvised advance across the shingle. However, a further advance up the bluffs just east of Les Moulins is too weak to have any effect and is forced back down. To their left, mainly between the draws on the Easy Green/Easy Red boundary, the 116th RCT support battalion lands without too much loss, although they do become scattered and are too disorganized to play any immediate part in an assault on the bluffs. At the eastern end of Easy Red another area between strongpoints allows G/16 and the support battalion to escape complete destruction in their advance up the beach. Nevertheless, most of G/16's 63 casualties for the day come before they reach the shingle bank. The other 2nd battalion company lands in the second wave; H/16 comes in a few hundred yards to the left, opposite the E-3 draw and are put out of action for several hours.

1030 Lieutenant Sidney Brinker commanding LCT30 and Lieutenant E. B. Koehler commanding LCI554 come ashore with all guns blazing at enemy strong-points, ramming their 400-ton craft through the beach obstacles.

1100 US soldiers enter Vierville-sur-Mer.

1130 Major 'Chet' Hansen returns to the *Augusta* and reports to Bradley: 'Disaster lies ahead.' Eisenhower issues an order to the Allied Air Forces to bomb 'Omaha' Beach at 1330 hours but fortunately, the order cannot be carried out.

1200 German defences are penetrated in four places. US troops begin to move inland, although the beach is still under heavy fire.

1330 Gerow signals Bradley, 'Troops formerly pinned down on beaches… advancing up heights behind beaches.'

1335 352nd Division reported to have thrown the Allies back into the sea from 'Omaha'. Observing the build up of shipping off the beach and in an attempt to contain what are regarded as 'minor penetrations' at 'Omaha', a battalion is detached from the 915th Regiment being deployed against the British to the east. Along with an anti-tank company, this force is attached to the 916th Regiment and committed to a counter attack in the Colleville area in the early afternoon. It is stopped by 'firm American resistance' and heavy losses are reported.

1400 The first beach exit is cleared. By early afternoon the strong-point guarding the D-1 draw at Vierville is silenced by the navy. But without enough force on the ground to mop up the remaining defenders, the exit cannot be opened. Traffic is eventually able to use this route by nightfall and the surviving tanks of the 743rd tank battalion spend the night near Vierville. The advance of the 18th RCT clears away the last remnants of the force defending the E-1 draw. When engineers cut a road up the western side of this draw, it becomes the main route inland off the beaches. With the congestion on the beaches thus relieved, they are re-opened for the landing of vehicles by 14:00. Further congestion on this route, caused by continued resistance just inland at Ste-Laurent, is bypassed with a new route and at 17:00 the surviving tanks of the 741st tank battalion are ordered inland via the E-1 draw.

1600 Tanks and vehicles begin moving inland from 'Omaha'. The F-1 draw, initially considered too steep for use, is eventually opened when engineers lay down a new road. In the absence of any real progress opening the D-3 and E-3 draws, landing schedules are revised to take advantage of this route and a company of tanks from the 745th tank battalion are able to reach the high ground by 20:00.

2000 Ste-Laurent and Colleville captured. Approaches to the beach exits are cleared, with minefields lifted and holes blown in the embankment to permit the passage of vehicles. As the tide recedes, engineers are also able to resume their work of clearing the beach obstacles and by the end of the evening, 13 gaps are opened and marked.

By nightfall Pockets of US forces cover an area approximately five miles wide by 1.5 miles deep. (At the start of the day it had been hoped that by nightfall V US Corps might have a beachhead 16 miles wide and 5-6 miles deep). Following the penetrations inland, confused hard-fought individual actions push the foothold out barely a mile and a half deep in the Colleville area to the east, less than that west of Ste-Laurent and an isolated penetration in the Vierville area. Pockets of enemy resistance still fight on behind the American front line and the whole beachhead remains under artillery fire. At 21:00 the landing of the 26th RCT completes the planned landing of infantry, but losses in equipment are high, including 26 artillery pieces, over 50 tanks, about 50 landing craft and 10 larger vessels. (Of the 2,400 tons of supplies scheduled to be landed on D-Day, only 100 tons are actually landed. On D+1 1,429 tons of stores were landed). 2,500 Germans are taken prisoner. US casualties are the highest of all the beaches. (Casualties for V Corps are estimated at 3,000 killed, wounded and missing. The heaviest casualties are taken by the infantry, tanks and engineers in the first landings. The 16th and 116th RCT's lose about 1,000 men each). The 29th Division has 2,440 casualties, the 1st Division, 1,744, most of these in the first two hours. These are the highest American losses in one battle since the Battle of Antietam Creek in north-west Maryland in the American Civil War on 17 September 1862 when the Confederate forces of General Robert E. Lee were defeated. [12] The 352nd Division suffers 1,200 killed, wounded and missing; about 20% of its strength. The last reserve of the 352nd Division, an engineer battalion, is attached to the 916th regiment in the evening. It is deployed to defend against the expected attempt to break-out of the Colleville - Ste-Laurent beachhead established on the 16th RCT front.

Midnight Generalleutnant Dietrich Kraiss, commander of the 352nd Division, reports the total loss of men and equipment in the coastal positions, advises that he has sufficient forces to contain the Americans on D+1 but that he will need reinforcements thereafter, only to be told that there are no more reserves available.

---

12   The Bloodiest Day in American history resulted in 22,719 casualties; 12,401 to the Army of the Potomac and 10,318 to General Lee's Confederate forces.

'Few, if any, of the troops actually crossed the beach during the early hours of the forenoon. The supporting destroyers and gunfire-support craft stood in as close to the beach as the depth of the water would allow and engaged all the defensive installations which they could locate. Despite this, however, little progress had been made prior to 1100 when there was still considerable machine-gun fire, sniping, artillery and mortar fire on the beaches between the exits and opposite the exits the condition was critical. A number of enemy strong-points in the beach were still holding out and our troops were not able to move inland. The first encouraging news came at 1100 from a message to Commander Transport Division.

'In the early hours of the afternoon General Bradley knew from the signals coming in that the Americans were indeed making ground; the Big Red One was coming through.

'Had a less experienced division than the 1st Infantry stumbled into this crack resistance, it might easily have been thrown back into the Channel. Unjust though it was, my choice of the 1st to spear-head the invasion probably saved us 'Omaha' beach and a catastrophe on the landing.

'Although the deadlock had been broken several hours sooner, it was almost 1.30 pm when V Corps relieved our fears aboard the *Augusta* with the terse message: 'Troops formerly pinned down on beaches Easy Red, Easy Green, Fox Red advancing up heights behind the beaches.'

Rear Admiral John L. Hall Jr., Commander Task Force 124 (the 'Omaha' Beach Assault Force) strongly disapproved of the amount of air and naval bombardment used. Hall was recorded saying, 'It's a crime to send me on the biggest amphibious attack in history with such inadequate naval gunfire support.'

'We got twelve miles from Normandy and stopped. They lowered us down by hydraulic lift into our landing craft. We sat in our landing craft and never looked over the side until we got ready to get off that thing. When we landed in that water, we started to circle. That water was so rough. The guys were seasick. I saw water spilling up over the sides of the LCVP,[13] but believe me, I didn't raise up to look over it. It was splashing in on us from shells busting and rifle fire hitting our boat. But I never raised up. None of us did. We had been told there was a sand bar about 50 yards off shore. [We were also told] if our coxswain on our landing craft let that ramp down, don't let him do that. Make him go over sideways, but don't let him let the ramp down because people will drown. Well, that came to pass. A lot of people drowned that way. When we hit the sandbar, our platoon sergeant raised up and said, 'Hey, no, go over that thing sideways. It's a sandbar.' The guy twisted the landing craft around. When we got off, the water wasn't up to my knees. The tide was rising a foot every ten minutes and we had to get in damn quick because high tide would cover up the obstacles and we would be blown out of the water. They were firing at us with everything. When I hit that sand I got behind any obstacle I could. Guys would try to

13   A British landing craft for personnel and vehicles.

get behind stones as big as coconuts, anything you could get behind, maybe even as small as a baseball. You'd try to keep the bullets away.

'We were in the second wave. When we got to the beach, there were 2nd and 5th Rangers piling in with us at the same time. We had a regimental commander named Charles D. Canham and he went in leading us. He was our colonel. There he was firing. He got his rifle shot out of his hand and he reached down and used his .45. He was about 55 years old and was the bravest guy and one of the finest leader. We had lots of leaders. Our platoon leaders, our platoon sergeants, we had good leaders. There's no question. If we hadn't had good leaders, we would have never made it off of 'Omaha' Beach.

'My boat team was the first one to go over the sea wall; I saw some of my friends die. In my boat team of thirty men we had only lost about five or six men. We were lucky. God knows we were. We followed the line that the engineers had laid out and we got through. We went up the hill then went parallel to 'Omaha' Beach through this little town. Mingled in with us were the 2nd and 5th Rangers. They were scattered about and so forth. Of course, there was a lot of scattering about on 'Omaha' Beach. I dare say we were on the beach an hour and half with bullets were flying. Bullets nicked off of my helmet. One went through my ammo belt, but we moved out. We were following our leaders. The day after I walked up the beach and saw guys that you couldn't get your two hands between lying on the beach dead. They were there with their eyes open, their rifles out ready. They were solid in death.

'The first man I saw from my company to die was Gene Ferrara. He was the kid we teased about carrying $700-$800 in his wallet. I landed and told him to move up. He moved up and then I got ready to move up, too. We were going leaps and bounds, trying to get cover and get behind the sea wall. I moved up ahead of him and happened to look back. The tide was beginning to take him back; he had been killed.

'That night, as we started the digging in, we couldn't fire a shot. We couldn't do anything. I would dig a little while and my buddy, Jim Macy. He was sent back to the States, but he later died from wounds. I'd dig a while, sit and watch with my rifle across my lap. I began crying. I cried like a baby. He looked at me and he said, 'Felix, why are you crying?'

'Look, I've been thinking about how close to death and the things that I've seen today.'

'I don't know how we made it through it all. We could see Germans maybe two or three hundred yards away. We just kept quiet, so that they wouldn't see us. There weren't enough of us to defend anything. We just tried to lay low. Jim would say, 'Felix, I know exactly how you feel.' Then he would do the same thing.

'Each one of us had our own little battlefield. D-Day was D-Day and it was awful. It was chaotic. No one can realize it until they were right there to see it. But you hear so many tales about it. We were well trained, we had good leaders and the Lord God Almighty was with us.'
Felix Branham, 116th Infantry, 29th Division.

'I was assistant driver on a swimming tank. 'Armour usually followed the infantry in an invasion but we were going to sail in to the beach before our soldiers and take out the German machine-gun nests. In the water, our tanks just looked like small assault boats. We would be a big surprise for the Germans when we came out of the surf.

'In sight of the beach, my tank was the first to launch from the LCT. The other three tanks never made it into the sea. The canvas screens which kept the waves out and kept the swimming tanks afloat had been ripped on each one, so they stayed on board.

'The sea was pretty heavy, we'd never practised in that kind of weather and I'm not sure why they let us go. The swell was really big. One moment you'd ride a crest and get a view of the beach, the next you'd be at the bottom of a trough and see water all around you. The motor driving our twin propellers was working quite well, but the struts holding up the canvas screen started to buckle. I was bracing the strut on our right side but I was in no doubt we were in serious trouble. We were the first tank to sink. It went straight down with a big gulp, dragging a couple of guys down with it. They floated back up, but one of our life rafts didn't work at all and the other only half-inflated. The water was really cold and we just had to wait for the LCT we'd left only minutes before to pick us up again. Of the 32 tanks to launch out to sea, 27 sank.

'That lost firepower could have made a big difference to the soldiers fighting on 'Omaha'. The LCT sailed right up to the beach to drop the other three tanks and then we were taken back out to sea.'

24-year old Private First Class Bill Merkert, 741st Tank Battalion. The command group of the 741st tank battalion lost three out their group of five in their efforts. Additionally, the commander of the 743rd tank battalion became a casualty as he approached one of his tanks with orders. When naval gunfire was brought to bear against the strong-points defending E-3, a decision was made to try to force this exit with tanks. Colonel George Taylor ordered all available tanks into action against this point at 11:00. Only three were able to reach the rallying point and two were knocked out as they attempted to go up the draw, forcing the remaining tank to back off. According to the commander of the 2nd battalion, 116th RCT, the tanks '... saved the day. They shot the hell out of the Germans and got the hell shot out of them.' Only five tanks of the 741st tank battalion were ready for action the next day.

'On the morning of June 6 we were up before dawn on the deck of the *Chase*. I carried my lightweight typewriter strapped to my back, encased in a raincoat for waterproofing. My other impedimenta included a blanket, a canteen of water, a couple of boxes of K-rations and a notebook and pencil. I was to go ashore in the same landing craft with Brigadier General Willard Wyman, assistant division commander of the 1st, whose job it was to help organise the troops on the beach. His partner in this job was Brigadier General Norman Cota, assistant commander of the 29th Infantry Division.

'The first and second waves of troops - scheduled to land at 6.30 and 7.00 am - had been thrown into disorder. Boats swung from their courses and drove through gaps wherever they could find them. This was possible because between 7 and 8 am the tide rose eight feet in the Channel. But units landed far from their assigned sectors. Commanders were separated from their troops. Sections were fragmented. And those who landed were pinned to the beach by heavy machine gun, artillery and mortar fire.

'We rode the rising tide through one of the gaps and waded ashore at 8 am. As far as I could see through the smoke of battle, troops were lying along a shelf of shale. Ahead of us stretched mined sand dunes to the bluffs where the Germans were sheltered in their trenches, bunkers and blockhouses. There was no cover for the men on the beach. The Germans were looking down on them - and it was a shooting gallery.

Don Whitehead, *A correspondent's view of D-Day, 1971.*

'There were thousands of ships and airplanes. About 0300 the planes flew over. First they dropped bombs and next came the paratroopers. About two or three miles out from the beach, destroyers and cruisers sprayed the beachheads with gunfire. We were in the first wave to hit Normandy. We hit the beaches at high tide at 0530. After dropping the anchors we set down the ramp to let the soldiers off. We couldn't leave until high tide so we dug fox holes, removed the wounded and waited for the trucks to unload our ship. The crew aboard the LCT was the captain, Lieutenant John D. Allen from Youngstown, Ohio, boatswain (me), two electricians, two machinist mates, three or four gunners mates, one signal man and the cooks. One name I remember was Thaddeus Kadinsky from Pittsburg, Pennsylvania. Three boys had the last name of Green and were from Texas.

'After the tide came back in, we pulled our ship off the beach and went back to the Merchant Marine ship to reload. Some of the landing craft would hit sandbars. Thinking they were on the beach, they hurriedly jumped out. Many sailors were drowned. On the third wave, we carried in a ship that General George S. Patton was on.

'The enemy had pillboxes up in the cliff. They were loaded with guns, supplies and ammunition. There were tunnels running to the pillboxes. The only way our soldiers could get to the problem was to send up two tanks at one time. The first tank would be hit, but the next one would get up there and shoot the enemy before they could reload.

'After the beachhead was secured, we went through these tunnels. One soldier had his left arm shot off above the elbow. Still, he helped us load the wounded. We carried the wounded out to the hospital ship. A bulldozer came and dug trenches and buried the dead.'

James Hollis Bearden boatswain, *General George O'Squire.* 'A few months later, a few of us sailors decided we wanted to go see Paris. We stole a jeep off the ship. It was in a box and we had to assemble it. Since Navy personnel was not allowed in Paris, we borrowed some of the soldier's uniforms, dressed in them and took off for Paris. We were on the outskirts of Paris when we were stopped and asked for our identification. Needless to say, we never saw Paris. When the MPs saw our Navy ID's, we were placed in confinement until our ship's captain could be notified. We were there for five days before returning to the ship. I stayed in the Navy till the war was over. The only time I came home during these three years was after I finished boot camp.'

'On my boat, the USS *Chase*, the population fell into three categories: the planners, the gamblers and the writers of last letters. The gamblers were to be found on the upper deck, clustering around pair of tiny dice and putting thousands of dollars on the blanket. The last-letter-writers hid in corners and were putting down beautiful sentences on paper leaving their favorite shotguns to kid brothers and their dough to the family. As for the planners, they were down in the gymnasium in the bottom of the ship, lying on their stomachs around a rubber carpet on which was placed a miniature of every house and tree on the French coast. The platoon leaders picked their way between the rubber villages and looked for protection be the rubber trees and in the rubber ditches on the mattress.

'We also had a tiny model of every ship and low on the walls were signs giving the names of the beaches and the specific sectors: 'Fox Green,' 'Easy Red' and others, all parts of the 'Omaha' beach. The naval commander and his staff had joined the gymnasium and they were pushing the little ships around in order to reach the beaches that were painted on the walls. They pushed them, around very expertly. In fact, the more I looked at these bemedaled gents playing on the floor, the more I was filled with terrific confidence.

'I followed the proceedings on the gymnasium floor with more than polite interest. The USS *Chase* was a mother ship which carried many assault barges which it would release ten miles off the French coast. I would have to make up my mind and choose a barge to ride in and a rubber tree to hide behind on the shore. It was like watching a lot of race horses ten minutes before starting time. In five minutes the bets would have to be placed...'

Robert Capa. Having been with the 1st Infantry Division in Sicily he spent a difficult night on board USS *Chase* trying to decide whether he should accompany one of the assault companies from the 2nd Battalion or go in with Colonel Robert Taylor's Regimental Headquarters after the first waves of infantry.

'I would say that the war correspondent gets more drinks, more girls, better pay and greater freedom than the soldier, but that at this stage of the game, having the freedom to choose his spot and being allowed to be a coward and not be executed for it is his torture. The war correspondent has his stake - his life-in his own hands - and he can put it on this horse or that horse, or he can put it back in his pocket at the very last minute. On the one hand, the objectives of Company 'B' looked interesting and to go along with them seemed to be a pretty safe bet. Then again, I used to know Company 'E' very well and the story I had got with them in Sicily was one of the best during the war. I was about to choose between Companies 'B' and 'E' when Colonel Taylor... tipped me off that regimental headquarters would follow close behind the first waves of infantry. If I went with him, I wouldn't miss the action and I'd be a little safer. This sounded like a real favourite - an even money bet - two to one to be alive in the evening... I was a gambler. I decided to go in with Company 'E' in the first wave.

'Our pre-invasion breakfast was served at 3:00 am. The mess boys of the USS *Chase* wore immaculate white jackets and served hot cakes, sausages, eggs and coffee with unusual zest and politeness. But the pre-invasion stomachs were preoccupied and most of the noble effort was left on the plates.

'At 4 am we were assembled on the open deck. The invasion barges were swinging on the cranes, ready to be lowered. Waiting for the first ray of light, the two thousand men stood in perfect silence; whatever they were thinking, it was some kind of prayer.

'I too stood very quietly. I was thinking a little bit of everything; of green fields, pink clouds, grazing sheep, all the good times and very much of getting the best pictures of the day. None of us was at all impatient and we wouldn't have minded standing in the darkness for a very long time. But the sun had no way of knowing that this day was different from all others and rose on its usual schedule. The first-wavers stumbled into their barges and - as if on slow - moving elevators - we descended into the sea. The sea was rough and we were wet before our barge pushed away from the mother ship. It was already clear that General Eisenhower would not lead his people across the Channel with dry feet or dry else.

'In no time, the men started to puke. But this was a polite as well as a carefully prepared invasion and little paper bags had been provided for the purpose. Soon the puking hit a new low. I had an idea this would develop into the father and mother of all D-days.

'The coast of Normandy was still miles away when the first unmistakable popping reached our ears. We ducked down in the puky water in the bottom of the barge and ceased to watch the approaching coastline. The first empty barge, which had already unloaded its troops on the beach, passed on the way back and the boatswain gave us a happy grin and the V sign. It was now light enough to start taking pictures and I brought my first Contax camera out of its waterproof oilskin. The flat bottom of our barge hit the earth of France. The boatswain lowered the steel-covered large front and there, between the grotesque designs of steel obstacles sticking out of the water, was 'Easy Red' beach.

'My beautiful France looked sordid and uninviting and a German machine gun, spitting bullets around the barge, fully spoiled my return. The men from my barge waded in the water. Waist-deep, with rifles ready to shoot, with the invasion obstacles and the smoking beach in the background - this was good enough for the photographer. I paused for a moment on the gangplank to take my first real picture of the invasion. The boatswain who was in an understandable hurry to get the hell out of there, mistook my picture-taking for explicable hesitation and helped me make up my mind with a well-aimed kick in the rear. The water was cold and the beach still more than a hundred yards away. The bullets tore holes in the water around me and I made for the nearest steel obstacle. A soldier got there at the same time and for a few minutes we shared its cover. He took the waterproofing off his rifle and began to shoot without much aiming. The sound of his rifle gave him enough courage to move forward and he left the obstacle to me. It was a foot larger now and I felt safe enough to take pictures of the other guys hiding just like I was.

'It was still very early and very gray for good pictures, but the gray water and the gray sky made the little men, dodging under the surrealistic designs of Hitler's anti-invasion brain trust, very effective.

'I finished my pictures and the sea was cold in my trousers. Reluctantly, I tried to move away from my steel pole, but the bullets chased me back every time. Fifty yards ahead of me, one of our half-burnt amphibious tanks stuck out of the water and offered me my next cover. I sized up the situation. There was little future for the elegant raincoat heavy on my arm. I dropped it and made for the tank. Between floating bodies I reached it, paused for a few more pictures and gathered my guts for the last jump to the beach.

'Now the Germans played on all their instruments and I could not find any hole between the shells and bullets that blocked the last twenty-five yards to the beach. I just stayed behind my tank, repeating a little sentence from my Spanish Civil War days. *Es una cosa muy seria. Es una cosa muy seria.'* - This is a very serious business.

'The tide was coming in and now the water reached the farewell letter to my family in my breast pocket. Behind the human cover of the last two guys, I reached the beach. I threw myself flat and my lips touched the earth of France. I had no desire to kiss it.

'Jerry still had plenty of ammunition left and I fervently wished I could be beneath the earth now and above later. The chances the contrary were becoming increasingly strong. I turned my head sideways and found myself nose to nose with a lieutenant from our last night's poker game. He asked me if I knew what he saw. I told him no and that 1 didn't think he could see much beyond my head. 'I'll tell you what I see,' he whispered, 'I see my ma on the front porch, waving my insurance policy.'

'Ste-Laurent-sur-Mer must have been at one time a drab, cheap resort for vacationing French schoolteachers. Now, on June 6 1944, it was the ugliest beach in the whole world. Exhausted from the water and the fear, we lay flat on a small strip of wet sand between the sea and the barbed wire. The slant of the beach gave us some protection, so long as we lay flat, from the machine gun and rifle bullets, but the tide pushed us against the barbed wire, where the guns were enjoying open season. I crawled on my stomach over to my friend Larry, the Irish padre of the regiment, who could swear better than any amateur. He growled at me, 'You damn half-Frenchy! If you don't like it here, why the hell did you come back?' Thus comforted by religion, I took out my second Contax camera and began to shoot without raising my head.

'From the air 'Easy Red' must have looked like an open tin of sardines. Shooting from the sardine's angle, the foreground of my pictures was filled with wet boots and green faces. Above the boots and faces my picture frames were filled with shrapnel smoke; burnt tanks and sinking barges formed my background. Larry had a dry cigarette. I reached in my hip pocket for my silver flask and offered it to him. He tilted his head sideways and took a swig from the corner of his mouth. Before returning the bottle he gave it to my other chum, the Jewish medic, who very successfully imitated Larry's technique. The corner of my mouth was good enough for me too.

'The next mortar shell fell between the barbed wire and the sea and every piece of shrapnel found a man's body. The Irish priest and the Jewish doctor were the first to stand up on the 'Easy Red' beach. I shot the picture. The next shell fell even closer. I didn't dare to take my eyes off the finder of my Contax and frantically shot frame after frame. Half a minute later, my camera jammed - my roll was finished. I reached in my bag for a new roll and my wet shaking hands ruined the roll before I could insert it in my camera.

'I paused for a moment... and then I had it bad.

'The empty camera trembled in my hands. It was a new kind of fear shaking my body from toe to hair and twisting my face. I unhooked my shovel and tried to dig a hole. The shovel hit stone under the sand and I hurled it away. The men around me lay motionless. Only the dead on the water line rolled with waves. An LCI braved the fire and medics with red crosses painted on their helmets poured from it. I did not think and I didn't decide it. I just stood up and ran toward the boat. I stepped into the sea between two bodies and the water reached to my neck. The rip tide hit my body and every wave slapped my face under my helmet. I held my cameras high above my head and suddenly I knew that I was running away. I tried to turn but couldn't face the beach and told myself, 'I am just going to dry my hands on that boat.'

[Eventually, Capa followed a medic team carrying a stretcher to a waiting craft; ahead of him most of the medics were cut down by machine gun fire]. 'I reached the boat. The last medics were just getting out. I climbed aboard. As I reached the deck I felt a shock and suddenly was all covered with feathers. I thought, 'What is this? Is somebody killing chickens?' Then I saw that the superstructure had been shot away and that the feathers were the stuffing from the kapok jackets of the men that had been blown up. The skipper was crying. His assistant had been blown up all over him and he was a mess.

'Our boat was listing and we slowly pulled away from the beach to try and reach the mother ship before we sank. I went down to the engine room, dried my hands and put fresh films in both cameras. I got back up on deck again in time to take one last picture of the smoke-covered beach. Then I took some shots of the crew giving transfusions on the open deck. An invasion barge came alongside and took us off the sinking boat. The transfer of the badly wounded on the heavy seas was a difficult business. I took no more pictures. I was busy lifting stretchers. The barge brought us to the USS *Chase* the very boat I had left only six hours before. On the *Chase* the last wave of the 16th Infantry was just being lowered, but the decks were already full with returning wounded and dead.

'This was my last chance to return to the beach. I did not go. The mess boys who had served our coffee in white jackets and with white gloves at three in the morning were covered with blood and were sewing the dead in white sacks.'

Capa was helped aboard by the crew of the *Chase* and he took photos of the wounded and dying men lying on the crowded decks. Then his head started to swim, things became confused and he suddenly passed out. He was taken to a bunk and a label was hung around his neck.

'**Exhaustion case. No dog tags.**' The *Chase* **eventually reached England on the evening of Wednesday 7 June when Capa committed his ten rolls of film to a waiting courier who sped them by train to John Morris at** *Life* **magazine in London's Piccadilly for developing.** [14]

'Seven days later, I learned that all the pictures I had taken on 'Easy Red' were the best of the invasion. But the excited darkroom assistant while drying the negatives had turned on too much heat and the emulsions had melted. Out of 106 pictures in all, only eight were salvaged. The captions under the heat-blurred pictures read that Capa's hands were badly shaking.'

Robert Capa photographed five wars, including the Spanish Civil War and French Indo-China in the early 1950s. He was 41 years old in 1954 when he stepped on a land mine at Thai Binh, after taking pictures of French combat troops. He died a short time later. His epitaph: 'If the picture isn't good enough, you're not close enough.'

'No one remembers the date of the Battle of Shiloh. But the day we took Fox Green Beach was 6 June and the wind was blowing hard out of the north-west. As we moved in toward land in the grey early light, the thirty-six-foot coffin-shaped steel boat took solid green sheets of water that fell on the helmeted heads of the troops packed shoulder to shoulder in the stiff, awkward, uncomfortable, lonely companionship of men going to battle.

'As the boat rose to a sea, the green water turned white and came slamming in over the men, the guns and the cases of explosives. Ahead you could see the coast of France. The gray booms and derrick-forested bulks of the attack transports were behind now and, over all the sea, boats were crawling forward toward France.

'Those of our troops who were not wax-grey with seasickness, fighting it off, trying to hold on to themselves before they had to grab for the steel side of the boat, were watching the *Texas* with looks of surprise and happiness. Under the steel helmets they looked like pikemen of the Middle Ages to whose aid in battle had come some strange and unbelievable monster.

'There would be a flash like a blast furnace from the 14-inch guns of the *Texas* that would lick far out from the ship. Then the yellow brown smoke would cloud out and, with the smoke rolling, the concussion and the report would hit us, jarring the men's helmets. It struck your ear like a punch with

14   When Morris finally received them at around 0900 he passed them to a darkroom assistant - 16-year-old Dennis Banks - telling him to develop them as fast as he could. Banks put the films into a drying cabinet, turned up the heat and closed the doors but the heat was too much and it melted the pictures; only eleven frames were salvageable. Eleven frames could be rescued - they were grainy and some were a little blurred but there was no doubt that they captured the hour of the attack. At 3.30 am, less than six hours before the 9 am deadline, Morris rushed round with them to the military censor's office and joined the queue. Growing ever more worried, he was delayed by the censor until 8.45 am. With just 15 minutes to reach the dispatch rider who'd be taking official documents to a waiting aircraft, Morris raced to Grosvenor Square and found the courier with just one minute to spare. Capa returned to 'Omaha' on 8 June and made his way to Bayeaux, he learnt about the darkroom accident but Capa took the news well. As Morris said, 'Capa was a gambler and knew that some you win, some you lose.' Capa's photos of D-Day were published in *Life* magazine on 19 June. *D-Day 6.6.44* by Dan Perry (BBC Books 2004).

a heavy, dry glove.

'Then up on the green rise of a hill that now showed clearly as we moved in would spout two tall black fountains of earth and smoke.

'Look what they're doing to those Germans.' I leaned forward to hear a GI say above the roar of the motor. 'I guess there won't be a man alive there,' he said happily.

'That is the only thing I remember hearing a GI say all that morning.'

Ernest Hemingway (45), who crossed to 'Omaha' Beach in the *Empire Anvil* before climbing down the ship's rope ladder into a landing craft, only to be transferred to another ship, up and down another rope ladder and finally into the small, crowded landing craft, describing the scene for his *Collier's* readers. From the landing craft Hemingway scanned the horizon with his field glasses, picking out the Coleville church steeple as a guide. The coxswain could not decide if the route into the beach was clear of mines; the lieutenant was not sure if this was Fox Green or if they should put ashore. Finally, confused and frustrated, they began the run into the beach where Hemingway could see that 'the first, second, third, fourth and fifth waves lay where they had fallen, looking like so many heavily laden bundles on that flat pebbly stretch between the sea and the first cover.'

'...the gliders landed, bringing with them besides much needed men, much needed medical supplies and anti-tank guns and howitzers. The gliders crashed into the hedgerows that lined the too small fields, into houses, barns, churches, and the Germans - who were again organized, after the initial surprise of the night - were ready for them. The medics found themselves landed in marshes where the water was from three to seven feet deep; under shellfire and small arms fire, they ferried their equipment out on life rafts and set up a tent hospital within 2 hours. In an airborne operation, the troops are necessarily surrounded, so the safest place to put a hospital is at the centre of the fighting. The hospital was less than a mile from the front, and the front was circular.'

Martha Gellhorn. On D-Day plus one, maybe two, against all regulations, she crossed the Channel in a 'snowy white' hospital ship with its 'many bright new red crosses painted on the hull and painted flat on the boat deck'. She simply went down to one of the ports, boarded and hid in the toilet until the ship was under way. On her return she was arrested, confined to an American nurses' training camp outside London and told that she could go to France with the nurses when they were ready. She climbed the fence, hitched a ride to a military airfield and flew to Naples. She had already written her husband Ernest Hemingway a note, having being told that he was livid on hearing that she had reached France when he, although he had crossed the Channel in an LST on D-Day, had not been allowed ashore.

'It was difficult to make our way through the stakes that had been sunk as obstructions, because there were contact mines fastened to them that looked like large double pie-plates fastened face to face. They looked as though they had been spiked to the pilings and then assembled. They were the ugly, neutral grey-yellow colour that almost everything is in war.

'We did not know what other stakes with mines were under us, but the ones that we could see we fended off by hand and worked our way to the sinking boat.

'It was not easy to bring on board the man who had been shot through the lower abdomen, because there was no room to let the ramp down the way we were jammed in the stakes with the cross sea.

'I do not know why the Germans did not fire on us unless the destroyer had knocked the machine-gun pillbox out. Or maybe they were waiting for us to blow up with the mines. Certainly the mines had been a great amount of trouble to lay and the Germans might well have wanted to see them work. We were in the range of the anti-tank gun that had fired on us before and all the time we were manoeuvring and working in the stakes. I was waiting for it to fire.

'As we lowered the ramp the first time, while we were crowded in against the other LCV(P) but before she sank, I saw three tanks a coming along the beach, barely moving, they were advancing so slowly. The Germans let them cross the open space where the valley opened on to the beach and it was absolutely flat with a perfect field of fire. Then I saw a little fountain of water jut up, just over and beyond the lead tank. Then smoke broke out of the leading tank on the side away from us and I saw two men dive out of the turret and land on their hands and knees on the stones of the beach. They were close enough so that I could see their faces, but no more men came out as the tank started to blaze up and burn fiercely.

'By then we had the wounded man and the survivors on board, the ramp back up. And we were feeling our way out through the stakes. As we cleared the last of the stakes and Currier opened up the engine wide as we pulled out to sea, another tank was beginning to burn.

'We took the wounded boy out to the destroyer. They hoisted him aboard it in one of those metal baskets and took on the survivors. Meantime, the destroyers had run in almost to the beach and were blowing every pillbox out of the ground with their 5-inch guns. I saw a piece of German about three feet long with an arm on it sail high up into the air in the fountaining of one shell burst. It reminded me of a scene in Petrushka.'

Ernest Hemingway's account of a trip to Fox Green opposite Colleville to pick up the wounded. When the German machine-gun fire picked out their landing craft, Hemingway dropped down and the lieutenant took the LCVP back out to sea.[15] Like Capa, this was Hemingway's fifth war since 1918. In WWI he had been an ambulance driver. Hemingway and Martha Gellhorn divorced early in 1945 and he married Mary Welsh, who reported the war for the London *Daily Express* and *Life* magazine. Hemingway committed suicide in 1961.

'Wherever troops hit France on those 'Omaha' beaches - Dog, Easy, and Fox - they took terrific punishment, as, feet slipping in the shifting sand, men stumbled through gray wave caps which raced over them to slap them

15 *Hemingway The Final Years* by Michael Reynolds. (W. W. Norton & Company 1999.

down with their too-heavy equipment, toss them on the beach, suck them back, toss them on again among the nightmare of jumbled equipment, smashed boats, drowned and broken bodies... Easy Red' was a small beach at the mouth of a wooded gully... Gun emplacements laced the slopes on each side, with summer villas converted into pillboxes. Woods were tunnelled under and fortified so the Germans could and did fight their way back through them for miles without ever having to come into the open... From the sea the view was as unmenacing-looking as the Normandy landscape... Only [later] it became visible - visible as a wall of fire so withering that it cut men down in drifts which will forever haunt the memories of those who had to fight their way in over them.

'One of the big tank landing ships attempted to beach - there were only ten allowed on all the 'Omaha' beaches on D- Day because that was all we dared risk losing - finally made shore as a machine gun in the cliffs above chattered while the big doors in her bow yawed slowly open. When, eventually, the first tanks debarked, the drivers cried and vomited as they had to drive over the bodies of their buddies.'

Iris Carpenter, an English war reporter for the *'Boston Globe'* and daughter of a wealthy movie magnate, who wrote this report after the landing as men who were there described it to her. (Her husband, at the time of the retreat from Dunkirk, piloted the family yacht back and forth across the Channel, retrieving soldiers). [16]

'I was the first person to leave the LCI (L) after beaching. The craft had ramps on each side of the bow for purposes of discharging the passengers. Shortly after I left the craft, the right ramp was blown away by an enemy shell which caused numerous casualties, both on the craft and in the water... My first awareness that what we were doing was real was when an SS-millimetre shell hit our LCI (L) and machine gun fire surrounded us. The Germans were in their pillboxes and bunkers high above the beach on the bluff and had an un-obstructed view of what we were doing.

The atmosphere was depressing. The top of the bluff behind the beach was barely visible; the sound of screeching 12-inch and 14-inch shells from the warships USS *Texas* and USS *Arkansas* off shore were new sounds never heard by us before; the stench of expended gunpowder filled the air and landing craft with rocket launchers moved in close to the shore and spewed forth hundreds of rounds at a time onto the German defences. The sea was rough. Purple smoke emanated from the base of the beach obstacles as the UDT prepared to detonate another explosive in the effort to clear a path through the obstacles to the dune line - this was the state of affairs as the platoon made its way to the dune line, oh so many yards away.

'Using the obstacles as shelter, we moved forward over the tidal fiat, fully exposed to machine gun fire. We finally reached the dune line. All of C-8 including Commander Carusi and his staff made the long trek of five hundreds yard safely. God was with us! Three days later, however,

16 *The Women Who Wrote the War* by Nancy Caldwell Sorel (Arcade Publishing, New York 1999).

Commander Carusi took a bullet through his lung and had to be evacuated. A great leader to be sure.

'Having reached the high water mark, we set about organizing ourselves and planning the next move as we had done so many times during our training period. The principal difference was that we were pinned down - with real machine gun fire - with very little movement to the right or the left of our position and absolutely no movement forward...

'I believe the most dramatic event that I experienced that morning was when an Army officer came to me and asked that I, as the beachmaster, pass the word over my powered megaphone that the soldiers were to 'move forward'. The men of C-8 have speculated that the officer was Colonel George Taylor, who landed at 0830...

'After I gave the order, an Army sergeant pushed a 'Bangalore' torpedo through the barbed wire at the top of the dune, exploded it and opened a gap in the mass of barbed wire. He then turned to his men and said 'Follow me'. He did not order his men forward, but he led them, which was the sign of a leader. The men rushed through the gap onto the flat plateau behind the dune line to the base of the bluff, a distance of some fifty yards or so through heavily mined areas. Many lost their lives or were seriously wounded.'

Lieutenant Commander Joseph P. Vaghi USNR from Bethel, Connecticut, was the beachmaster - or 'traffic cop' - as he put it, for Easy Red Sector. He landed with his platoon C-8 at 0735 hours when the tide was at full-ebb. He and his men had a 500-yard open beach to cross before reaching the cover of the sand dunes. It was his first combat.

'Late in the afternoon of the 5th, the ship's engines started again and we headed toward France. As our little ship neared the Normandy coast we could hear the heavy pounding sounds of the explosions. An announcement was made earlier that no-one was allowed on deck so we imagined what must be happening as the ship shook with each explosion, making the hull ring as if it were a kind of giant muffled bell. The tension was growing and our voices were ominously silent when someone over the PA system cautioned us to hang on to something solid as the driver was going to ram the ship as close to the shore as possible. He also said we were off course by a hundred yards or so from the assigned landing point and that one of the sailors would attempt wading ashore with a rope attached to an anchor that we might use to steady ourselves in the surf. He wished us good luck and we made for the hatches to the deck, our platoon going up and off the starboard ramp. On deck at last there was no mistake of this being a full blown war. Huge explosions seemed to be going off everywhere. I wondered if they were mines or artillery shells. As I hastened down the ramp I glanced at my watch. It was 08:20.

'I stepped into what seemed like four feet of water and inflated my waist belt with the CO2 activated release, just in case the water went too deep. We were all carrying extra ammunition. I had two bandoleers of rifle ammunition plus my own supply of carbine cartridges and twenty pounds of TNT in a waterproofed burlap package we called a satchel charge. My carbine in its green plastic waterproof envelope was not immediately functional until I reached the shore, which worried me some. Wading single file through the water I attempted some ridiculously humourous remarks just to relieve the growing tension I suppose. I think it went something like 'Hey Guys, we best get the hell out of here; looks like they don't want us!' I couldn't see much beyond the beach as heavy smoke covered the high ground ahead. It covered the entire area blowing from West to East.

'As I got to the beach I flopped down, not on sand as I expected, but on smooth rocks everywhere and I crawled forward between two tanks at the water's edge, about 50 or so yards apart. The one to my left appeared to be on fire but both were firing their 75mm guns. Wounded and dead seemed to be scattered everywhere. My god, I discovered I was crawling on rocks slippery with blood and a chap to my right seemed to be cut in half and held together only by his clothing. Tearing off the protective plastic cover of my carbine, I immediately unfastened my inflated waist belt enabling me to get an inch or two closer to the ground. I could see what were artillery rounds bursting in a line towards me from the right in about five seconds intervals. I decided I must get out of there and crouching, I ran forward about 20 feet, when a shell burst behind me. Looking back at that instant I saw one hit the very ramp of the LCI I had left moments earlier. The utter confusion added to the frightening situation. Here the frightening realisation that there was a distinct possibility I might not get off the beach alive added to my confusion. The almost continuous explosions of both incoming, as well as the navy fire were terrifying! Which direction should I move toward? Then I spied my platoon sergeant 50 feet or so ahead, who signalled us to the higher ground. There, where a gap had been opened in the barbed wire, we were attempting to reach a more sheltered spot on the rising slope of the beach.

'My next thoughts were for the mines and stepping through a small shell crater was one, half exposed and I leapt over it. Another fluttering swish of an incoming shell made me dive to the ground. It burst terrifying close behind me. As I tried to get up, I discovered I couldn't move a muscle. I realised I was completely paralysed. I could only hear someone shout, 'Anyone hurt?' But, not feeling any pain, in seconds I could move again. Working my way forward and still on my stomach, something seemed to be tugging on my pack. Looking back, no-one was close and I continued to crawl forward. Glancing back at the beach I saw huge eruptions and smoke filled debris hurtling skyward. I was glad to be this far off the beach. By God, this was all too frightening a business. Our assault regiment, the 116th Infantry, appeared to have been decimated. I felt the whole German Army was firing at me. Some of the fire hitting us was coming directly from prepared positions inland.

'The trench works we were encountering were producing prisoners but obviously not Germans. They resembled Orientals and might possibly have been Japs. They were held in little groups on this slope of the hill. A destroyer not far off in the channel was firing into these entrenchments and the defenders were surrendering after grenades were thrown in. It was there I noticed my right hand drenched in blood. I felt nothing and couldn't imagine what caused it. I saw it was nearly sliced open between the thumb and forefinger. I wrapped my handkerchief around it and continued working my way up the steep slope. To our right was a rather deep draw and some of us tried taking it to avoid the incoming shells, but it was under the fire of inland artillery. I noticed one huge crater obviously made by the navy's big guns, as there, partially buried, was the nose fuse of what must have been a 16-inch shell. I thought then how I'd love to have it for my collection back home. But as German artillery was falling in that area I decided to lose interest in it. Somebody later would have a dandy souvenir.

'Crossing the draw to the right and higher ground, we reached a crest with smoke from grass fires that were as thick as fog. We couldn't see any Germans and our platoon sergeant made some attempt to organise our group. The platoon leader was missing and I suspected him to be a casualty. It was now mid-afternoon. Creeping forward ever so cautiously, I tripped a Bouncing Betty mine. It popped into the air and I hit the ground expecting to be blown to bits. It fell back to earth with a thump, a dud probably failing to explode after several years in position. We were well spread apart some 20 or 30 yards and I hesitated to move in any direction. When encouraged by another, I followed in his footsteps until we believed we were out of the minefield. The people with the mine detectors were still making their way up the steep slope. We got down and started digging in to wait for the platoon to re-group.

'German artillery shells continued, though sporadically, overhead on their way to the beach. From here I had a good view of the beach area and saw one ship on fire and some tanks making their way up hill. There were many aircraft that seemed to fill up the sky; fighter planes with their black and white stripes - just as we had been told they would be marked back in the briefing back in England. There appeared to be thousands of them flying back and forth over the beaches and were a reassuring sight.

'It was difficult to hold my shovel to dig and a medic bandaged my hand while asking what happened. I told him I had no idea and he went on. Engineers began marking lanes through the mine field with white tape as things began to quieten down. I didn't like the way my white bandage on my hand showed up and covered it with my blood soaked OD handkerchief. It made too much of a target, I imagined. Greatly fatigued, I just lay there wondering if the war would last much longer. In a short time we were up and moving inland. Our Lieutenant appeared as if from nowhere and our platoon seemed intact again. But confusion continued and communication with our commanders did not apparently exist. We reached a farmyard surrounded by apple orchards. Rifle companies on either side were not finding any Germans and we cut through a farmer's yard on to a road leading south. We were following some distance ahead in the vicinity of the road and an army fighter plane dove toward the location strafing and bombing the area.

'Approximately a half-hour later we came to a German tank that had been burning, its crew scattered about the ground. All appeared dead and badly burned. Among the bodies there on the road was a bare white foot standing upright. It was cleanly severed from its owner and not even bloody. How awful things were getting. This tank must have been hit by the fighter plane strafing ahead. A German soldier called 'Kameraden' from the bushes at the roadside. Ted Schwanke in our squad spoke to him in German and learned that he had been badly wounded and was asking for help. We could do nothing for him. Schwanke told him the medics would be along shortly. Rifle fire further up the road drove us into the woods prevented any determination of just where the fire was coming from. By now the rifle ammunition was running critically low and the extra bandoleers we carried were collected and distributed.

'It was here, under a big tree growing on the hedgerow that the Communication's Platoon Lieutenant took the sergeant's rifle and binoculars, saying he was going to climb up into the tree to get the bastards. I reached up to pull the Lieutenant back, saying 'That's not a good idea Lieutenant' or something to that effect. Glaring back at me he continued up and found a good firing position and fired two or three rounds. He screamed 'God, I'm hit!' and came crashing down on the other side of the hedgerow. The sergeant and I dove through the hedge and pulled him back in the cover of the hedge. He was shot through the chest. We called for a medic who gave him some morphine. The company was moving out and we had to leave the Lieutenant with others. What a thorough waste, I thought. All the money spent on commissioning this guy and he's trying to act like a Sergeant York! Didn't last a day. What a terrible waste. He died that evening.

'It was late afternoon as we followed a hedgerow in a single column of squads. We were all very tired. It had been an exhausting day and we had eaten nothing, although I do not recall being hungry. An explosion some yards to the rear of the squad caused a now instinctive flop to the ground. After a minute or so we got going again. Word passed that a grenade dangling from a man's pack strap had come loose releasing the safety pin. Several casualties and a cry for medics immediately followed. I thought, 'my God, they'd come this far without a scratch and now a stupid accident has probably killed someone'. There was an awesome quiet as we made our way along a sunken road bordered by high hedgerows. It was getting close to dusk and we rested a few minutes. The Battalion commander came up indicating to our Lieutenant that he was looking for a place to set down the weapon company's mortars. They went through an opening in the hedge and while scouting the adjacent field, German mortars began falling where Colonel Blatt and the mortar section were. The Germans must have had the field under observation. The Colonel was mortally wounded by the mortar fire. We were now some three miles inland and we were told the Colonel was carried on a litter back to the beach where he died that night of June 6th.

'It was now dark and our company crawled into a kind of ditch beside the hedgerows that concealed us with overgrown trees and bushes. Dead tired, I lay there but sleep wouldn't come. Just where did this road lead that we were lying alongside? Would the Jerries be using this road in an attack? Listening for tanks and excepting for my buddies near me in this ditch, I felt very much alone in this awful place. A few pulled their jackets over their head for a smoke. The familiar sound of incoming shell broke the stillness and I braced for the explosion. Feeling the impact when it thumped into the earth, I was relieved that it must have been a dud. Perhaps sabotaged by the forced labour we heard about. That one would surely be followed by more, but nothing came and complete silence continued.

'God, what a good feeling I thought after such a miserable day. Sleep came in little doses as the night wore on. First, German planes flew low heading for the beach and their bombs suggested that the beaches were getting a hell of a pasting. Much better to be here in the front lines for now. Later a lone plane flying along the very road we were next to, unloaded a terrifying load of anti-personnel bombs that exploded with a staccato roar, apparently hitting no-one as I listened for cries for medics. Again, silence and more dozing. Footsteps on the road now startled me. I imagined they were Jerry's hobnailed boots coming down the road. 'Christ sake' I thought is everyone asleep? Somebody, or maybe the whole German Army is marching up the road. I poked a couple of my buddies.

'Ya hear that?' I asked.

'Oh hell, it's probably some damn Frenchman in his wooden shoes' was his reply.

'Yep, it was the sound of two feet, nothing more, as they faded away. How could this be? I thought. The biggest invasion in all history has taken place and now in the middle of the night some French farmer clomps nonchalantly along the pavement as he probably done for years.

'This then ended my first day for a combat infantry soldier - trying to get some sleep in a ditch a few miles inland from a beach known hereafter as 'Omaha'.'

John Hooper, 29th Infantry Division, HQ Company, A&P Platoon, 1st Battalion, 115th Regiment. 'Some days later, rain called for me to open my pack and remove my carefully folded raincoat. What a surprise! It had been shredded into ribbons! It appeared that two or three bullets had entered the top of my pack almost parallel to my prone body. Entering just below my mess can pouch where I stored my K-rations, passing through the folds in my raincoat. Yep, there were pencil sized holes just under the flap that secured the mess can pouch. We had stored our mess kits along with blankets, an extra pair of shoes and a shelter - half in our barracks bags back in England to be trucked by the Battalion HQ people. I got soaked locating a raincoat from one who would no longer need it.'

'I was an infantry platoon leader. My unit was assigned to land on 'Easy Red' in the second wave. We rushed down the ramp of the LCI into water about knee deep and ran up to the beach to re-assemble there. There were dead bodies floating in the water and many on the beach. Some tanks had been hit by artillery. The confusion on the beach made it impossible for me to get my bearings. Death and wreckage were everywhere. German mortar shells were still hitting the beach. The noise from the planes, boats, artillery explosions and gunfire was almost unbearable.

There was a red-headed fellow with a very white face looking up at me in a kneeling position on the beach. I stepped back from the sight and was given a push by a man kneeling on the ground behind me. He yelled, 'Do you want to get us both killed?' He was in the process of disarming a land mine. I gestured and muttered something about the red-headed fellow in front of me. The soldier exclaimed, 'Don't worry about him, he's dead! Just watch where you put your feet.' I then came out of my daze and was very alert to everything around me.

'We all lined up and started up the hill, one after another, following the soldiers that were removing the mines. There were explosions all around us but I couldn't see anyone firing guns at us. There were uncovered land mines on both sides of the path so we knew we had to watch our step. It seemed to take a couple of hours to get up the hill. Before we went over the top of the hill, I looked back and contemplated the scene before me. Hundreds of ships and boats were circling in the Channel. LCIs and LSTs were landing men and tanks. With planes soaring overhead, big shells bursting on land and sea and the beach littered with men and machines, I thought of the millions of dollars and thousands of lives being spent to wage war and the tragic cost and horror of it all. At the top of the hill we had to cross a mine field, after which we dug in for a counterattack, which never came.

'For the next several weeks I led my platoon, moving forward during the day and digging foxholes for the night. It was very tedious fighting from hedgerow to hedgerow. After about six weeks, we dug in and held the line. Finally, our unit was relieved from the front lines and allowed to rest for a few days. I was able to take my first shower since D-Day - it was wonderful! One day after I was relieved, the man who replaced me in my foxhole was killed during a German counterattack. At that time and following several other close encounters with death, I felt that my Heavenly Father had blessed me and spared my life for a reason.'

2nd Lieutenant H. Smith Shumway, Company 'B', 18th Infantry Regiment, 1st Infantry Division, born in Salt Lake City, 'Utah' on 27 November 1921. When the USA entered the in 1941 he was 20 years old and was hoping to serve as a full-time missionary for the Church of Jesus Christ of Latter-day Saints (Mormons). On 27 July, a few miles to the west of St. Lô, his life changed forever. He was walking on a narrow sunken road bordered with hedgerows, about one meter behind a tank when he stood on anti-tank mine. He was blinded and he lost the right side of his chest, calf and thigh muscles from one of leg and had shrapnel wounds over his entire body. He later proposed to his college sweetheart, Sarah Bagley by saying, 'If you'll sort the socks and read the mail, I can do the rest.' They were married on 1 September 1948 in the Mormon temple in Salt Lake City, 'Utah'. They had eight children and 40 grandchildren.

'We hit 'Easy Red' in advance of the first wave of infantry at 06:00 under a rain of sniper fire from the enemy. Since late 1943 the 299th had trained at Fort Pierce, Florida to blast out concrete pillars, deadly mine-tipped angle beams and logs and great steel cross arms called 'hedgehogs.' I was in charge of eight armoured bulldozers. Miraculously, they all got ashore in running order. Shells started falling around me. I was near a blown-out landing craft. I hit face down. Shell fragments slashed the back of my pant legs. It was like I'd cut myself on barbed wire. I found a tank with a dozer blade mounted in front. The crew had bailed out. So I climbed in it and ran it, clearing obstacles. Finally, I ran over a mine. It blew a tread. There were fires everywhere. A wrecked landing craft, still loaded with tanks, burned fiercely. Ammunition exploded. There was shellfire, noise, confusion and bodies all around. I was one of the lucky ones. I never thought I would live through it. I overheard a corporal talking to an officer. He said that there were six men left in his entire infantry company of more than 200 and he was the highest ranking person. He was in Command. Part of our crew began clearing the beach of bodies but there was no place to put them. Orders came down to dig a temporary mass grave. I had one of my dozers do it. The driver kept going back and forth until he had a big enough trench. The Chaplain and I gathered men to collect the bodies. They all got sick leaving only the Chaplain and me to finish. Then the bodies were stacked in there like cordwood and covered over with sand. I understand it was the first American graveyard in Normandy WWII.'

Warrant Officer James W. Tucker, 299th Combat Engineer Battalion. It was three days before they moved off the beach. Half of the 299th Engineers were killed or wounded on 'Omaha' Beach. Those who survived were to move inland on 9 June. The 'Famous 299th Combat Engineer Battalion' received the Presidential Citation for Outstanding Gallantry on D-Day. James W. Tucker went on to fight through the Battle of the Bulge, into Germany and win five battle stars and a Bronze Star. His Bronze Star Citation says: 'In a two week period, Warrant Officer Tucker, by his marked ingenuity and untiring efforts, converted eight heavy tractors into armour protected equipment to be used in removing underwater and beach obstacles... in the face of sporadic artillery, mortar and small arms fire, he personally led his crew onto the invasion beach and supervised the removal of numerous obstacles. By his technical knowledge, fortitude and devotion to duty, Warrant Officer Tucker reflects credit upon himself and the military service.' In 1957 James Tucker went back to 'Omaha' Beach with his family. He told them about it while the kids played in the German pillboxes. They visited the cemetery nearby. From a bronze plaque, he read the names of the 299th's dead. He could recall every one of them. James W. Tucker was buried in Arlington National Cemetery with full military honours in 1983.

'We left the LST at 0400 hours. The sea was still very rough, making us about three hours later than planned. The ground swell were estimated to be about fourteen feet which lifted the ramp of the LST high above the water and made it very difficult to launch our DUKW. The driver, Jim Mildenberger from Minnesota, waited until the ramp was taking on water enough to float us. He then gunned the motor and headed off the ramp onto the sea. An LCVP which was to lead us to shore came alongside and hailed us to follow him. That was the last we ever saw of them. Another LCVP at our rear was to follow us but he became lost to our view behind the high waves. From then on we were on our own. Our ride to the shore was very risky due to the weather and not knowing for sure if we were really going in the right direction, which really overburdened our already frustration. We were being passed by LCIs and LCTs loaded with men of the 1st and 29th Infantry division who were to make the assault as the first wave of the invasion, so we knew we were headed in the right direction.

'At 0620 hours Colonel Talley said to break radio silence with a message to the Ancon, 'At line of departure, everything is GO'. More and more we were being passed by small boats carrying men to the beach among them were LSMs which were carrying DD-4 tanks. We heard later, even though the tanks were waterproofed with the floatation gear deployed they were unable to operate in such deep water. Only five of them made it to the beach. We learned later only our DUKW was the sole survivor off LST 176. Our twin DUKW on the other ship also made it but later that day it received a direct hit and burned, killing one man and wounding two others. The two Jeeps carrying our radios were also victims of the sea and were drowned out.

'We attempted several landings on the beach. Finally at high tide we tried again, the water being high was to our advantage it helped us miss the underwater obstacles. These underwater barriers had mines and other explosives attached to them and if hit or bumped by a DUKW or other boats the damage would be devastating and final. There were many soldiers in the water bogged down by their two water-soaked blanket roll packs, rifle and ammunition. Most were trying to stay afloat by swimming but there were many others in the water that could swim no more.

'To give directions to the driver of our DUKW I lay on the nose of the vehicle and gave hand signals to help guide us around the obstacles. I could see the mines and explosives attached to the obstacles, we were truly blessed that we made it through this maze. What with the mines, heavy machine gunning, artillery and rifle fire our route was very precarious. Our DUKW had five gallon cans of gasoline strapped to the sides of our boat cabin, because of the incoming fire we decided to dump the cans overboard into the water. This proved to be one of our better decisions because our DUKW did receive machine gun fire through the walls of the cabin. We finally made it to the shore but for a short time only. Our antennae stuck up in the air about 15 feet making our presence a prime target. The infantry men on the beach let us know in no uncertain terms that we were not welcome in their area. They waved us off and I can still hear very clearly, 'Get that ******* radio out of here.' We withdrew from the beach and ran parallel to the shore for a distance of approximately 300 feet. From that distance we could observe more accurately the activity on the beach. We sent many radio messages to the Ancon advising General Gerow of the situation concerning both men and supplies. We also made a run to Pont-du-Hoc a little south of us where the 2nd and 5th Ranger Battalions were scaling the cliffs. On our way we heard a message from them, 'We need ammunition and reinforcements, many casualties'. One of our destroyers also intercepted this message and sent a small boat loaded with small arms ammunition racing for the base of the cliffs.

'On our way Colonel Talley called attention to two small boats drifting aimlessly near shore. We checked them they were loaded with ammunition and supplies. We found both drivers dead. The destroyer sent two seamen to take over and complete the mission. We returned to 'Omaha' beach. The number of LCIs and LCTs were increasing to about 50 and more arriving all the time. The situation on 'Omaha' previously was very much in doubt. We landed again, Col Talley's journal notes: 'It was impossible to distinguish the living from the dead and in moving up and down the beach it was necessary to step over men without knowing or expressing concern over their condition'. We finally found a spot on the beach where we were tolerated. During this time there was continual machine-gun fire and incoming shells from German rifled 88 cannons. They could shoot on line for a distance of 600 yards very accurately.

'Colonel Talley, Jim Mildenberger and myself were on shore trying to burrow in a low ground depression to keep us from being hit. Jim caught some shrapnel in his back and right shoulder. I found a Medic who came and evacuated him to England. I later learned that Jim refused discharge to the States and returned to France for duty. Equipment and soldiers were arriving in large numbers crowding the beach. Casualties were mounting because of the cross-fire from one end of the beach to the other. I remember seeing a bulldozer coming off the ramp of an LST with his blade up. As he cleared the ramp heading for shore shells ricocheted off the blade. The operator kept right on moving oblivious to all action and started up the slope from the beach with the blade held high. He was followed by infantrymen who fanned out behind him. We were on our way to victory. While on the nose of our DUKW looking for underwater obstacles, I had lost my helmet. On the beach I noticed a helmet lying next to a lieutenant from the 1st Division. He didn't need it anymore. I took his helmet and wore it for the rest of my stay in Europe.

'I wonder who he was?'

I. J . Degnan, Security Control Officer, V Corps' Information Detachment.

'Our LST was dragging its bow anchor due to wind and sea so rough the crew dared not open the bow door. Later the heavy stern anchor was dropped, the bow anchor was lifted and we swung about with the bow downwind where the door could be safely opened. Each passing swell brought water almost over the sill of the ramp, then lifted the end of the ramp 14 or 15 feet above the water, only to submerge it when the ramp went down. We drove onto the ramp and were signalled to disembark. We cleared the ramp at 04:00. I was still dirk. We were nearly 3 hours behind schedule and 12 miles from, shore. Our radio operators, cooped up in a small boxlike cabin, became desperately seasick, but it affected their operations only when they had to go out to vomit into the sea. To facilitate secure communications, we had prepared a 'one-time' code consisting of the letters of the

International Phonetic Alphabet: 'Able, Baker, Charlie,' etc. Each letter had a special meaning. Copies were given to all headquarters concerned. Other messages would be encoded by machine.

'We went on the air on schedule at 0600 and transmitted 'Peter Item King', meaning DUKW #1 afloat. Soon we met empty LCTs returning from the direction of the beach. By their numbers we knew they had carried DD tanks. We were surprised that the tanks had been launched in the rough water but reported the passage of the returning LCTs without comment. Later we learned that of 64 DD tanks, eight reached the shore and four survived the day.

'As we approached the beach, we saw small units of the 1st Division on our extreme left hugging the vertical cliff to escape grenades being dropped on them by the enemy on top the hill. I made several attempts to land, but the three long antennas extending nearly 15 feet into the air above the DUKW drew such intense machine gun and mortar fire that I would withdraw. In any event, we could see little from the beach, whereas we had a complete panorama while at sea. The bullets hitting the sea around us reminded me of hail.

'I was in almost continuous radio contact with headquarters on the Ancon in the channel behind us. At 0900, I sent the message: 'From 1,000 yards off Dog and Red I see several companies of the 16th Infantry on Easy, Red and Fox Beaches. Enemy fire still effective. LCTs shifting to Dog. About 10 LCTs standing by to land. Obstacles appear thicker than in photos. LCI-85 hit and smoking after unloading. Have seen two LCTs burn. Count ten tanks on Fox. Landing resuming on Dog.' [17]

'Quickly the situation changed and the landing stopped, altogether. I radioed General Gerow that the landing had stopped and more than 100 landing craft were milling around like a herd of cattle before a storm and dared not approach the beach due to heavy artillery and mortar fire. In another message I said I believed the Germans were using a church steeple at Vierville as an observation post. This message was passed by hand from DUKW #2, Lieutenant Colonel Kilburn Houston in charge, to destroyer which immediately fired two salvos at the church steeple, cutting it off at the roof line and blowing if apart. Effective German artillery and mortar fire ceased, shortly thereafter and the landing resumed.

'I landed shortly thereafter and within fifty feet of where I had gone ashore, met General Millard Wyman, commanding the 1st Division troops. He told me that he had no radio communications; that he had either lost his radio equipment or his operators. I sent a message for him and as we lay on the ground, mortar shells struck nearby. Six of us were lying close, together. Of these, three were wounded and three unhurt. My driver, Private James Mildenberger, lying beside me, was hit by a shell fragment which otherwise would have hit me. I was unhurt save for some loss of hearing. 'While on the beach, I learned that DUKW #2 had received direct hit and burned, killing one man and wounding two others two Jeeps carrying the

17   This message is in the Situation Report of V Corps for about 0920, 6 June 1944.

small radios had landed in deep water were drowned out. A hue and cry arose from the men on the beach nearby to get the radio out, since it was drawing fire. We turned to the water. I later learned that the 29th Division too, were without radio communications, so that DUKW #1 was the only radio in operation. This station sent a message every fifteen to twenty minutes for nine hours and later served as the communications centre on the beach for several days after the landing.

'Within an hour I was able to report a patrol of our troops on the skyline and shortly thereafter an entire platoon moved up a gully. Enemy small arms fire had slackened. Only a few poorly aimed mortar shells were falling. Units reorganized and advanced according to plan.

'The destruction of the church steeple and shelling of German trenches and concrete emplacements by the Navy, plus the actions of a few tanks and more important, the gallantry of brave men had broken the enemy resistance. Before noon, I sent Message No. 21 to General Gerow: 'Troops moving up slope of Fox, Green and Red Beaches. I join you in thanking God for our Navy.' [18]

'In late afternoon a German bombardment from heavy long-range guns destroyed nearly two-thirds of our equipment ashore. V Corps asked me if they should continue to send equipment and I said, 'No.' That bombardment caused especially heavy losses its the Engineer Group commanded to Colonel John O'Neill charged with destroying the obstacles on the beach. Losses in this group were almost 50% of the entire command. 58% of his officers and nearly 42% of his enlisted men were either killed or wounded on D-Day. Elsewhere, by noon First Lieutenants commanded battalions and Sergeants commanded companies.'

Colonel B. B. Talley. In July, 1944 a Special Order of the First Army awarded the Distinguished Service Cross to 33 individuals, including Colonel Talley. The other members of his team each received the Silver Star for gallantry in action. This was second only to General Jimmy Doolittle's participants in the raid on Tokyo on 18 April 1942 as the largest group of which all were decorated. (Doolittle received the MoH for this action when B-25 bombers attacked the Japanese capital from carriers in the Pacific).

'Five men were assigned to DUKW #2, myself included, two radio operators, one driver, one assistant driver and a crew chief. Major Sterling Abernathy in command and an Army observer Colonel Ralph W. Zwicker with no command authority. At about 04:00 the morning of 6 June we assembled in the cargo hold of LST 54 and readied DUKW #2 for launch. Up to this point we had no idea where we were going to land or when. The doors opened, the ramp dropped and we were in the water and on our way. For most of the way in Joe Amato and I were outside with the others watching the naval bombardments, rockets, air bombing as we sloshed on in. The seas were high, approximately six feet and the Duck was much slower than its top speed of 5mph.

'We finally reached the point, about 06:00, when we were to begin

---

18 Colonel Talley's message books are in the Museum of the Invasion at Arromanches, open at this message.

monitoring the radio traffic and both Amato and I had to get inside and go to work. The conditions inside of the HO (a hut-like enclosure mounted in the cargo area) were far from ideal. It was hot. Everything was swinging and sliding due to the high seas and we were sick! I had never been seasick, before or since, but made up for it on that voyage. The worst part was that we could hear all of the gunfire and noises but, of course, had no idea of what was going on outside of the HO or where we were in proximity to the beach. In spite of this we did our job and copied all traffic between Duck #1 and the Ancon. We tried to land three times and were driven off each time by artillery and small arms fire. I am sure that our pair of 15 foot antennae had a lot to do with that. In each landing attempt we received damage to the Duck but no casualties. As our job was to provide communications, Colonel Talley ordered us to cruise parallel to the beach, observe and report until it became safer to land and set up the command post. We complied with these orders until about 0930 or so. It was then that the damage we had incurred during the landing attempts caught up with us and the Duck was taking on more water than the pumps could handle and the rudder had been severely damaged to the point that the Duck was almost impossible to manoeuvre. Amato and I were ordered outside and told that he and I, along with crew chief Sergeant John James would be put ashore and Major Abernathy and Pfc's Robert J. Rasmussen and Robert L. Halseth, the drivers, would try to get the Duck ashore before it sank. If they did not make it to shore, we were ordered to find Colonel Talley's CP and join up with them. The drivers somehow manoeuvred the heaving Duck up to the stern of a knocked-out LCT and the three of us managed to jump onto it without killing ourselves. The Duck took off along the beach looking for a way through the obstacles to land before sinking. We, on the LCT, ran down the length of it, waded in, made a mad dash for the high water mark, where there was some minimal shelter and dug in. We laid there, in our holes, for what seemed like an eternity with nothing to really do except to watch and duck. About the time that we were talking of taking off and finding Colonel Talley's CP, the Duck came rolling up the beach with water pouring out of all of her battle wounds. As dire as the situation was, it was a funny sight. Major Abernathy ordered us to stay away from the Duck as, with all of the burning vehicles around it, he felt that it would look to the German guns as if it was knocked out. No argument from us. In the meantime he would search out Colonel Talley's CP and obtain further orders and return.

'About 45 minutes after the Major left, Colonel Zwicker appeared and asked me if I shouldn't be in the Duck monitoring the radio traffic. I relayed on to him the orders that we had received from the Major. He countermanded those orders and ordered Amato and I into the Duck and to get the radio operational. I tried to again explain our orders but he became adamant that we get the Duck operational. Deeming it poor judgement to argue with a full Colonel, especially under combat conditions, Amato and I climbed aboard. But before we could fire up the radio, the power units had to be started. We had two gasoline generators on the stern of the Duck. The equipment could be run on one generator but we usually kept both of them operational so that in case we lost one, we would not shut down the radio. I climbed up on the Duck - the deck was about six feet from the ground - worked my way back to the stern and tried to start the generator motors, feeling like the main attraction in a shooting gallery. These engines started with a rewind lanyard, just like a lawn mower motor and the first one mercifully started with about two pulls. The second one would not start, no matter how many times I pulled. I started to check to see if we had gasoline and found that most of the gas tank was missing! Some place along the line, that day, something had destroyed it. We'd operate on one. Amato and I got the receivers and the transmitter fired up and we were in business and quite busy what with the landings in full swing and the resulting heavy radio traffic.

'After a half hour or so, Sergeant James appeared at the doorway and informed us that we had been ordered, by Colonel Zwicker, to move the Duck - reason unknown. We moved about 40 or 50 feet and were struck by a mortar round that landed on the port side of the Duck and exploded the gasoline tanks that lined each side of the HO. The explosion was horrendous and knocked both Amato and I unconscious. When we regained consciousness we were buried under a spare parts chest that was once fastened to the HO wall behind us. There was huge hole through the wall of the HO just to the right and behind me. Through this I could see that we were on fire. We heaved the chest off of us, smashed the door open and jumped off the Duck onto the beach. Once outside, we started to search for the rest of the crew. We found Halseth on a stretcher, mortally wounded and to die in a hospital in England on June 8th. We found James sitting on a stretcher being treated by medics for terrible burns on his face and back. That also was the end of his war. We could not find Rasmussen or Colonel Zwicker. Rasmussen was found later by one of the other members of the team with a very bad head wound. He was evacuated to England and later rejoined the Battalion. The Colonel turned up at the CP unharmed.

'After making sure that our guys were being cared for, Amato and I took off up the beach and eventually found Colonel Talley and the rest of the team. We reported that we were out of action and gave our casualty report. For the rest of the time we remained on the beach, then left to rejoin our Battalion on the 8th, we helped man the radio on Duck #1 and performed any other duties that were required of us.'

Robert R. Chapman, Technician 4th Grade, Information Team, 56th Signal Battalion.

'My LCT was loaded with jeeps, command cars, several soldiers and a 32-ton Sherman tank. The distance to Fox Red was 110 miles. Because I could only make 5 knots with the load, I had to leave 26 hours before my scheduled time to hit the beach. Crossing the Channel was awesome, ships in front and back over the horizon as far as the eye could see. At night, we could only see a faint blue light of the ship ahead to follow and guide us. The sea was heavy but because of the excitement, I didn't get seasick. Many in the crew felt sick so the staff officer stepped forward and volunteered to wash the dishes and secure the galley. This delighted the crew. Before daylight I remember seeing flares in the sky and thought, they were our airplanes being shot down. My thoughts were 'Hey you (Germans), we are the Americans, lay down your guns and run'.

'We reached the rendezvous area on time and proceeded to the line of departure. At this point, we were now 2000 yards off the shore. I expected the other LCTs to fall in line to hit the beach. They weren't reacting as if they were preparing for the run so I used my megaphone to ask another skipper what was going on. His answer, 'They're all scared to go in'. This disgusted me so much I didn't even answer and ordered the helmsman to steer towards the beach and I ordered the engines at full speed. We crossed the bow of the battleship Arkansas and could see her 14' shells that she was firing from her big guns. After each shell was fired it was necessary to eject the smoke that came from the powder. This smoke engulfed us and was so dense I couldn't see my hand in front of my face.

'We were now ready to do what we were there to do, what we were trained for and ready to carry out our orders. I could see smoke and fire ahead of us but the surprise that startled me was that a house was still standing there. It was damaged but still standing. I choose to station myself on the conning tower for a good vantage view. I was so confident that nothing was going to stop us. I felt the beach was secure from all I heard at the briefing. I expected to go in, unload, back off and continue my assignment. I never looked back. So far, all was perfect, the timing and our position. A lieutenant colonel that was in charge of the soldiers rushed up the ladder to the conning tower and said, 'You can't go in there. Look at our boys'. I was vexed and ordered him off the conning tower. Now we were closer. I took a better look and I could see the soldiers were face down on the shingle of the beach. They were hugging the ground with only a slight sand dune to protect and hide them. I could see the soles of their shoes. As Ernie Pyle said, 'Our boys are holding on with their finger nails.'

'It was easy to see that I couldn't discharge the jeeps and other vehicles since the beach was not secure. I decided to offload only the tank and back off with the other vulnerable equipment. Our approach was perfect when one of the crew called to ask permission to open fire. I asked, 'To fire at what'? He said, 'They are firing at us from that house' Open Fire. One of my crew was standing and gawking. With my megaphone, I call out to him to lay low. The electrician, who was manning the anchor winch thought I said, 'Let go.' And down went the anchor. The anchor goes down to stabilize the craft and help us when we need to back off the beach. I wasn't ready to release the anchor just yet. Since it was down there was nothing I could do. I figured I could drag it, any way we were close enough to lower the ramp and let the tank off load. Just then, like a bolt of lightning, a shell hit the port gun wounding the gunner and loaders. The force of the blast wounded and knocked the electrician to the deck below. I dashed off the tower, ran across the cat walk, to assess the damage. In these few split seconds I looked down to the deck below and saw the electrician was chalk white. The gunner and others lay on the deck wounded. I rushed back to the control tower and then in front of me another shell hit. This was another direct hit into the wheelhouse. The door flew open and the five men stationed at the controls came pouring out. All wounded. Blood everywhere. Another shell hit us on the port side. I dashed inside and like I had three arms and hands I thrust the engines in reverse, operated the wheel and tried to operate the radio all at the same time. I got the craft turned around and headed out to sea but couldn't make any headway. Another shell hit us on the starboard side. More wounded .I thought it was the anchor holding me back. I ran to the cable cutter to cut us loose. My peripheral vision saw two fires, one at mid ship and the other forward. No time for fires. Let somebody else put them out.

'I had to keep us from drifting back to the beach. I went to the cable cutter above the anchor chock to sever the 1' cable. With a sledgehammer, I started to pound the cable cutter with all my strength. More shells hit us-the tracers gave evidence that some missed. Before I was able to cut the cable a seaman ran to me and told me the engine rooms were flooded. Someone took the hammer to finish the job. I ran below to get to the hatch that was the access to the generator room. I stepped over a decapitated body. Blood all over the deck and bulkheads. At the hatch to the auxiliary room, one of the motor macs was standing on the ladder and I asked him to go down and see what the situation was. He looked at me and said, 'People drown down there'. I said 'Yes God people drown'. I was furious. For some reason, he did not have his helmet on and I grabbed him by the hair of his head and pulled him up and off the ladder. I went down and saw that the water was waist high in the generator room. I then saw a break in the bulkhead where water was pouring in from the engine room. I knew then that the water level was higher and the engines were under water. Back up topside, over the body and this time noticed one of the solders sitting in his jeep, his entire midsection shot away. I thought of his family. Too late to stop the cable from being cut, we were now lifeless with no power and no way to stop us from floating back to the beach. I grabbed a seaman and went over the bulkhead on the port side where a spare anchor was stored. An 88 had embedded itself in the stalk of the anchor almost breaking it in half. If I tied a rope to it and pushed it off the side, would it hold? Anyway, it was too heavy for the two of us so we gave up. The 3' hose that was lashed to the outward side of the bulkhead was pulverized. The bulkhead had hundred of pit marks. Did a machine gun do this? The craft had now turned and left us exposed to the beach and for the first time, I felt I was in danger. I got to the lee side of the bulkhead in a hurry.

'We still had the problem of floating back into the beach. In my desperation I grabbed a throw line, a rope about the size of a clothes line with a knot called a monkey fist on it and stood on the bow hoping someone would take it and tow us out. Not a single craft was heading toward the beach. It was helter-skelter and mass confusion. Not one was willing or made an effort to help.

'We continued to drift with the current and our bottom finally settled to the east under the cliffs. The unsinkable sank on the beach. The cliff protected us from enemy fire; however we had a new fear, that grenades could be hurled at us from above our heads. One of our destroyers was firing toward the top of the cliff, duelling with an enemy tank that was above us. The 5' shells shook the ground and made earth and rocks fall. The water at the ramp was about 3 feet deep so we were able to get the tank and vehicles ashore. The big problem was the wounded. I ran west to where there was more of a chance to get help. The cliff at my back protected me from gunfire. I looked for anything to come in. One lone LCVP was coming towards me to offload its soldiers. When it got close enough for me to throw a baseball to it, it hit a mine and all aboard want flying through the air like rag dolls. Farther west, it was too menacing. Dejected, I ran back to my craft to try to make the wounded as comfortable as possible. I then learned that the body I had been stepping over was the staff officer. All of us on board had coveralls on to protect us from a gas attack, sailors and soldiers looked alike. For that reason, I didn't recognize him. Still keeping a lookout for help, I saw a lone LCVP come into the beach about 75 yards east of us. I got to him, exhausted from running in knee deep water, before he could get away, I prevailed upon him to come to the seaside of my craft and take the crew to a hospital ship.

'The base of the cliff was now jammed with wounded soldiers seeking protection. However, the tide was coming in and they would soon be under water. I waded ashore and explained to a medical doctor, who was administrating to them, that they would not be able to stay there. I showed him where the high water mark was and that the water would rise to it. He agreed to bring as many as we could get on the forward half of my craft. We put them down on the hard steel deck, shoulder to shoulder head to feet and there they spent the night. When the high tide came in the waves would splash over the bulkhead and many were wet all night. The lucky ones got to sleep in the forward part of the living quarters. We didn't have much more than band aids to doctor with and many spent the night with open wounds. Some whimpered, some cried, one asked for his mother, most were silent and sombre. When some asked for drinking water, I had to step over bodies to bring it to them.

'The morning brought some calm to our part of the beach. However the tide and current brought in and deposited the ones that didn't make it. The beach was so littered that it was literally impossible to walk freely. I could not take three steps without stepping over or around a precious dead American soldier.'

Ensign Joseph Alexander, Officer in Charge LCT 856. 'That morning the 1st US Infantry Division needed all the help it could get. I like to think that my little LCT number 856 did its part. We got most of our cargo ashore, battered but at a tremendously high price. I like to think that we distracted the enemy. I like to think that the time the enemy spent on pounding us with their 88s was precious time our boys used to get a better hold on the beachhead. Soon after all this happened, the fighting turned in our favour and that day made history.'

'We started the engines at 0300 and with others departed the harbour. We ran up the English Channel, made our turn and headed for Red Beach. By now everyone knew that this was going to be a tough day. We wanted to land; others wanted us kept off the beach. We were to be in 6th wave, but ended up earlier. We needed to get in to spot where we could off load vehicles. We moved over. A German 88 fired over us and small arms fire was sweeping our bow. One vehicle got off but couldn't make it to the beach. We raised the ramp to the water's edge to make a better landing. I noticed several wounded men in water. The CO moved us over closer to them and I was instructed to lower the ramp more and then John E. Foulk and I went down the ramp and pulled the men we could reach on board. We collected 20 bodies. After off loading the Army men and gear we went to Hospital Ship to off load the wounded. Then we did our job of off loading all the supplies and moving them to the beach. We ran day and night till the storm hit. Some of us at a later date got to make the trip to Paris. Great.'

Ralph E. Gallant, Motor Machinist's Mate 2/c, LCT(6) 546. In November he returned to USA and was then sent to Pacific where he took part in the invasion of Okinawa.

'Oh God it looks like Tarawa'
Captain Bill Friedman, S-1, 16th Infantry Regiment, 1st Infantry Division, who went ashore on Fox Red at 0810 hours had recalled the horrific images from the American newsreels of the terrible island battle in the Pacific in November 1943 and remembered images of dead Marines floating in the surf and the thousand fatal casualties suffered.

'This type of operation is chaos incarnate at the best of times but 'Omaha' was turning into something much worse. As the ramp went down the chaos was evident all around us. It looked like God had taken all the debris of the world and thrown it onto that beach. During the run in seeing the DD tanks being launched and trying to make headway through in the rough seas was terrible to watch. They just went to the bottom. Landing craft on their sides, turned the wrong way... it was like a very strange spectator sport. It was surreal.

'I had gone off the ramp into deep water. It was up to my chest. As we moved forward I must have been on a ridge of sand because the men around me began to go under and I had to help them stay above the waves. After going about 6 to 8 feet, I felt firm ground beneath me... I then moved quickly to the shingle and just lay down and joined that great big long pile of men on the shale. We were totally immobilized. I did not know what to do, or where to go. I remember looking at the sea and the water was red, there were bodies and equipment just rolling in the surf. Along the line of men on the shingle I saw people jerking as they were hit with the impact of bullets and shrapnel. Somehow it didn't count. I was reassured because I was shoulder to shoulder with other men. There was something reassuring about having warm, familiar human bodies next to you... even if they were dead... you were not alone... they provided comfort and sometimes even cover from the bullets. At one point I was still lying down and shouting in the ear of the Regimental 54. He was a major. My mouth was next to his ear; it was so noisy that he could not hear me otherwise. While I was trying to make myself understood above the din, a bullet struck him dead. It had hit him in the centre of his helmet... our faces were inches away when it happened... it could have been me.

'I was in that mass of living and dead when I saw Colonel George Taylor move back from the main line of men and stand up. He started walking up and down the line shouting at the men 'move up' and 'move out'. This had a great effect on me. I remember getting up and starting to shout and scream trying to get the men moving, I didn't hurl myself forward at the defile; I guess that I should have done so. What I did do was urge other men forward.

'While doing this, I remember a funny incident on that terrible morning when I approached three soldiers lying down together absolutely rigid. As I did so bodies were being struck by bullets all around us. These three soldiers would not move so I pulled out my pistol and they looked at me, a distraught Captain waving nothing more threatening than his pistol. I wanted them to go forward to attack up the draw and one of them shouted at me, 'Captain are you out of your fucking mind?'

'Once we got to the base of the bluffs we were relatively safe. We were quite well protected from view and from the enemy's fire. I don't think that they expected anyone to get off the beach because once we started moving up hill and clearing their positions it became just a matter of time. The positions really did not have any depth to them. That's when I saw my first Germans they were either dead, or already prisoners.

'That evening Colonel Taylor sent me to find General Huebner about the time that the 18th RCT began to move up. I found the General and I said 'Colonel Taylor sends his respects' and presented my report. The general had tears in his eyes and all he could say was 'you did it... you did it!' He was deeply moved by the all too-evident sacrifice. Later that night I fell asleep in a farmyard around Colleville. I recall a sense of being purged.

'I had been frightened in battle before D-Day and again many times afterwards. But that day I was not frightened. I was simply convinced that we had absolutely no influence or control over our fate. No action we could take would have stopped a bullet. It was surreal.

'When I was awakened next morning; it was by French women who gave me some Camembert cheese to eat and Calvados to drink. I had survived D-Day.

'For the next two days we pretty much just licked our wounds and tried to find out who was alive. We now had to reconstruct the Regiment. I recall the endless reports that I had to complete and the arrival of the fresh reinforcements. I also recall that I was under cover somewhere around Colleville. It was quiet and I was not under fire.'

'After we left Weymouth to cross the Channel I spent time going over the map that I had of the beach where we were to land. I had been briefed and had seen a sand table 'mock up' of the beach area. During the crossing - to see so many ships and boats of every size and shape was unbelievable. There were thousands so close that at times you could hear the men talking on the next boat. Every ship and craft was packed with men. Some of the smaller craft were having a hard time staying afloat in the very heavy weather. Many men were seasick... The 16th Infantry Regiment of the 1st Division was the only 'first wave' assault unit on D-Day with combat experience. It didn't help much. I had been with the 16th in North Africa in 1942 and in Sicily in 1943. Nothing I had seen in all those battles would compare with what we encountered at 'Easy Red' on June 6, 1944.

'I was sick from the time I was loaded into the Higgins boat from the LCI as was everyone else. There were so many men throwing up all over the boat and each other that we could hardly stand. The boat to our left got hit and burst into flames. Many of the men on that boat were on fire. All that could went overboard. I remember one was burning all over - even his shoes were burning. Those who got into the water were drawn under by the weight of their equipment and never seen again. There were so many craft and with the seas running from 4 to six feet the entire wave that I was in was drifting away from where we were to have landed. The boat on our right blew up and most of the troops on board were killed.

'We were under intense fire from machine guns, rifles, mortars and artillery all from both flanks as well as from dead ahead. Our heavy gun support from the battleships was halted because they could not tell how far our troops had advanced. We could hear the machine gun shells hitting the ramp and side of our boat. We (I) knew when we lowered the ramp we would walk into a death trap, but there was no other way. Those support Navy vessels that could fire sent shells so close over our heads that we could hear the shells pass and I am sure I felt the wind from a few. We continued to get enemy fire from 105s, 88s, 40mm mortars and machine guns. The enemy had mined the area and these mines were exploding. It was indescribable. I said to Corporal Herbert Meyer, 'If there is a hell this has to be it'. I was so sick that I didn't care if I died. I just wanted to get off that damn boat. There were so many dead and wounded in the water that our boat was going over them. The DD tanks were going right to the bottom as they drove off the ramp from their craft. Many of the tank crews went down with the tank. Some crewmembers did get out and were floating in the water.

'As we neared the beach I saw all the obstacles and wondered how any of us would ever reach the beach...'

Staff Sergeant Ray Lambert, in a medical section with the 2nd Battalion, 16th Infantry RCT. The 32 DD tanks of the 743rd Tank Battalion were not launched because of the rough sea but the 741st Tank Battalion destined for the eastern half of 'Omaha' had begun launching their 32 DD Shermans 6,000 yards out from the shore.

'On one of the landing craft, the fourth tank tore its canvas on a gun mounting as it moved along the deck. Its commander was a sergeant called Sertell. He stopped to see what damage had been done and while he was stopped everybody on the landing craft, including him, watched the three tanks in front of him go under. The naval officer on the bridge advised him to stay on board and told him that his orders had been that if the last tank was damaged he should land it later in the day. But Sertell insisted on going. He said he thought his bilge pump could keep down the water from the leak. He drove down the ramp and sank. Later in the day, the same landing craft was hailed by a small patrol-boat which handed over a body to be taken back to England and the body was Sertell's.

'Two of the tanks reached the beach under their own power. Three more were saved by an accident. One craft launched its first tank and watched the tank commander and gunner desperately bracing their backs against the bulging canvas to try to stop it collapsing under the pressure of the waves. Their struggle only lasted half a minute.

'But the landing craft had lurched when the first tank went off it and the second ran backwards into the third and fourth and all three of them tore their canvas so badly that they could not possibly have floated. The ensign commanding the landing craft decided on his own responsibility to make for the shore: and he fought his way in all alone and landed the three last tanks.'

Dawn Of D-Day.

'As they neared shore, troops of the 18th had no impression that any progress had been made from the beach: The beach shingle was full of tractors, tanks, vehicles, bulldozers and troops - the high ground still held by Germans who had all the troops on the beach pinned down - the beach was still under fire from enemy small arms, mortars and artillery. The first units of the 18th came in where the original gap had been left by the assault waves and they found an enemy pillbox still in action on the right of the E-1 draw. They immediately attacked it but were stalled until naval fire was laid on. A destroyer only 1,000 yards off shore was brought on the target in four rounds and the pillbox quickly surrendered. This cleared the last enemy defences in front of the E-1 draw and it was quickly opened for movements off the beach.'

Lieutenant Colonel Derrill M. Daniel, commander of the 2nd Battalion, 26th Infantry.

'Two destroyers moved in incredibly close, so close we could almost yell to their crews, so close Germans were hitting them with rifle bullets. They fired broadsides directly at us, it seemed and while their shells were just above our heads, plus the thunderclaps of their 5-inch guns, it was almost as terrifying as the German artillery. Their gunfire was amazingly accurate.'

War correspondent Gordon Gaskill.

'We would hit 'Omaha' Beach at Dog Green strip, near the seaside town of Vierville-sur-Mer. The 16th Infantry Regiment of the 1st Infantry Division would be on our left and the 5th Ranger outfit on our right. The British and Canadians were on the left side of the 1st Division, so we were to land on the west flank of 'Omaha' Beach. We saw photos of the Germans preparing the defences. They were taken in May 1944 by our P-39 planes over the beach. Having my college education and a good background in American history and wartime battles, I realized that it was not going to be easy and I did not expect to come back alive. I wrote as such to my sister in New York City to get the mail before my parents and to break the news gently to them when she received the telegram that I was no longer alive.

19   By David Howarth (The Companion Book Club 1959).

'Many of my thirty buddies went down as they left the LCA. I got a bullet through the top of my helmet first and then a bullet aimed at my heart hit the receiver plate of my M-1 rifle. I waded through the waist-deep water, watching many of my buddies fall alongside of me. The water was being shot up all around me and many a bullet ricocheted off the water-top at me. Clarius Riggs, who left the assault boat in front of me went under, shot to death. A little in front of me, I saw Private Robert Ditmar of Fairfield, Connecticut hold his chest and heard him yell, 'I'm hit, I'm hit!' I watched him as he continued to go forward. He tripped over a tank obstacle and as he fell, his body made a complete turn and he lay sprawled on the damp sand with his head facing the Germans, his face looking skyward. He seemed to be suffering from shock and was yelling, 'Mother, Mom...' as he kept rolling around on the sand. There were three or four others wounded and dying right near him.

'Sergeant Barnes got shot down right in front of me and Lieutenant Donaldson. Sergeant Clarence 'Pilgrim' Robertson had a gaping wound in his upper right corner of his forehead. He was walking crazily in the water, without his helmet. Then I saw him get down on his knees and start praying with his rosary beads. At this moment, the Germans cut him in half with their crossfire.

'Fragments from an 88-millimeter shell hit me in my left cheek. It felt like being hit with a baseball bat, only the results were much worse. My upper jaw was shattered; the left cheek was blown open. My upper lip was cut in half. The roof of my mouth was cut up and teeth and gums were lying all over my mouth. Blood poured from the gaping wound. I washed my face out in the cold, dirty Channel water and managed somehow not to pass out. I got rid of most of my equipment. I was happy that I did not wear the invasion jacket. I wore a regular Army zippered field jacket, with a Star of David drawn on the back and 'The Bronx, New York' written on it. Had I worn the invasion jacket, I probably would have drowned.

'In order to get my equipment off, I had to try to unbuckle the life preserver, which was under my arms and going up near my neck. I accidentally squeezed the carbon dioxide capsules and my life preserver pulled my arms up and I was out of the six inches of water that I was in and made a perfect target. The water was rising about an inch a minute as the tide was coming in, so I had to get moving or drown. I had to reach a fifteen-foot sea wall, two hundred yards in front of me. I crawled forward, trying to take cover behind bodies and water obstacles made of steel. I got another rifle along the way. They were zeroing in on me though and a bullet went through the thick steel rails of the tripod-shaped obstacle that I was behind. I continued forward in a dead-man's float with each wave of the incoming tide. Finally, I came to dry sand and there was only another hundred yards or maybe less to go and I started across the sand, crawling very fast.

'Patched up and woozy from the loss of blood, I joined the remnants of various companies as they moved up through a captured beach exit towards Vierville. On the way up, at about ten o'clock in the morning I was wounded in the left foot while crawling. I tried to bandage it myself. I took the shoe off and saw a big hole in the dorsum of my left foot. Shells started to land, so I ripped the bandage off and pulled the shoe back on and dove for protection in a hedgerow. Sergeant John Frazier of Company 'A' seemed to be shot in the back and was paralyzed, couldn't move. I later found out his legs were shattered. While leaning over him, a mortar shell landed and I got shot in the left side of the head through the helmet into my scalp. I guess the helmet saved my life. Blood came streaming again over my left ear and down on to my face. I dragged Sergeant Frazier to cover behind a wall. As it got dark I became very trigger-happy and started to fire at anything that moved in front of me. I got another bullet through the face. I was not in any severe pain, though, because we were the first American troops ever to be allowed to carry our own morphine. We each carried a grain of morphine in a little toothpaste tube. All you had to do was shoot yourself under your skin and squeeze and you could be relieved of pain.

'I went up on the hill just above the exit; there was a ditch off to the left-hand side. I saw four or five soldiers there, Rangers. I said to them: 'Where is the front line?' He said, 'This is the front line. There are Germans over there and they've got machine guns, so stay down.'

'I was overtaken by fatigue. You have to remember I had not slept for two nights and all of the day. My clothes were still wet and that chemical-impregnated material smelled to high heaven. My lips were parched and I could hardly close my mouth because it was full of sand and other debris from the artillery pounding we had taken on the beach. One of the Rangers said 'Sergeant, why don't you catch a little nap here. I'll stay awake for a couple hours, then I'll wake you and then maybe I can get a little sleep.' So, I lay down. There was a burst of machine-gun fire and it was pretty close to my head. I just moved over a little bit and thought 'Well, he can't get me here.' And I fell sound asleep.

'Later they took me out and put me in a stretcher and I saw a huge statue - I think in retrospect it was a church silhouetted in the darkness. They then laid me out on the sand in a stretcher, amongst a line of stretchers containing some of my wounded buddies. They gave me some more morphine and I went to sleep. The next morning German snipers opened up on the beach, including the wounded. I got shot in my right knee, in the stretcher. Finally at about 3pm on 7 June, I was taken off the beach out to an LST. There, a Navy doctor took my clothes off and cleaned up my wounds.'
Private Harold Baumgarten, Company 'B', 116th Infantry Regiment.

'We were awakened at 2:30am and we had chow: wieners, beans, coffee and doughnuts. By 4:00am the ship had stopped and all the men climbed up on deck. It seemed strange, but the men seemed a lot different, more cheerful than they were before. There was a lot of handshaking, 'See you in Berlin' and 'Watch out for those French girls' and kidding like that. Our equipment consisted of impregnated OD uniform, treated to prevent gas, our assault jackets containing four fragmentary grenades, one smoke grenade and one phosphorous grenade. Each of us had one quarter pound of TNT and sixty rounds of M-1 ammo plus three bandoliers around our necks.

The Germans held their fire until the first landing craft reached the shore. Up to that moment I was hoping that the defending guns had all been knocked out by the sea and air bombardment. This hope died 400 yards from shore. The Germans began firing mortars and artillery. To try to explain the absolute chaos to anyone who wasn't there would be impossible. Fire rained down on us, machine-gun, rifle, rockets from the bunkers on top of the cliff I saw assault boats like ours take direct hits. The boats were zigzagging to avoid being hit, which fouled up all the plans. Our boat dropped its landing ramp somewhere near Les Moulins and my lieutenant, the first off, took a shot in the throat and I never saw him again.

'As ranking non-com, I tried to get my men off the boat and make it somehow under the cliff I saw men frozen in the sand, unable to move. My radio man had his head blown off three yards from me. The beach was covered with bodies, men with no legs, no arms - God, it was awful. It was absolutely terrible.'

Sergeant Harry Bare, 29th Division, 2nd Battalion, 116th Infantry Regiment.

'I thought that the British cheer that went up as the battalion passed was for the departure of troublesome guests and not for heroes leaving on a crusade... no bands played: no girls waved handkerchiefs while struggling to choke back tears. The closest to a send-off was a leathery old dockworker who croaked, 'Have a good go at it, mates.' It was like loading for a Slapton Sands exercise except for the pounds of equipment we carried. We clambered into tugs to be ferried out to our transport, the SS *Thomas Jefferson*. The accommodations were spacious for a troop-ship. The oppressive crowding, so much part of army life, thins out markedly the closer the approach to battle. We had a last dinner that was quieter than usual and there was no special talk of the morrow. There was probably more than the usual number of private prayers launched that night as the realisation grew that this was not going to be another exercise and that in the dawn, metal would be flying both ways. There was no bravado, or even the normal crap game. An engineer officer played an accordion, but there was no singing. Some of us talked with a British navy frogman who, several times, had gone in on 'Omaha' Beach from a submarine to examine its rows of obstacles. He could tell us little that we did not already know from our study of the terrain model sand aerial photographs but it was curious to talk with a man who had already trod with apparent ease the stretch of sand we were making such a titanic effort to reach.

'At 2am I was woken by the ship's gong sounding Reveille. Breakfast in the ornately-decorated salon was unreal: bacon and eggs on the edge of eternity. By 4am, waiting for the first ray of light, the 2,000 men stood in perfect silence. Whatever they were thinking, it was some kind of prayer. Men helped each other into the open-topped, rectangular steel box that we were to ride into battle. It had a motor and rudder at one end and a hinged ramp at the other. The men sorted themselves into their long-rehearsed places and then suddenly, with a rattle of chains and a screech of wire cable, the craft began to move slowly down the Jefferson's side. It was met by a rising swell that slackened the cables and dropped us with a crash as it rolled on. The next move brought us fully into the waves. By some miracle we were not slammed into the ship's side, the propeller caught and we followed a shepherding launch out to join other craft, circling as in some strange conga line in the dark, with red and green riding lights appearing and disappearing in the troughs of waves that were four or five feet high... it seemed that we would surely swamp.

'Where Channel and shore met was a wavering, undulating line of dark objects. Some of the larger ones, recognizable as tanks and landing craft, were erupting in black smoke. Higher up the beach was another line of smaller forms, straight as though drawn with a ruler, for they were aligned along a bank of shingle stone and seawall. Scattered black forms were detaching themselves from the surf and labouring toward the line.

'It was now apparent that we were coming ashore in one of the carefully registered killing zones of German machine-guns and mortars. The havoc they had wrought was all around in an incredible chaos - bodies, weapons, boxes of demolitions, flamethrowers, reels of telephone wire and personal equipment from socks to toilet articles. Hundreds of brown lifebelts were washing to and fro, writhing and twisting like brown sea slugs. The waves broke around the disabled tanks, bulldozers and beached landing craft that were thick here in front of the heavily defended exit road... The beach rose above me, steep and barren. There was a wide stretch of sand being narrowed by the minute by the tide, then a sharply rising shingle bank of small, smooth stones that ended at the sea wall. Against the wall were soldiers of the first assault team. Some were scooping out shelters; a number were stretched out in the loose attitude of the wounded; others had the ultimate stillness of death; but most were sitting with their backs against the wall. No warlike moves were apparent.'

Captain Charles Cawthon, Commanding Officer, HQ Company, 2nd Battalion, 116th Infantry. He lost over half his ranks. 'Together we had been through months and years of wartime confusion and strains; marched countless tedious miles; lived in mud and dust, heat and cold. I knew their problems... and they knew mine... then it all came down to this brief first day of battle on the coast of Normandy and, for so many of them, it all ended. For the rest of us, what has been since has not been the same.'

'Everybody went off the sides. It was bedlam, chaos and it took a while to get it all sorted out and under control before we realised we've got to get organised, get across and get on top of the hill and get dug in. The first person I saw got wounded was a guy who was trying to run across the beach from the craft just to our right. He was staggering and looked like he had a lot of baggage - he was he was just kind of lumbering across. He was about 25 yards away from me and he got shot. The bullet hit him and he went down in a runnel of water. I watched the water turn red. He was screaming for a medic and one of our medics went over to help him and the medic got shot. Both of them were screaming and I wanted to go out there and help them but I knew if I did I'd get shot so I just lay there. Within 3 or 4 minutes it just went silent so I guess they died. That was the second shocking thing that I saw that day. Then it was just people all around screaming because the water was over their head and getting hit and artillery getting closer and closer to where we were. We knew we had to go. We didn't have any choice. We couldn't stay where we were. We couldn't retreat because there was nowhere to go back there. So the only option was straight ahead.

'When you run over unconscious men, or men lying on their bellies, it's tough to keep your balance. There is no room. You go into the water, but the water is washing bodies in and out. Everywhere there are body pieces - a testicle here, a head there, an ass here. Crap all over the place. Intestines, intestines, intestines. That's what 'Omaha' beach was.'

Corporal Samuel Fuller, 16th Regiment, US 1st Infantry Division.

'I don't think I knew what courage was until I was on 'Omaha'. Our company commander was brought back and he had no legs... and he just asked the doctor, who showed up from somewhere, 'I want to ask you a question and I want you to tell me the truth. If I've got a chance, I'll stay awake, I'll fight. If I haven't, I'll go to sleep.' I often wondered if he made it... I saw so many heroes that day; they just couldn't make enough medals for them all.'

John Hamilton, a radio operator.

'As if this were the signal for which the enemy had waited, all boats came under criss-cross machine-gun fire...As the first men jumped, they crumpled and flopped into the water. Then order was lost. It seemed to the 'men that the only way to get ashore was to dive head first in and swim clear of the fire that was striking the boats. But, as they hit the water, their heavy equipment dragged them down and soon they were struggling to keep afloat. Some were hit in the water and wounded. Some drowned then and there...But some moved safely through the bullet-fire to the sand and then, finding they could not hold there, went back into the water and used it as cover, only their heads sticking out. Those who survived kept moving forward with the tide, sheltering at times behind under-water obstacles and in this way they finally made landings.

Within ten minutes of the ramps being lowered, Company 'A' had become inert, leaderless and almost incapable of action. Every officer and sergeant had been killed or wounded...It had become a struggle for survival and rescue. The men in the water pushed wounded men ashore ahead of them and those who had reached the sands crawled back into the water pulling others to land to save them from drowning, in many cases only to see the rescued wounded again or to be hit themselves. Within 20 minutes of striking the beach Company 'A' had ceased to be an assault company and had become a forlorn little rescue party bent upon survival and the saving of lives.'

Account by the US War Department's Historical Division of the 1st Battalion, 116th Regiment, which directly assaulted Dog-Green and which experienced the severest fire of all on 'Omaha', from a bluff commanding the western end of the beach and from the Vierville exit.

'The first ramps were dropped at 0636 in water that was waist deep. As if this had been the signal for which the enemy waited, the ramps were instantly enveloped in a crossing of automatic fire which was accurate and in great volume. It came at the boats from both ends of the beach. Company

'A' had planned to move in three files from each boat, centre file going first, then flank files peeling off to the right and left. The first men tried it. They crumpled as they sprang from the ship, forward into the water. Then order was lost. It seemed to the men that the only way to get ashore with a chance for safety was to dive head-first into the water.'

Private Howard L. Gresser

'That many were lost before they had a chance to face the enemy. A few had jumped off, trying to follow the SOP and had gone down into water over their heads. They were around the boat now, struggling with their equipment and trying to keep afloat. In one of the boats, a third of the men had become engaged in this struggle to save themselves from a quick drowning. Some of them were hit in the water and wounded. Some drowned then. Others, wounded, dragged themselves ashore and upon finding the sand, lay quiet and gave themselves shots, only to be caught and drowned within a few minutes by the on-racing tide. (Murdock) But some men moved safely through the bullet fire to the sands, then found that they could not hold there; they went back into the water and used it as cover, only their heads sticking out above it. Others sought the cover of the underwater obstacles. Many were shot while doing so. Those who survived kept moving shoreward with the tide and in this way finally made their landing. Others who had gotten into the sands and had burrowed in, remained in their holes until the tide caught up to them, then they, too, joined the men in the water.'

Pfc Gilbert G. Murdock.

'I was 10 minutes behind the first wave. My officer, Captain Zappacosta, told me to stick my head up over the side of our landing craft. All I could see was bodies, smoke and fire. All the men of the first wave were either dead or wounded. The beach was supposed to have been bombed out, giving us craters to hide in, but there wasn't a hole there. We would be sitting ducks for the German heavy machine guns.

'The ramp went down and we ran out. I tripped and fell sideways off the ramp and went under the water. I was carrying our radio and I struggled to get it off before it dragged me down. When I surfaced, Zappacosta was shouting that he was shot. He sank down in water that was just full of blood. There was nothing I could do for him. People were dropping in the water like you wouldn't believe. I was the only man not hit. My sergeant was wounded. He raised himself up to talk to me and he was immediately hit full in the head by German machine-gun fire.

'I began to make my way body to body up the beach. The Germans stopped shooting at me - I guess an incoming landing craft must have been a better target. 'There were bodies, body parts, men blown apart and still alive, hollering.

I was amazed how bad a man can be hit and not die straight away. I was scared all the time but I kept going. I had no rifle and even my shirt had been ripped off. I reached the shelter of the sea wall and from there I'd run back out on to the beach to get bodies. Some of them were still alive when I dragged them back and a medic would try to help them.'

18-year old Private First Class Robert L. Sales, infantry radio operator, 29th Division, Dog White Sector.

'Baker Company, which is scheduled to land 26 minutes after Able and right on top of it, supporting and reinforcing, has its full load of trouble on the way in. So rough is the sea during the journey that the men have to bail furiously with their helmets to keep the six boats from swamping. Thus preoccupied, they do not see the disaster which is overtaking Able until they are almost atop it. Then, what their eyes behold is either so limited or so staggering to the senses that control withers, the assault wave begins to dissolve and disunity induced by fear virtually cancels the mission. A great cloud of smoke and dust raised by the mortar and machine gun fire has almost closed a curtain around Able Company's ordeal. Outside the pall, nothing is to be seen but a line of corpses adrift, a few heads bobbing in the water and the crimson-running tide. But this is enough for the British coxswains. They raise the cry: 'We can't go in there. We can't see the landmarks. We must pull off!'

In the command boat, Captain Ettore V. Zappacosta pulls a Colt .45 and says: 'By God, you'll take this boat straight in.' His display of courage wins obedience, but it's still a fool's order. Such of Baker's boats as try to go straight in suffer Able's fate without helping the other company whatever. Thrice during the approach, mortar shells break right next to Zappacosta's boat but by an irony leave it unscathed, thereby sparing the riders a few more moments of life. At 75 yards from the sand, Zappacosta yells: 'Drop the ramp!' The end goes down and a storm of bullet fire comes in.

Zappacosta jumps first from the boat, reels ten yards through the elbow-high tide and yells back: 'I'm hit.' He staggers on a few more steps. The aid man, Thomas Kenser, sees him bleeding from hip and shoulder. Kenser yells: 'Try to make it in; I'm coming.' But the captain falls face forward into the wave and the weight of his equipment and soaked pack pin him to the bottom. Kenser jumps toward him and is shot dead while in the air. Lieutenant Tom Dallas of Charlie Company, who has come along to make a reconnaissance, is the third man. He makes it to the edge of the sand. There, a machine gun burst blows his head apart before he can flatten.

Private First Class Robert L. Sales, who is lugging Zappacosta's radio (an SCR 300), is the fourth man to leave the boat, having waited long enough to see the others die. His boot heel catches on the edge of the ramp and he falls sprawling into the tide, losing the radio but saving his life. Every man who tries to follow him is either killed or wounded before reaching dry land. Sales alone gets to the beach unhit. To travel those few yards takes him two hours. First, he crouches in the water and waddling forward on his haunches just a few paces, collides with a floating log - driftwood. In that moment, a mortar shell explodes just above his head, knocking him groggy. He hugs the log to keep from going down and somehow the effort seems to clear his head a little. Next thing he knows, one of Able Company's tide walkers hoists him aboard the log and, using his sheath knife, cuts away Sale's pack, boots and assault jacket.

Feeling stronger, Sales returns to the water and from behind the log, using it as cover, pushes toward the sand. Private Mack L. Smith of Baker Company, hit three times through the face, joins him there. An Able Company rifleman named Kemper, hit thrice in the right leg, also comes alongside. Together, they follow the log until at last they roll it to the farthest reach of high tide. Then they flatten themselves behind it, staying there for hours after the flow has turned to ebb. The dead of both companies wash up to where they lie and then wash back out to sea again. As a body drifts in close to them, Sales and companions, disregarding the fire, crawl from behind the log to take a look. If anyone of them recognises the face of a comrade, they join in dragging the body up onto the dry sand beyond the water's reach. The unfamiliar dead are left to the sea. So long as the tide is full, they stay at this task. Later, an unidentified first-aid man who comes wiggling along the beach dresses the wounds of Smith. Sales, as he finds strength, bandages Kemper. The three remain behind the log until night falls.

Only one other Baker Company boat tries to come straight in to the beach. Somehow the boat founders. Somehow all of its people are killed - one British coxswain and about 30 American infantrymen. Where they fall, there is no one to take note and report.'
Official 116th Regiment account.

'I was in the green sector of 'Omaha' beach. The sea was very rough. When we got there the little hatch opened and bullets showered the people near the front of the boat. Then another craft landed next to us and the attention of the bullets turned to the then we got out…it was over so quickly I never knew how lucky I was.'
Tom Bradley.

'As the ramp went down we were getting direct fire right into our craft. My three squad leaders in front and others were hit. Some men climbed over the side. Two sailors got hit. I got off in water only ankle deep. I tried to run but the water suddenly was up to my hips. I crawled to hide behind the steel beach obstacle. Bullets hit off of it and through my pack missing me. Others hit more of my men. Many were hit in the water, good swimmers or not. Screams for help came from men hit and drowning under ponderous loads... There were dead men floating in the water and there were live men acting dead, letting the tide take them in.'
A soldier in the 1st Battalion, 116th Infantry on the western part of 'Omaha'.

Captain Wozenski's company suffered numerous casualties in reaching the fire-swept invasion beach. Boldly, he moved along the beach, at the risk of his life, to reorganize his battered troops. The reorganization completed, he courageously led his men through heavy machine-gun and small-arms fire across the beach and toward an enemy-dominated ridge. Demoralizing fire from a powerful installation on the ridge threatened to stop the attack. Ordering his men to deploy to the flanks of the enemy position, Captain Wozenski, with great valour, advanced alone to within 100 yards of the emplacement. With cool and calm efficiency, he engaged the fortification single-handedly with rifle fire to divert attention of the enemy from the flanking movement. Upon observing this valiant soldier, the enemy directed the fire of its machine guns on him, but

Captain Wozenski, with complete disregard for his own safety, continued the harassing fire until his men reached their positions safely. His inspired troops charged the strongpoint vigorously and completely destroyed it, inflicting numerous casualties upon the enemy...'

Citation, Captain Edward F. Wozenski, 16th Infantry, who received the Distinguished Service Cross for his conduct on 'Omaha' Beach.

'The journey across that Channel, 12 miles, we were up in it, we were gonna be on the water at least 4½ hours. And so it was everybody immediately became seasick. There was a foot of water in the bottom of the boat and we had to take the bilge pumps but they couldn't evacuate the water fast enough so we had to use our helmets to bail the water. Everybody was seasick. I'd never been sick before and some of my buddies had filled their puke bags already so I gave my puke bag and my Dramamine tablet away. Then I got sick. Woosiness became stomach sickness and then vomiting. What caused me to get sick was the cold. It was probably in the 40s, the wind was blowing and we were soaking wet. I was just shivering. I went into my assault jacket and found a gas cape that we had in case of mustard gas and got under it to shield myself from the wind and the water. Of course lack of oxygen under the cape caused me to get really got sick and I came out from under that thing. I started vomiting and I just pulled my helmet and vomited in my helmet, threw it out and washed the helmet out, vomited some more and that's the way we went in. At this point death is not so dreadful. My thinking, as we approached the beach, was that if this boat didn't hurry up and get us in, I would die from seasickness. I didn't care what the Germans had to offer, I wanted to get on dry land. Nothing is worse than motion sickness, except maybe 88 mms and MG-42 machine-guns.

'About 200 or 300 yards from shore we encountered the first enemy artillery fire. Near misses sent water skyward and then it rained back on us. The British coxswain shouted to step back, he was going to lower the ramp and we were to disembark quickly. I was stationed near the front of the boat and heard Sergeant Willard Norfleet counter, 'These men have heavy equipment and you will take them all the way in.' The coxswain begged, 'But we'll all be killed!' and Norfleet unholstered his .45 Colt pistol, put it to the sailor's head and ordered, 'All the way in!' The craft proceeded ashore, ploughing through the choppy water until the bow scraped the sandy bottom.

'About 150 yards from shore I raised my head despite the warning from someone to 'Keep your heads down!' I could see the craft to our right taking a terrific licking from small arms. Tracer bullets were bounding and skipping off the ramp and sides as they zero'd in on the boat, which touched down a few minutes before we did. Had we not delayed a few minutes to pick up the survivors from a sunken craft, we might have taken the concentration of fire that boat took. Great plumes of water from enemy artillery and mortars kept spouting close by.

'We knew then that this was not going to be a walk-in. No one thought that the enemy would give us this kind of opposition on the water's edge. We expected 'A' and 'B' Companies to have the beach secured by the time we landed. The reality was that no one else had set foot in the sector where we touched down. This turned the boys into men. Some would be very brave men, others would soon be dead men, but all of those who survived would be frightened men. Some wet their breeches, others cried unashamedly and many just had to find it within themselves to get the job done. This is where the discipline and training took over.

'As we approached the beach the ramp was lowered. Mortar and artillery shells exploded on land and in the water. Unseen snipers concealed in the cliffs were shooting down at individuals, but most havoc was from automatic weapons. The water was turning red from the blood. Explosions from artillery gunfire, the rapid-fire from nearby MG-42s and naval gunfire firing inland was frightening.

'I was stationed on the left side of the craft and about fifth from the front. Norfleet was leading the right side. The ramp was in the surf and the front of the steel craft was bucking violently up and down. As my turn came to exit, I sat on the edge of the bucking ramp, trying to time my leap on the down cycle. I sat there too long, causing a bottleneck and endangering myself as well as the men who followed. The one-inch steel ramp was going up and down in the surf, rising as much as 6 or 7 feet. I was afraid it would slam me in the head. One of our men was crushed by the ramp, killing him instantly. I guess a wave had caused the landing craft to surge forward and it just smashed and killed him. It was a terrible sight and a terrible shock to everybody to see that man a healthy young man one-minute and the next minute he's smashed to smithereens. You couldn't tell what he was.

'From then on it was screams and hollering and people drowning and getting hit and fear. There were dead men in the water and there were live men as well. The Germans couldn't tell which was which. It was extremely hard to shed the heavy equipment and if one were a weak swimmer, he could drown before inflating his Mae-West. I had to inflate mine to get in, even though I was a good swimmer. I remember helping Private Ernest McCanless, who was struggling to get closer in, so he wouldn't drown under all the weight. He still had one box of precious 30 cal. One of the dead, Mae-West inflated, had turned a dark colour.

'There were dead men floating in the water and there were live men acting dead, letting the tide take them in. I was crouched down to chin-deep in the water when mortar shells began falling at the water's edge. Sand began to kick up from small-arms fire from the bluffs. It became apparent that it was past time to get the hell away from that killing zone and across the beach. I don't know how long we were in the water before the move was made to go. I tried to take cover behind one of the heavy timbers and then noticed an innocent-looking mine tied to the top, so I made the decision to go for it. Getting across the beach became an obsession. The decision not to try never entered my mind.

'While lying half in and half out of the water, behind one of the log poles, I noticed a GI running from right to left, trying to get across the beach. He was weighted with equipment and looked as though he was having a difficult time running. He was probably from the craft that touched down about 50 yards to our right. An enemy gunner shot him as he stumbled for cover. He screamed for a medic. One of the aid men moved quickly to help him and he also was shot. I will never forget seeing that medic lying next to that wounded GI and both of them screaming. They died in minutes.

'The tide was rushing in and later waves of men were due, so we had to get across. I believe I was the first in my group, telling Pfc Walfred Williams, my Number One gunner, to follow. He still had his 51-pound machine-gun tripod. I had my rifle ready to fire, safety off and had also fixed the bayonet before disembarking.

'I gathered my courage and started running as fast as my long legs would carry me. I ran as low as I could to lessen the target and since I am 6 feet 5 inches I still presented a good one. I had a long way to run - I would say a good 100 yards or more. We were loaded down with gear and all our clothes were soaking wet. Can you imagine running with shoes full of water and wet wool clothing? As I ran through a tidal pool with about six or eight inches of water, I began to stumble. I finally caught my balance and accidentally fired my rifle, barely missing my foot. I continued on to the sea wall. This is the first time I have admitted the embarrassment of inadvertently almost shooting myself!

'Upon reaching the sea wall I looked back for the first time and got a glimpse of the armada out in the Channel. It was an awesome sight to behold. I also saw that Williams, Private 'Sal' Augeri and Private Ernest McCanless were right behind. I didn't see Norfleet until later. Augeri had lost the machine-gun receiver in the water and I had got sand in my rifle. We still had one box of MG ammo but I don't believe we had a weapon that would fire. The first thing I did was take off my assault jacket and spread my raincoat so I could clean my rifle. It was then I saw bullet holes in my raincoat. I didn't realise until then that I had been targeted. I lit my first cigarette. They were wrapped in plastic, as were the matches. I had to rest and compose myself because I had become weak in the knees. It was a couple of days before I had enough appetite to eat a K-ration.

'All the squad crossed the beach unscathed except Private Robert Stover and Medic Private Roland Coates, both of whom were killed. I don't know what happened to either of them. Stover was behind me in the boat and I didn't see him in the water or on the beach. (Coates died of wounds on 7 June.) I didn't see Coates' fate, but knew Stover was a poor swimmer. A minor wound or accident could cause drowning in the rough surf.

'We landed in column of companies. Company 'A' about 0630, Company 'B' some ten to fifteen minutes later and Company 'D' about 0710, though we probably all were late. We hit the eye of the storm. The battalion was decimated. Hell, after that we didn't have enough to whip a cat with.'

Sergeant John R. Slaughter, 116th Infantry, 29th Division; a National Guard Division. The leading companies of the 1st Battalion were A, B and D, recruited and based respectively around the Virginian towns of Bedford, Lynchburg and Roanoke.

'I remember well the devastating impact on my family when we received telegrams two days in a row stating that my two brothers were killed or missing in action on D-Day. Shortly after we got the telegrams my mother received a letter from a Corporal Creighton in West Virginia saying that on D-Day plus one that he was walking on a beach in France and he spotted a Bible in the sand. And, as anyone would do, he picked it up. Having thumbed through it, he found my mother's name. He was also very careful to word the letter to say, 'By now you have probably heard from your son and he is fine.' I think he was even clever enough not to send it for some time to make sure that she had received word that my brother was all right. She has always treasured the Bible so much. She said that, next to her son, she would have wanted to have his bible.'

Lucille Hoback Boggess who was 15 years old in June 1944, living on her family's farm near Bedford, a small town of 3,000 people, which lost 23 men on D-Day, 22 of these from Able Company, 116th Regiment. There were three sets of brothers in Company 'A'. Raymond and Bedford Hoback were killed. Raymond was wounded and lay on the beach. Then when the tide came in he was washed out to sea and drowned. His body was never found but he was carrying a Bible and it washed up upon the sand. On the Saturday the family got a telegram that Bedford was killed and then on Sunday they got another one saying that Raymond was too. There were two Parkers killed.

'The closest relative I had at D-Day was a twin brother. Ray was on a boat of an even number and I think mine was number five. When we were loading off the large boat to go on the smaller one, he was standing alongside and he stuck his hand out for me to shake. I said, 'I'll shake your hand in Vierville-sur-Mer at the crossroads there in the night or this morning sometime.' And he just sort of dropped his head. He had a feeling that he wasn't going to make it and he just kept telling me that. But, anyway, he just dropped his head. And the lieutenant with him couldn't understand that either. That has haunted me quite a bit since that happened, because I should have shaken his hand. I was just so sure that we were going to meet there, but he wasn't.'

Private (later Technical Sergeant) Roy Stevens, 116th Infantry Regiment, 29th Infantry Division. Company 'A' was loaded into seven boats. Roy Stevens' boat was number five; his brother Ray's was number two. These and the four other boats carried 30 men each; a seventh boat, which was to land 19 minutes after the others, carried 17 men including Lieutenant Elisha Ray Nance and vital communications equipment. 'The Bedford Boys: One small town's D-Day Sacrifice' by Alex Kershaw (Simon & Schuster UK Ltd 2003).

Bedford boy Lieutenant Ray Nance, 28, managed to get a few hours' sleep. He awoke at 2am, dressed in full combat gear. He had not even removed his boots. Nearby were five fellow officers from Company 'A'. By lunchtime, three of them would be dead. In the non-commissioned men's berths, a few dozed fitfully. Most sat in silence, alone with their thoughts. Others lay in bunks writing last-minute letters home. After breakfast, Ray Nance gathered his kit and climbed up a gangway. A heavy canvas curtain stopped light seeping on to the deck from below. Nance stepped through and into pitch blackness. He went to the rail and looked out at the dark waters, swelling ominously.

Suddenly, he noticed Captain Taylor Fellers at his side. Fellers had, like Nance, grown up on a farm outside Bedford. The two were cousins. Fellers (29), was tall and thin. He was suffering from a sinus infection and looked tired and concerned. Before embarking for France, Fellers had confided in Nance, telling him that very few would come back alive. Fellers had studied the Allied intelligence and concluded that Company 'A' was being sent to face certain slaughter. Fellers and Nance both looked out to sea. 'We stood there awhile,' recalls Nance. 'We didn't say a word, not a single word to each other. I guess we'd said it all.'

'Now, hear this!' called a loudspeaker. 'All assault troops report to your debarkation areas.' As 34 Bedford boys emerged from below into the darkness, Nance touched every one of them lightly on the arm. 'It was a gesture, a goodbye. They were the best men I have ever seen in my life.' The men included husbands, three sets of brothers, pool-hall hustlers, a couple of Lotharios, a minor-league baseball player and several quiet young men who missed their mothers and dreamed of home cooking. The Bedford boys checked weapons and kit, exchanged scribbled home addresses and wished each other luck. 'This is it, men,' a loudspeaker blared. 'Pick it up and put it on, you've got a one-way ticket and this is the end of the line.'

The country boys who died on 'Omaha' Beach, The Week', **14 June 2003.**[20]

'551 LCA Flotilla had trained with US Rangers in Scotland and we presumed we would be taking them into 'Omaha' beach on 6 June. We were surprised when we heard we were taking the 116th Infantry Regiment on board the SS *Empire Javelin,* as they were a National Guard Regiment from Virginia - pleasant friendly country lads but not assault troops. My task as leader of the first wave of six LCAs was to land Able Company at Vierville-sur-Mer at 0630 so they could secure the pass leading off the beach for the following troops to move inland. The beach at 'Omaha' had cliffs all the way along it and couldn't take vehicles. The vehicles had to go through a pass, which was at Vierville-sur-Mer and it was the job of the 116th Regiment to capture that pass so that all the vehicles, guns and heavy equipment could get off the beach.

'Captain Taylor Fellers, the Officer Commanding Able Company, confided to me his misgivings of the task he had been given. His troops had never seen action and he wondered how they would react under fire. He asked me if I could go flat out for the beach and give his troops covering fire as they advanced up the beach. I assured him that if I saw any Germans I would certainly open fire on them with my machine guns.

'I wasn't very pleased to be woken up at half-past three on the morning of 6 June because my call was for four o'clock. But Able Seaman Kemp, who woke me, said, 'Please, sir. Would you go along to the flotilla office? There's

20 See also: *'The Bedford Boys: One small town's D-Day Sacrifice'* by Alex Kershaw (Simon & Schuster UK Ltd 2003).

been a change in time; they want you to go earlier'. So I went along to the flotilla office and I was told then that the time of launching had been brought forward from 4.30 to four o'clock because of the rough seas. So I scrambled to get ready, got all my equipment, got my guns, snatched something to eat and went up on deck.

We were supposed to take in two LCAs from HMS *Prince Charles* carrying US Rangers but we had to leave before they arrived and they followed us in.

'At four o'clock it was still dark, pitch black and the ship was rolling. It had already come to anchor at its point about fourteen, fifteen miles off the Normandy coast but it was rolling in the very heavy seas and it didn't seem to me as though the sea had abated much since the previous day. Certainly there was quite a sea on, roaring along the side of the ship and we were going from side to side.

'When I arrived on deck the American troops were already there. They'd been called early and were waiting to be loaded. Previously we had been working with Rangers who had previous experience of landings and were a pretty tough group, a tough-looking lot, they looked as though they could take care of themselves. Now the 116th were a very pleasant lot, like country boys, they looked like Somerset farm lads; very pleasant, very open, wanting to be friendly, though we didn't have much chance of speaking to them.

'The LCAs were bound into the side of the ship so it was a fairly easy process for the troops to step from the deck, even though it was rolling a bit, on to the deck of the LCA. Then they'd go down into the well of the boat and sit down as they'd been instructed and as they'd practised on exercises. So they all got on board and sat down in their three rows, with a terrific amount of kit, ready for launching into the sea.

'They were very quiet when they got on board. They weren't talking very much amongst themselves. It was probably going into the boat, which was a bit unnerving and they weren't encouraged to make a lot of noise on board because we had to carry out our communications, so they were talking in whispers amongst themselves. But they weren't high-spirited. I think they were realising that this was it. They were thinking, you know, 'How am I going to react? What's ahead of us?' What talking there was, it was quiet and subdued.

'Whether the commanders passed this down to their troops, I don't know, but all the commanders, all the leaders of the invasion force, were told that a third of us were expected to lose our lives in the first wave. And originally my wave was to go in an hour before any other wave approached the beach so we were given the tag of the 'suicide' wave among the flotilla. It was jokingly given, I think, but we were proud to accept that, although we all expected to come back.

'We formed up in our formation of two columns and set off in the direction of the beach according to the course that we'd worked out and the speed we'd worked out and we had an American patrol craft with us as our escort. About five miles off the beach he left us. Just after that I came across a group of LCT's [landing craft tanks] carrying DD tanks, which were to land ahead of us. This was the first I had heard about these tanks and I told Taylor Fellers that they would never make it on time as they were wallowing in the heavy seas. We left them behind and never saw them again.

'About 0600 it began to get light and we could make out the French coast. It was a strange experience to be out in front facing goodness knows what. The bombardment stopped and there was only the sound of the sea and wind. Then we heard a terrific noise. Some LCT(R)s appeared and launched all their rockets into the sea well short of the beach. A terrific firework display but absolutely useless and I shook my fist at them. They'd come all the way from England to the Normandy coast and shot their rockets up in the air and disappeared and I wasn't all that pleased because I was beginning to make out pillboxes on the beach and it looked a pretty formidable beach for the troops to take. At that moment, just before I gave the order to form up, an LCG, a landing craft with guns, opened up and hit one of the pillboxes from about a thousand yards out. It really let rip.

'I was just about to give the signal to go into line abreast from two columns when LCA 911 immediately behind me sank by the bows. Petty Officer Stewart waved at me. I shouted back at him that we would be back to pick them up. I don't know whether he heard it. Everybody had life jackets on and they were bobbing about in the water but I had instructions, I had to get there on time and I didn't have room. My instructions were quite clear. 'Don't pick up anybody from the water. Get to the beach on time.' But it went against the grain to leave people in those seas with life jackets and the Americans with all the equipment they had with them. It really did hurt to go on but I had to do it. We then went into line abreast and made full speed ahead for the beach.

'We were told that the beach would have craters on it so that the troops would be able to shelter. It was going to be a wide sandy beach with obstacles but the American air force the night before was supposed to bomb the beach and cause craters and the bombardment was also supposed to do something of that sort. But there were no marks at all. There was a virgin beach stretching for three hundred yards with not a sign of any place where the troops could shelter: they had to cover an open beach with the Germans waiting for them in the darkness of the cliffs. Although at half-past six it was lightish, it was still a grim, depressing sort of morning and the cliffs looked very foreboding and sinister and we knew that Germans were there because they were popping mortars at us.

'I spoke to Taylor Fellers and said, 'There's the beach, where exactly do you want to land?' He said, 'I want to land to the right of the pass, just there and I want the other group to land to the left of the pass so that when we go up the beach we can converge on the entrance to the pass.' So I gave the order to go full speed ahead, we saw the beach ahead of us, we made for the spot and we crunched to a halt, because the beach was very shallow, about 30 yards from the shoreline. I didn't expect to hit it just there, so there was a bit of a shudder, we all staggered a bit. The ramps were lowered and the troops who had been sat down in three rows filed off as arranged, Taylor Fellers leading the way. I wished him good luck as every sailor has great respect for the troops he carries. He was followed by the middle rank, followed by the port, left-hand, rank, followed by the right-hand rank. This was as practised. But they had to go out in single file because it was a narrow door and they plunged into surf and they were going up and down and they had to keep their weapons dry so they had to hold them over their heads. One minute the surf was round their ankles, the next minute it was under their armpits and we had to keep the boat steady as they were getting out to assist them in their disembarkation. It took some time for the troops to disembark as the craft was bouncing up and down in the heavy surf and the soldiers were hampered by the amount of kit they carried. They had certainly come to stay.

'Surprisingly, because we were particularly vulnerable, the Germans held their fire at this point. We couldn't fire back because we were so involved in keeping the boat straight and the troops were in the water without being able to get at their firearms. There were a few mortars popping around us but nothing else opened up. It was almost an unearthly silence while the troops got out. And I was surprised that when they got out of the craft and made their way in single file on to the beach they didn't go charging up the beach. Originally I was going to cover them with my machine guns as they went up the beach but they didn't go. They lay down in a firing line along a ridge parallel to the shore with their rifles pointing toward the Germans hidden in the cliffs who were popping off mortars at us. The obstacles were about fifty yards up the beach and then a further two hundred yards from the obstacles were the cliffs. Nothing, no craters, no shelter, did they have.

'As there was nothing more I could do at the beach we pulled off and my coxswain said, 'Sir, there's some of our blokes on the beach.' I said, 'There can't be,' but there were. They were from the Rangers' craft that had been hit by four mortars as it went in - sank the craft, killed a number of the Rangers and wounded some of the crew - and they were on the beach waving frantically at me to go and pick them up. Obviously they didn't want to be there and I don't blame them. I was toying with the idea of leaving them because my first thought was for those poor people floating about in the water, Petty Officer Stewart and his crew and all the American troops relying on their life jackets to keep them afloat in this terrible sea. But I couldn't leave the naval ratings on the shore so I went in and picked them up.

'Then I went back to where the 911 had gone down and where all the Americans were floating about in the water. I found then that the naval people had been picked up by an American patrol craft going by but he'd left all the Americans still floating about. So we picked them up, one by one, which was difficult because they were quite big blokes and they had all this kit which was soaking wet and the LCA has about two or three feet of free board to haul them up. In most cases we had to cut their kit off them with seamen's knives to haul them aboard. I thought we'd rescued everybody but they told me that their radio operator had gone to the bottom because he had his radio equipment, which was very heavy, on him. But everybody else on that boat was picked up. I then returned to the *Empire Javelin* with as many soldiers as I started with.

'We made sure people went to the sickbay to get their wounds dealt with. And then I don't remember a thing after that. I must have flaked out. I must have gone and had something to eat but I don't remember it. Don't remember talking to anybody at all. In fact the next thing I remember was when the *Empire Javelin* entered Plymouth Harbour to the sounds of the sirens of all the ships. We'd lost a third of our craft in Normandy and they could see the vacant spots on the davits where the six LCAs had been and they knew where we'd been and they really gave us a welcome I shall never forget.

'It was some time before I heard that Taylor Fellers and all the men in LCA

910 had been killed. Practically everyone else in that first wave we landed at 0630 was wiped out shortly after landing. When I left Company 'A' on this ridge, some 300 yards away from the Germans, the tide was lapping at their feet. They couldn't stay there long, the tide was coming in - it comes in at a rate of knots on that beach, it really does flood in. They had to move and, as they went up the beach, the Germans with their machine guns opened fire and wiped them out. Practically were wiped out. There were very few survivors by the time the second wave came in. Practically all of Company 'A' had perished within minutes of walking up the beach. As they walked up the beach they were just sitting targets, well, standing targets and down they went, mowed down by machine guns. They didn't have a chance. It's lived with me ever since. I can still see those fresh-faced boys getting out of the boat. It comes back to me from time to time, you know, that I was a link in their death. I know I had to do my job, they had to do their job, but I was in some way responsible for putting them there and it does haunt me from time to time. It does haunt me. I still see their faces.

22-year old Sub-Lieutenant George 'Jimmy' Green RNVR, Divisional Officer, 551 LCA Flotilla from the *Empire Javelin*. (On 9 May 1941 Ordinary Seaman Green participated in what King George VI called 'the most important single event in the war at sea' - the capture of U-110 by HMS *Bulldog* and what remained of its crew and equipment, including an 'Enigma' cypher machine with the 9 May settings still on its rotors and several code books). Jimmy finally left the Royal Navy in 1946 and he subsequently re-mustered in the British Army, retiring as lieutenant colonel.

'Within 7 to 10 minutes after the ramps had dropped, Company 'A' had become inert, leaderless and almost incapable of action. The Company was almost entirely bereft of Officers. Lieutenant Edward N. Gearing was back where the first boat had foundered. All the officers were dead except Lieutenant Elisha R. Nance who had been hit in the head as he left the boat and then again in the body as he reached the sands. Lieutenant Edward Tidrick was hit in the throat as he jumped from the ramp into the water. He went on to the sands and flopped down 15 feet from Private Leo J. Nash. He raised up to give Nash an order. Him bleeding from the throat and heard his words: 'ADVANCE WITH THE WIRE CUTTERS!' It was futile, Nash had no wire cutters. In giving the order, Tidrick himself a target for just an instant, Nash saw machine-gun bullet cleave him from head to pelvis.

In those first 5 to 10 minutes when the men were fighting in the water, they dropped their weapons and even their helmets to save themselves from drowning and learning by what they saw that their landing had deteriorated into a struggle for personal survival, every sergeant was either killed or wounded. It seemed to the others that enemy snipers had spotted their leaders and had directed their fire so as to exterminate them. A medical boat came in on the right of Tidrick's boat. The Germans machine-gunned every man in the section. Their bodies floated with the tide. By this time the leaderless infantrymen had foregone any attempt to get forward against the enemy and where men moved at all, their efforts were directed toward trying to save any of their comrades they could reach. The men in the water pushed wounded men ahead of them so as to get them ashore. Those who reached the sands crawled back and further into the water, pulling men to land to save them from drowning, in many cases, only to have them shot out of their hands or to be hit themselves while in these exertions. The weight of the infantry equipment handicapped all of this rescue work. It left many unhelped and the wounded drowned because of it. The able-bodied who pulled them in stripped themselves of their equipment so as to move more freely in the water, then cut away the assault jackets and the equipment of the wounded and dropped them in the water.

'Within 20 minutes of striking of the beach, Company 'A' ceased to be an assault company and had become a forlorn little rescue party bent on survival and the saving of the lives of the other men.'

Extract from the official 116th Regiment account. Edward N. Gearing (20) 'just a kid with a buzz cut' had been to a military academy in Virginia.

'Early on 11 June, Roy Stevens and the other men from his landing craft returned to Dog Green on 'Omaha' without so much as getting their feet wet. In just four days, the beach had been transformed into a bustling port, through which tens of thousands of reinforcements and countless armoured vehicles were now pouring. Roy Stevens and fellow Bedford boy Clyde Powers decided to visit a makeshift graveyard near the village of Colleville sur Mer. The graveyard was lined with several rows of crosses. From each cross dangled a dog tag. Stevens walked to a section for men with names beginning with 'S'. He scraped some mud from a dog tag. It belonged to his twin brother Ray. In shock, he walked on, looking at more dog tags on more crosses. One bore the name of Jack Powers, Clyde's brother. 'We didn't know what to say to each other,' remembered Stevens. 'I felt like crying, but couldn't.'

'The Bedford Boys: One small town's D-Day Sacrifice' by Alex Kershaw (Simon & Schuster UK Ltd 2003). In England when they had gone to boat stations, Roy Stevens had seen an 'obviously distressed Jack Powers, the powerfully built, normally unflappable ex-Ranger whose brother Clyde was in Roy's boat team.' Roy had been surprised by Jack's behaviour. Jangling nerves had got the better of him.

'It was waist deep when we went in and we lost, I'd say, probably one third between getting off the boats and to the edge of the water and then probably another third between there to the base where you get any protection at all, because it was straight down and they were zeroed in there. They're very, very good defensive soldiers, but they're not trained the same... they're trained to think how they're told to think and Americans are more independent, they can think on their own resources and this makes a lot of difference in a battle. Most, except myself, were seasoned men, they knew what to do... there were landing craft blown up in the water, lying in the water, they never got in... direct hits... bodies of men who didn't even get into the sand and there were a lot of them lying on the sand... there was crossfire from pillboxes... the beach here cost an awful price in men, good men... it was a job that had to be done and we were allotted to it. That's it. You do what you have to do.'

18-year old Private Lee Ratel, 16th Infantry Regiment, part of the 2nd wave that landed on 'Omaha' Beach.

'I was a medic in the second wave. Being a medic was dangerous work. Of the 96 men in the medical corps of my regiment, half of them died on D-Day. When our large landing craft beached, the Germans had zeroed their guns on the ramp. I was the last man and thought about staying aboard and letting it take me back to England, but I felt I couldn't do that to the boys. I wasn't going to go down the ramp where men were getting shot, so I dived over the side since I could swim pretty well. God must have been looking out for me. The landing craft backed on to a mine and exploded. If I'd been on it I'd have been dead.

'On the beach, the first wave had really taken a beating. It was pitiful. But I was told to get off the beach and let the navy medics care for the wounded. I didn't want to leave my friends who had been hit, but I ran like a rabbit.

'We proceeded toward the beach and many of the fellows got sick. The water was quite rough. It was a choppy ride in and we received a lot of spray. Our boat was one of six of Company 'A' in the first wave and when we got to the beach, or close to it, the obstacles erected by the Germans to prevent the landing were fully in view, as we were told they would be, which meant the tide was low.

'We didn't get far inland, about 1,000 yards. The Germans were putting up heavy resistance. We lost lots of men to snipers - including another medic who I had to fix up. The Germans climbed trees to shoot at us. We weren't used to that, but you learn pretty quick when you're under fire. I had to be on my knees to fix people - you couldn't do it lying down. To make myself less of a target, I'd drag the wounded behind a hedge.

'We came to a little church [Ste-Laurent] and there were snipers firing from the steeple. We called in artillery from the ships and three shells screamed overhead like freight trains. The church came down.

'A lot of the people who got hit you couldn't do anything for; lots of them got hit in the head. I did fix up about ten of our guys on D-Day. One had been hit by a mortar and his foot was hanging off - the heat sears the wound so they don't bleed too much. He lives near me and I still see him sometimes and he thanks me.'
24-year old Corporal Maxwell Moffatt, 115th Regiment, 29th Division.

'It was around 05:00 that we approached the area where the LCTs were to form columns to approach the beach for landing. At about 05:30 I was given the order from the Skipper, Lieutenant (JG) Hamilton Adams, to hoist flags that indicated forming one single column. Upon lowering the flags the LCTs were to break away and head for their respective landing area. The LCT 538 was the lead craft in the column of 8 LCTs. The 538, 539, 540, 541 and the 542 were to land at Easy Red and 543, 544 and the 545 were to make landing on Fox Green. We were all to land at around H-hour. The shelling and machine gun fire coming from shore was so heavy that it made it very difficult to make a good landing to be able to allow the troops to leave the craft. The ramp was lowered but it was immediately raised as we had to back off without any vehicle having a chance to leave the LCT. In the short time that we were at the landing site we had been hit several times by 88mm gunfire along with machine gun fire and all this caused the loss of several crew members.

'To add to our woes, as we were backing off the beach, the current caused us to drift into an obstacle with a mine attached to it. The explosion caused damage to two or three watertight compartments on the bottom of the LCT and the flooded compartments almost caused us to get hung up on the beach. We did finally get off the beach and started looking for another area in which to land but with the bottom compartments flooded it caused a bad starboard list and prevented us from making a landing close enough to shore to allow the vehicles to safely disembark. When we finally did get to another area, most of the vehicles were blown up before they got on the beach. It was total chaos with bodies floating around and body parts flying through the air. LCT 539 skippered by Lieutenant (JG) Linwood Rideout made landing to our port side and their initial landing was no better than ours. They also suffered direct hits from the 88mm guns and took casualties as well. The 539 also had to retreat from that area and look for another place to make the landing. LCT 540 skippered by Lieutenant (JG) Fredrick Nye Moses rammed the beach and suffered nine direct hits from the 88s, which killed the Skipper along with several other crew members.

'We were able to resume our mission after engineers repaired the compartments and went out to the anchorage area where the Liberty ships were anchored to start bringing troop reinforcements and supplies to the beaches. This we continued to do until night fall.

'One of the things that I will always remember was that horrible whining noise of those German 88 projectiles whizzing over our heads. Believe me there was an awful lot of other noises. Easy Red was directly under some real menacing shore battery. The Germans were hitting us with great accuracy so much so that it made you think they were looking right down at us. It was thought that they were using the church steeple in Vierville as an observation post. Our Skipper got a message from a tank commander on the beach asking if we could help by getting a message out to the ships to destroy the steeple. I signalled the nearest ship to us which happened to be the destroyer Harding and I relayed that request. It took a few moments for them to get approval from the higher up but when it finally came we could see the guns begin to swing around toward the steeple and the shelling started and in no time the steeple was gone. Soon after that the shore battery shelling was very erratic. Later we found out that there were American casualties. Some of our troops had gotten through and had started firing on the steeple.

'As nightfall came down upon us it became apparent that our ground troops had made enough headway to make the beach area much safer to be around.'

Albert J. Berard, Signalman 3rd class, LCT 538.

'We departed Falmouth and formed Convoy B-3 under the command of Commodore Campbell Edgar, which was composed entirely of LSTs. We had the men of the 175th AT company along with other support personnel and a large US Navy medical team with two doctors. Our public address system carried the voice of General Eisenhower throughout the landing ship. Overhead the endless roar of aircraft engines drowned out any chances of a normal conversation. The C-47 troop transports carrying the paratroopers blinked their landing lights in a 'V for Victory'!

'As we neared the beach area Shells from the battlewagons *Texas* and *Arkansas* were going over our heads and sounded like speeding locomotives. Deadly 88mm shells landed in the water. At first I couldn't see the beach as there was a long trail of white smoke covering 'Omaha' Beach. Then we could see what appeared to be cord wood spread out the whole length of the beach but a second look with stronger binoculars revealed that they were the bodies of dead soldiers bobbing with the tide.

'Like angry bees, a swarm of P-38s, P-51 Mustangs and RAF Spitfires buzzed low over our heads and disappeared into the horizon in the direction of Vierville. I could see grey uniforms up on the bluffs near Pointe-du-Hoc then figures wearing our uniforms attacking in their direction. It looked like a see-saw battle for a while then there were no more grey figures moving. Our LST could not get in to land as there were still plenty of Teller mines and enemy machine gun fire was spraying the beach area. More splashed in the water near us as the 88s sought the range of ships anchored nearby. A tiny tugboat was hit and a geyser of storm spurted skyward.

'After a fruitless attempt to beach, we finally came in amid sporadic sniper fire and 88mm artillery. The first truck off our ramp and hit mines, setting another nearby vehicles afire. Soon, the sounds of horrible screams filled the air as men of the 175th struggled to free themselves from the roaring flames that had already consumed the bodies of their comrades. One of our officers pulled one of the helpless soldiers from the debris scattered beach area and dragged him onto the tank deck, laying him down where the medics began to feverishly tear the charred clothing from his body. A sergeant, his jacket ablaze lunged past the burning trucks and dove into a large pool of water, sending up a tiny cloud of steam. Our medics quickly got him aboard and began treatment. A large plume of black smoke rose from the burning trucks and could be seen far out into the English Channel. We shut the bow doors so that we no longer could witness the suffering of those men of the 175th AT who remained trapped in the conflagration. Their screams could still be heard the entire length of 'Omaha' Beach. The tide slowly and mercifully covered the blackened skeletons. The screams of those men trapped in the burning trucks on 'Omaha' Beach would continue to haunt me the rest of my life.'

Tony Leone, Seaman 1st Class, US Coast Guard LST 27.

'I was the rifle sergeant and followed Lieutenant Anderson off the boat and we did what we could rather than what we had practiced doing for so many months in England. There was a rather wide expanse of beach and the Germans were not to be seen at all, but they were firing at us, rapidly, with a great deal of small-arms fire. As we came down the ramp, we were in water about knee high and we started to do what we were trained to do - move forward and then crouch and fire. One of the problems was we didn't quite know what to fire at. I saw some tracers coming from a concrete emplacement, which to me looked mammoth. I never anticipated any gun emplacements being that big. I attempted to fire back at that, but I had no concept of what was going on behind me. There was not much to see in front of me except a few houses and the water kept coming in so rapidly and the fellows I was with were being hit and put out of action so quickly that it became a struggle to stay on one's feet. I abandoned my equipment, which was very heavy.

'I floundered in the water and had my hand up in the air, trying to get my balance, when I was first shot. I was shot through the left hand, which broke a knuckle and then through the palm of the hand. I felt nothing but a little sting at the time, but I was aware that I was shot. Next to me in the water, Private Henry G. Witt was rolling over towards me. 'Sergeant, they're leaving us here to die just like rats.' I certainly wasn't thinking the same thing, nor did I share that opinion. I didn't know whether we were being left or not.

'I made my way forward as best I could. My rifle jammed, so I picked up a carbine and got off a couple of rounds. We were shooting at something that seemed inconsequential. There was no way I was going to knock out a German concrete emplacement with a .30-caliber rifle. I was hit again, once in the left thigh, which broke my hipbone and a couple of times in my pack and then a bullet severed my chinstrap on my helmet. I worked my way up onto the beach and staggered up against a wall and collapsed there. The bodies of the other guys washed ashore and I was one live body amongst many of my friends who were dead and, in many cases, blown to pieces.'
Sergeant Thomas Valence.

'There were many brave men on 'Omaha' that day - Dutch Cota, Bill Wyman, George Taylor and scores of men whose names were never imprinted on the honor roll of 'Omaha' Beach. Under the guns of the enemy, they organised small units and established small islands of order in the chaos. In what seemed a formless, confused horde, there did emerge gradually a core of discipline. And even as the Germans believed they were winning this battle on the beach, units of infantrymen were working their way through the minefields and up the bluff.

'I remember vividly Private Vinton Dove of Washington DC. His name has remained with me to this day. He drove a bulldozer from a landing craft and then he began bulldozing a road from the beach as calmly as though he were grading a driveway at home. He sat there with only a sweatshirt to protect him from bullets and the shell fragments.

'The firepower of the navy was one of our salvations in those first few hours. I recall that we were about 200 yards west of a small draw on Easy Red marked on the maps as E-1 or Exit 1. A blockhouse had been built into the bluff above the dirt road that led inland. The German gunners manning an 88mm weapon had a clear field of fire to the west. They were firing at almost point-blank range at the landing craft and the troops trapped at the edge of the water.

'A radio call for help went from an army-navy beach team to a destroyer. We saw the destroyer come racing towards the beach and swing broadside, exposing itself to the fire of the batteries on the bluff. One shell from the destroyer tore a chunk of concrete from the side of the blockhouse. Another nicked the top. A third ripped off a corner. And then the fourth shell smashed into the gunport to silence the weapon. Always, in my mind, the knocking out of this gun was a major turning-point of the battle in our sector.

At 1.30 pm General Wyman moved from the beach and set up his first sheltered command post in the knocked-out blockhouse and this was where I wrote my first story of the landing. As I saw it, that was when the battle of the beach was won - seven hours after the first wave hit the beach.'

Don Whitehead, A correspondent's view of D-Day, 1971. At 08.00 hours, while Cota searched for a point to break through the wire towards the Les Moulins draw, just as LCIL 91 approached the beach, an artillery shell exploded on board, apparently hitting the fuel tank of a soldier carrying a flame-thrower. He was catapulted clear of the deck, completely clearing the starboard bulkhead and plunging into the water. Burning fuel from the flame-thrower covered the foredeck and super-structure of the ship... The LCIL, which was the 116th Division's alternative headquarters, continued to burn for more than 18 hours, during which her stores of 20 mm ammunition for the Oerlikon anti-aircraft guns continually exploded. Ten minutes later the LCIL 92 suffered a similar fate.

'Well it looks like the Rangers are going to have to get us off the beach.'

Brigadier General Norman 'Dutch' Cota, pinned down by the seawall on 'Dog White', to Lieutenant Colonel Maxwell Schneider, 5th Ranger Battalion. (Schneider's men, reinforcements for the attack on Pointe-du-Hoc, had not been needed and had therefore moved to Dog White as planned). Cota directed specialists armed with Bangalore torpedoes to blow vital gaps in the thick barbed wire just beyond the seawall. The first soldier through the wire was hit by a burst of machine-gun fire. 'Medico!' he yelled. 'Medico, I'm hit. Help me!' 'Finally he died after sobbing 'Mama', several times.' Others began to trickle then flood through the steep hillside.

'They're murdering us here! Let's move inland and get murdered!'

While Cota had decided to carry out a reconnaissance to the right of the exit off the beach, Colonel Charles D. Canham had gone to the left of the exit. Shortly afterwards he was shot through the right wrist but he just had it bandaged and put in a sling and carried on, 'clutching a .45 Colt in his bony left hand'. Canham shouted for officers to 'Get the hell off this beach! Go kill some goddamned Krauts!'A lieutenant colonel sheltering from the enemy mortar barrage shouted back, 'Colonel, you'd better take cover or you're going to get killed.' 'Get your ass out of there!' Canham screamed back. 'And get these men off this goddamned beach.' At 0830 Cota returned to join Canham at his improvised command post under the bluff. A mortar bomb killed two men next to Cota and blasted his radio operator 20 feet up the hill. They moved the CP rapidly but all communications had collapsed. Cota went up on to the bluff to see how the riflemen he had sent ahead were advancing. When he found them pinned down by machine-gun fire said, 'OK, now let's see what you're made of' and he led them in a charge. After helping take Vierville (where a group of men met Cota on the main street, 'twirling a pistol on his index finger like an Old West gunfighter' and greeting them with: 'Where the hell have you been, boys?') Cota returned to the landing area to help speed the flow of vehicles, including a bulldozer loaded with TNT needed up forward. On 7 June Cota and his men stormed

a house in Ste-Laurent occupied by Germans. In July he became commander, 28th Infantry Division.

Norman Cota penetrated inland on D-Day to a point the American front-line as a whole would not reach until two days later. He received the Silver Star and the Distinguished Service Cross and the British Distinguished Service Order, from Montgomery; and a 'hell of a bawling out' too - from General Bradley - for getting too far out in front.'

'Working their way to the top of the high ground overlooking the beach the 1st platoon, led by Lt. Spaulding, under covering fire of a platoon from Company 'G'... proceeded west to reduce the strong-point... consisting of AA Gun, 4 Concrete Shelters, 2 Pillboxes, 5 MGs pillbox by pillbox to wipe out the strongpoint covering the east side of Exit E-1. Extremely stubborn resistance was encountered in this strongpoint with its maze of underground shelter trenches and dugouts. A close exchange of hand grenades ensued and small arms fire until the 1st platoon cornered approximately 20 Germans and an officer who, overpowered, surrendered.'
S-3 Combat Report, 16th Infantry.

'Of our six assault landing craft only three made 'Omaha' beach. We were surrounded by casualties in the water. They were clinging to the various obstructions - anything they could find. On our way back out we pulled a wounded American soldier aboard. We were told that a serviceman's Bible with a steel-backed cover had deflected the bullet that hit him. On cleaning our craft we found a bloodstained cardboard case that had contained the Bible. I kept it as a souvenir.
First Lieutenant P. Clough.

'...*Arkansas* and the *Texas* were behind us as we were going in and these shells would sing their way right over the ship. It was such a din! Some of the targets were 8 and 10 miles inland. Every once in a while you would hear or see a big explosion way inland and we knew they had hit an ammunition dump or something. It was such a hectic thing, everybody firing this way, beach fire coming at you. They were firing at us from the pillboxes on the beach. You would hear the shells coming at you. You could hear them whirring by and when you saw them hit the water... well if you were in the wrong place, forget about it. Those German 88s were awful. Once you heard them bark and you were still alive, you knew they hadn't gotten you because that shell would be on top of you before the noise got there. We did get hit by shrapnel every once in awhile. When we got hit I was directly beneath one of the gun mounts trying to set up an aid station under gun No.4. As I was coming up the ladder, I heard this noise and then heard a fellow who was in the gun mount, say, 'Round and round she goes and where she stops nobody knows.' Evidently, a piece of shrapnel had gotten into the gun mount and wound its way around until it exited. I couldn't imagine how cool he was.'
19-year old Pharmacist Mate Frank R. Feduik, USS LST 338.

'0001 hours June 6, I was in a stateroom with about 16 other officers in full battle dress. Some officers lying on bunks getting 40 winks, others writing letters, others contemplating praying. I remember my distinct wish not to be killed on my niece's birthday. We all went on board about 0230-0300 to prepare to disembark down rope ladders to our LCI. Waiting to go we saw and heard the thousands of planes flying overhead across the Channel to bomb the various targets. We got General Eisenhower's message. At about 0400 we debarked down rope ladders, fully equipped, 65 pounds on our backs. Gas masks, first aid kits, Red Cross brassards on arm, no rank on shoulders and so forth, into our LCI. Litter bearers had litters. We circled for about one hour or so, always moving closer to shore. About one quarter mile from shore our Navy driver straightened out and went in. We landed 20 minutes after H-Hour, which was 0600. We were taking constant fire from batteries and pill boxes on shore. Machine guns, artillery and so forth. Our LCI was extremely lucky: no casualties. From what I saw, the others were not so lucky. Men and material in the choppy water, drowning, dying, yelling for help.

'Our ramp dropped open and we ran off in disciplined order, no panic. Training paid off. Waist deep in water. Rushed onto the beach, which was strewn with our dead and wounded, plus those floating in the water. Our medics became busy immediately, giving First Aid and so forth. Coming off the LCI, our radio man, Private Jerry Greene was shot through his thigh muscle and upper arm muscle. I used to sit with him every noon time we could in his radio car and listen to the 12:00 news. This one time I missed, the Nazi bastards vectored in on his radio and mortared it. He was mortally wounded. Nevertheless, with his radio on his back, he dragged a wounded buddy onto shore and saved his life. I rushed to his side, did what I could, jeeped him to the collecting company. All the way to the collecting company he was calling for his mother. They couldn't save him. He received a cluster for his Purple Heart and a Silver Star for his bravery on the landing on 'Omaha' Beach - the latter posthumously.

'We all tried to get to bottom of hill for protection. We were being fired on with everything conceivable, unmercifully and witheringly, from enfilade fire from above and to the right and left. In our distinguished unit citation award, first one given to any unit on 16th Infantry Regiment for the assault of 'Omaha' Beach, it is said we took 800 casualties, dead and wounded, that first day. Meanwhile, we could see to the north of us to Pointe-du-Hoc, the steep cliff on which our 29th Rangers were assaulting. For the first few minutes or so, they and our infantry were exchanging fire, until communications straightened that out. We were pinned down for about five or more hours. If the tide were coming in instead of going out, we would have been drowned.

'About 12 noon or so our first tanks came on shore. What a beautiful sight. About 1430 saw first Nazi prisoners, another beautiful sight. Also more men and material all up and down the beach were arriving, the remainder of our regiment. Meanwhile, Brigadier Dutch Cota, our assistant divisional commander, was all over the place after shouting those famous words. I heard them but forgot them anyway. Something like, 'No sense dying here, men. Let's go up on the hill and die.' And with these words he started to tap soldiers on their butts and said, '29 - Let's go!' Our divisional yell. And I was one of them. All the West Pointers I knew in my regiment did their duty and more and brought honour to the Academy. For instance, our regimental commander, Colonel Charles Durwood Canham[21] ran off the LCI ramp, took a bullet in his wrist, stopped to have it bandaged and never stopped leading his troops. Always in front. In fact, he was reprimanded for having his command post too far forward. Major Sidney V. Bingham,[22] wounded, taken to hospital, treated and ran out of hospital to be with his men. Major Bingham and I were standing on a hill. He was looking for snipers. One had just killed our new Colonel Phillip Doyle. All of a sudden I heard a ping, a bullet. I dove to the ground. He never moved. He said, 'What a lousy shot.' That's what I call cool.

'We went up the hill on the way to Vierville-sur-Mer, taking much fire. Saw many Nazi dead all the way. We arrived at liberated Vierville-sur-Mer and spent the night in trenches about five and a half feet deep, evacuated by retreating Nazis. We looked into the English Channel and saw our ships shelling inland, also our planes flying overhead. This by the way was going on all day. Air Force did tremendous job of flying sorties inland all day and night. Nazis had one plane: Bed Check Charlie. Useless. And so ended the first day for us; then to sleep.'

Captain Bernard S. Feinberg, 116th Infantry Regiment, 29th Division. 'We must have eaten on the attack in going forward. I ate fig bars. We had C-rations also.'

'All day there was a rumbling noise like thunder but no natural sounds at all. It was as if nature had simply stopped. Finally, my father plucked up courage to investigate and returned, elated. 'It's the Americans,' he said. That evening an infantry regiment set up camp in our fields and we took them milk and cheese. The GIs were only a few years older than me and they were like big brothers. To me they will always remain heroes.'

15-year-old Madeleine Hardy, a farmer's daughter living with her father and three sisters in Baynes, 11 miles from 'Omaha' beach.

'All hell was breaking loose as we pulled away from 'Omaha' Beach. It was 0630 and we were already on the way back home. Our job was done. We had been among the first servicemen in France on D-day, parachuting at 0003 to establish communications posts for the first units landing at 'Omaha' beach to report back. Formed from submariner volunteers, we were nicknamed 'Mountbatten's illegitimate children' and known as the 62nd simply because that comprised our number.

'We thought it was another practice run until a gunner on the Halifax bomber dropped the bombshell: 'Right; lads. This is 'It'. It's the second front.' We were dumbfounded. Complete with a few choice adjectives, the general response was 'Bloody roll on.' The plan had been to drop half a mile behind 'Omaha' Beach but we finished three miles further inland and had to snake our way back, avoiding pockets of German troops in the dark.

---

21 Later to become Brigadier General Assistant Commander 28th Division, then Major General Commander 28th Division, then retired as Lieutenant General.
22 Later colonel and retiring as brigadier general.

'We reached our target area at about 0415, working feverishly to set up camouflaged communications posts just off the beach and then crawling on our bellies across the sand to defuse mines with magnets, spanners and screw driver. The beach was generally deserted. A couple of sentries came by - I saw one smoking - but we had dug ourselves in and went unobserved. The first ships appeared on the horizon at about 0615 and a battleship blasted the enemy positions. Landing craft streamed in and men and machines poured off. Our job was done and we rushed aboard a boat, which took us back to Glenearn, an LCA carrier. We were then transferred to LCA 3904 and home to Portsmouth. As we pulled away, all hell was being let loose in the barrage of bombs and shells that were raining down on German coastal defences. I was glad to be out of there.'

Lenny Hickman, one of 'Mountbatten's illegitimate children'.

'We landed American troops and tanks on 'Omaha' Beach. We then ferried supplies from Southampton to Normandy for 19 days until we became beached in a storm. After five days food was getting scarce and we were living on herrings in tomato sauce. Eventually I could take it no longer. I grabbed the cook and said, 'Take some of those tins to the Yanks and see if you can swap them. Don't come back with those herrings - Or else!' He returned after 30 minutes with two five-gallon tins of pears, the first we'd seen since the war started. We were most grateful. The Americans must have taken pity on us.'

Royal Navy stoker Reg Lilley.

'As the landing craft reached the beach they were subjected to heavy artillery, mortar, machine-gun and rifle fire, directed at them from the cliffs above the beach. Men were hit as they came down the ramps of the landing craft and as they struggled landward through the obstacles and many more were killed or injured by the mines attached to the beach obstacles. Landing craft kept coming in with their human cargoes despite the heavy fire and continued to disgorge them on to the narrow shelf from which no exits had been opened. Several landing craft were either sunk or severely damaged by direct artillery hits or by contact with enemy mines.'

Official report, 16th Infantry. Captain Joseph Turner Dawson (1914-28.11.98), company commander for Company 'G', 2nd Battalion, 16th Infantry was one of the first officers to reach the top of the ridge overlooking 'Omaha' Beach and move inland. His unit landed in the second wave at the Easy Red sector. Instead He helped to find and clear a path up the mined bluffs. Once at the top, he led his men to his objective at Colleville-sur-Mer where he was wounded. For his actions he earned the Distinguished Service Cross. Dawson, who was born in Temple, Texas where his father, Joseph Martin Dawson was the minister of the First Baptist Church in Waco, continued to serve as commander of Company 'G' through the campaign in France, Belgium and finally, to Aachen, Germany. Company 'G' (along with Company 'I') held off German counterattacks for 39 days during the battle on, what was called in contemporary papers and is still called in US Army history, 'Dawson's Ridge.' This ridge sat astride the main route that for the German attempts to relieve the city of Aachen, which Hitler had ordered to

be defended at all costs. Company 'G' lost 117 out of 139 men during the battle for 'Dawson's Ridge.' For this action, Dawson's command was honoured with the Presidential Unit Citation. Dawson later served in the Office of Strategic Services (OSS).

'I was ashore before four o'clock in the morning. I immediately started work. I think the tide was making fairly well. There was a diver working below me and I had what is now known as snorkel gear if I needed it but I worked virtually on the surface. There's a pier at Arromanches and I was working to the seaward side of that, our craft was tied up under it and I went about my business. You had to be able to blow those charges but not before the bombardment started. Some of the bombardment, we think, was designed to land on the beach defences themselves and on the sand. Obviously some of them would fall in the water but that was a chance that had to be taken. The bombardment duly opened and we duly started blowing charges. The Germans would mistake them, we hoped, for the bombarding ammunition coming in. We didn't succeed in doing all of it.

'The Germans had done all sorts of things. They'd left in position a lot of the pre-war beach kiosks and things like that on the promenades. Only of course they were really pillboxes either painted to look like they were before or heavily reinforced. They did indeed open fire as soon as the landing craft appeared and I engaged what looked like a beach kiosk where I'd seen what I took to be an Oerlikon or heavy machine-gun muzzle emerging from the slot. I had it covered and I fired straight into it. I managed to subdue whatever was going on there, by which time the infantry landing craft were in.

'We'd heard an enormous amount of firing coming from our right - to use the civilian term, starboard to us - along the beach and it was, of course, 'Omaha'. We knew who was going in on 'Omaha' and some of the conveyance of the troops ashore was being carried out by the Royal Navy. This is not generally known but British naval personnel were also on 'Omaha' Beach. Some were there for the same reason as we were on 'Gold' and they were still on that beach along with United States' combat engineers, trying to disable explosives and mines, when the first wave of landing craft came in and came under very heavy fire from the German defences, which were very well sited.

'We were ordered up to give support. Well, we naturally thought that we were going up there to do what we'd been doing. We might get involved in fighting but the first, primary objective was to disarm whatever mines or explosives we could lay our hands on, to broaden the landing craft front so that you could get more landing craft in. Unfortunately, when we got there, there was an enormous fire-fight taking place and we had no alternative but to join in.

'We got in the water. Practically the first thing I became aware of was a lot of objects in the water and the peculiar colour of the water and the froth. I think everybody that was ever on that beach knows what I mean by this. The noise, the confusion, the stonk were overpowering. You had a heavy bombardment taking place in the sea. You had the cries and the screams, an awful lot of young men, bodies, nudging you in the water. I became, by turns, very afraid, then, as you do, you settle down and I became colder and more angry. The Germans were standing up shooting at them. They were throwing grenades down at them. I thought, 'This isn't right.'

'There was a landing craft which was abandoned. I crouched alongside it and I opened fire along with other people. I was aware that there were comrades of mine also in action and exchanging fire. I don't know how long this went on. I have no idea. I remember a lad clutching hold of my ankle. He was an American, badly bleeding. I had a knife on; I cut his equipment off him. The first landing craft that came in on the other side of me was fortunately a Red Cross one, one of ours, bearing ambulance marks. Not that the Germans cared about that, they fired at that as well; after all, they were defending their beachhead. I managed to get a few lads into there.

'A surprising thing happened: I don't know how long I'd been at it but I was given ammunition from Americans coming in. Seeing the weapon I was using, they dropped me off spare clips, a whole box of Remington ammunition. I noticed the flashes of course and some of them were 2nd Rangers, which upset me even more because I had trained with some of them. Now and again there'd be a little lull and I'd spot something that had been uncovered that looked suspiciously like a mine and I would deal with it if I could. I thought, 'I don't want some poor sod to tread on that.' There was enough going on as it was.

'Something comes over you. Your actions are almost automatic. I was clipped more than once by bullets or ammunition. It didn't seem to matter. Nothing really hit me. It was pinging and clanging off you like rain. Tracer flying in all directions. Grenades. None of them came near me fortunately but an awful lot of people were being killed on that beach. The Royal Navy decided not to put them in the water where they were told to but were driving them right up the beach and turning them round, to try and give them some cover to get off.

'This seemed to go on for an interminable time. Eventually the Rangers did it. Somehow they got off that beach. The other troops were still pinned down but the 2nd Rangers went up that damned cliff. They took an awful lot of casualties trying to do it.

'I found a bit of space and was able to get on with some mine clearance and one or two more of our mine people appeared but I think we took quite a few casualties along that beach. Then I was withdrawn from there and repaired to one of our depot craft to get cleaned up, get some food, get a bit of sleep and go back in again to my own beach, 'Gold' Beach, which by this time was secure. There was still fighting going on for 'Omaha' but they had more or less got a good foothold. But that was a terrible, terrible experience. Bear in mind that I had no idea I was going to be an infantryman when I joined the Navy and that's basically what I became for that time. I only thank my lucky stars that I knew how and when to use weapons.

'During the course of that particular day, that peculiar day, somebody tapped me on the shoulder and when I turned round it was a German. My Remington carbine was up his nose in an instant but he was only trying to surrender. He too was paralysed with fright; he'd been wounded; it turned out he was a German military policeman, a much older man than us, obviously conscripted into the army. I covered him so he wouldn't get hit again, I put him into one of the Red Cross landing craft, a Royal Navy one and our lads took care of him. Before he left he got something out of his tunic pocket and pressed it into my hand. It looked like an Iron Cross; it turned out to be a German police long-service medal, which I still have to this day.

'That's how action is. There's so much confusion; surprising things happen. You look along the beach and suddenly you see a whole warship, a minesweeper, she's struck a mine, she seems to go up in the air and disintegrate completely. People scream, they shout. They call out for mothers and Lord knows what. They all seem younger than you. I was eighteen.'

Leading Seaman Wally Blanchard, Landing Craft Obstacle Clearance Unit.

'Off 'Omaha' Beach all hell broke loose. Our LCT hit a mine when we were still a couple of miles from the beach and lost power. As a result we drifted onto the beaches with the tide and landed at 0530 with the demolition men, earlier than planned. We took fire from artillery and mortars and I got some shrapnel in my backside. It hurt, but it wasn't bad enough to stop me functioning. We had a tank on board but when the ramp went down it was hit and blew apart. I waded ashore with my medical equipment in about four feet of water. The scene was pretty bad. Scared? You bet. Some of the troops were pinned down under some cliffs. I reached them and did what I could for the wounded. At that time, they didn't care what colour my skin was. That's what I got my Bronze Star for.'

21 year old Waverly Woodson, 320th Barrage Balloon Battalion, detached to serve as a medic with the 49th Infantry and one of the handful of black American soldiers who landed on D-Day.

'At dawn we got ready and that is when it started to get exciting. I went on deck and saw British PT boats giving directions to the skippers like pathfinders. I saw a battleship; it was shelling and that was very impressive. It was not raining; it was overcast and chilly, but it wasn't that bad. I saw guys going down cargo nets into LCVPs, a lot of LCVPs circle and I saw the coast. The coast was just one strip of smoke. We were told to go down the hole and wait until the time came to hit the beach. We were scheduled in the third wave. At this point I, in my 23-year-old infantile mind, thought that this was going to be another Army operation. We were in the third wave. The first wave would be already half-way to Paris and we wouldn't even see any action. This was an Army operation, first wave was going to go on, roll right inland and we were in the third wave and we were going to miss out again. I had the impression that the Germans were beaten and that they had no air force left and that it was just a sort of a mopping up operation.

'OK, now it's about 7:30 in the morning and we are down in the hold. We hear that the engines are slowing down and then I heard a scraping along the side of the ship and I thought either we're scraping an obstacle or else were are under machine gun fire. About 10, 15 minutes after we heard this scraping noise, or maybe a little shorter, there was a tremendous explosion. A great bang, as if the ship had been hit with some gigantic steel hammer. I remember seeing a flash and hearing yelling, 'Let's get out of here!' Our hold started to fill with

Previous Page: The 4th Division en route to Utah.

Above: Troops embarking for Utah

Troops and vehicles coming ashore from LSTs.

B-26 Marauders in the 323rd Bomb Group at Earls Colne bombing enemy positions on Utah Beach on D-Day. (via Ross E. Harlan).

A camouflaged artillery position on the Atlantic Wall concealing a captured French 105 millimetre 1913 Schneider gun which could fire a 15.74 kilogram (34.7lb) shell to 1200 metres (13,130 yards).

HMS *Holmes* bombarding targets inland.

Right: A Browning .30 calibre machine gun crew from the 1st Infantry Division moves off past wreckage strewn along the shore. At the rear the GI is carrying ammunition boxes for the weapon.

Below: A wounded and dazed GI is attended to by a medic at the bottom of the cliffs.

British troops going ashore from an American LCT.

Above: Germans defending the Atlantic Wall digging in.

Right: Alarm! Alarm! A German propaganda picture used in *Signal* purporting to show the so-called impregnability of the defences on the Atlantic Wall.

Captain George Mabry's 8th Infantry Battalion shelter from artillery fire behind the seawall. Mabry was the first seaborne officer to report to General Maxwell D. Taylor commanding the 101st Airborne Division when at 11.05 they met in the sand dunes of Utah Beach.

Utah Beach after the landings.

Smoke rising from Utah Beach as construction units go in.

Liberated Italian soldiers who as prisoners of war held by the Germans had been constructing coastal defences on the Atlantic Wall wait for US landing craft to evacuate them from Utah Beach to England for repatriation to Italy.

A fully-laden M3A1 half-track followed by a number of trucks leave the beachhead on 7 May..

American troops in vehicles going ashore.

GIs mopping up inland..

Jack Culshaw and .... *'the body of a soldier wearing the uniform of a German trooper confronted us. A pair of jackboots lay tidily beside the body, his steel helmet a few feet away. I murmured, 'He was someone's son I suppose...'*

acrid smoke and the pipes were coming off the wall. The ship was on an angle on an incline. Lieutenant Churan gave the order, 'Bayonets out, cut off the bag of the guy in front of you and out the hatch.' My buddy Newman was one of the first to leave. I was one of the last. Churan was the very last to leave the compartment. We went out on deck and I saw my first casualties. There were guys lying on deck - sailors - and I thought, 'Why are they sleeping here?' I hadn't connected that these guys were dead. And then I went down the port side ladder and I had my helmet and my rifle and all three rifle grenades. I was supposed to be the rifle grenade guy. We didn't think of our pontoon at that point. We left it. I went into the drink and it was over my head. I struggled. I swam on my back towards the shore, about maybe 200 feet. I saw the beach and I saw the obstacles and I was back stroking and I saw water spouts in the water behind me and I felt solid ground.

'I landed right at the entrance of the Vierville beach road, right between where the road winds between the hills, between the cliffs. I crawled up on the beach. I was half-drowned and I saw nothing but dead Americans. I saw an American tank that had gone to the water's edge. It was right above the little seawall about three feet high, a gradual rise. Apparently the tank had been hit. I don't know if there were anybody alive in it. I crawled underneath the tank and then some other guys crawled up. Somebody yelled to me, 'Get out of here, they have this thing zeroed in.' I started crawling along the seawall toward the east. I saw a guy that was slit open. He was smoking a cigarette and the medic was administering to him. He had planted a rifle into the sand and he had a plasma bottle hanging from it, trying to save him. This guy was white and he was smoking and his guts and everything was just wide open.

'I found some of the previous waves. There were combat engineers, infantry, guys from the 116th and our guys. We were just lying there, we couldn't move around except crawl. I had my rifle but didn't know what to do. I didn't have my radio and I couldn't do my job.'The shelling was just horrible. German artillery just kept whining over my head and exploding in the water. There were landing craft that were being hit; guys were thrown up in the air. I saw one landing craft that was hit, the sides of the LCVP just collapsed and guys walked into the water. Guys were dragged ashore by other guys. I started to get very, very scared. I had never been that scared in my life before. I was talking like a normal guy and I was doing things; just the fear was basic, it was just underneath. It didn't prevent me from acting.

'Then I came across Master Sergeant Thomas J. Kochie, our platoon chief. In the meantime, during the hour or so that I spent, on the seawall, under this German fire, the LCI 92 drifted with the tide, it didn't sink; it drifted on the beach and burned. I could hear the small-arms ammunition on the boat exploding about 500 feet away. Kochie was a regular Army 30-year man. He was a soldier's soldier, he'd been in the Philippines, he'd been in Hawaii. He had been through it all. He went aboard LCI 92 and got all the equipment off. He got me my radio. He went despite the ammunition and despite the explosions. He also, I found out later, crawled onto the beach exit and started to kill Germans. While I was behind the seawall he gave me my radio and I tried it out and I remember there was a blue haze over the dials. The whole

thing was soaked and it didn't work. There was a blue haze over the dials and
it had burned out. I started to dig a foxhole and the pebbles kept falling back
into the hole. Finally I got the 245, opened it up and piled it full of pebbles to
be additional protection.

'About 12 o'clock, the machine gun fire kept up. The officers from the 29th
were going along the seawall and anybody they could see from their outfit,
they'd chase them over the top, 'Get going, go over the top!' I must admit that
I was glad I didn't have to do that; I wasn't trained for it. I stayed where I was
and next to me was a guy by the name of Mortimer Roth, a pfc in our platoon.
He was a so-called radio operator. He was the only guy in the United States
Army when we were called out to go on the trucks to go down to the beach
who turned out without a helmet. The whole platoon roared when Churan
asked him, 'Roth, where's your helmet?' He kept amusing me by counting the
shells; like they would whistle overhead and he would say, 'That's one of ours.'
Then there were some incoming, 'That's one of theirs.' He kept counting and I
yelled at him, 'Shut the fuck up!' At some point he had got burned by a
phosphorous grenade. He disappeared out of his foxhole, found a first aid guy
and ten minutes later he was back. He was smeared up in the face like with
white, like Coney Island sun cream. Later on he was evacuated. I don't know
what happened to him. I think he spent the entire war in the infantry in Europe,
whereas we were shipped to the Pacific.

'After I got rid of Roth I found my buddy Newman and he and I sort of
stuck together. We crawled around behind the seawall. It wasn't too healthy to
stand up straight. We kept moving further east toward the other end of the
beach, where the 1st Division had landed. We were still in the 116th sector. I
guess it could have been Easy Green. It seemed to us that it was somehow safer
to move down the beach. About 3 o'clock, they landed a British outfit on our
beach by mistake. This outfit came off an LCT with trucks and I guess they
were some sort of ordnance unit. They had repair trucks; we thought what the
hell are they doing here? The Germans started shelling them. The trucks and
soldiers were hit. Corporal Kelly from New Jersey left his foxhole and ran out
and rolled this guy in the sand to extinguish the flames. I thought that Kelly
should have gotten something for that. That's how we spent the afternoon
hours, just dodging the shelling.

About 3 or 4 o'clock, I was looking out toward the sea and I saw the Caen
promontory jutting out into the sea, into the ocean, it was so damn peaceful.
And I said to myself, 'What am I doing here? The Germans had a barbed wire
obstacle right along the seawall. It was pretty much shot through from our
bombardment and their own machine guns. It was in tatters, but some guy
pulled on the wire and a booby trap exploded further down. Things were
exploding all over, the noise was deafening and the stink of burning oil was
just overpowering. The tide was coming in and there were dead GIs and parts
of boats, cargo - all kinds of stuff - in the water. Toward evening Newman and
I moved back west toward where the LCI 92 had been beached, toward the
Vierville cut. Apparently inroads had been made onto the Vierville road.

'Newman and I went halfway up the bluffs, we crossed the beach and up the
hill about halfway. I saw a German MG-42 and I thought what a marvellous

weapon. It was like a Mercedes-Benz. It was well built and it had been abandoned. I also picked up a German steel helmet as a souvenir and I threw it away after five minutes because I had to run for it. When we moved west a burning barrage balloon came down right where I had my foxhole. That scared me.

'So we moved halfway up the hill and it was getting dark. Newman and I started to dig in. There was infantry and there were some officers from the 29th. We never thought that they would chase us off the beach because, despite the shelling and all, I thought that there were troops ahead of us, infantry, ahead of us on the foot roads and that was actually true. They would prevent a counterattack. I had made up my mind that if the krauts came I was going to defend myself. We saw a Heinkel twin engine bomber coming at us and he had the bomb bay doors open. He was no more than 1,000 feet up, very low. Two engines were howling and I saw the Iron Cross on the fuselage. All of a sudden Newman and I were in this foxhole together. The plane went right straight over us, didn't drop anything and every gun in the fleet, the machine guns on the LCVPs and the LSTs, opened up. Everybody was taking their rage out on this airplane. The thing went right through it, didn't seem to get hit and disappeared. We met others from my outfit, from the 293rd and one of them said, just some scuttlebutt, 'I just heard from an infantry colonel, there's eight men between us and the Germans.' So I thought, well, that's great. Troops had been coming in all day despite the shelling. That evening, there were already quite a few on the beach.

'In the morning, the shelling wasn't bad, but there was still a lot of sniper fire. We went onto the road, onto the Vierville road. We passed at the bottom of the hill more bunkers and from one a bunch of Germans came out with their hands up. They were white in the face from the reverberation of the shelling of the cement in the bunker. They were scared as hell. I spoke German to them but they didn't understand German too well, probably they were 'Beufegermanen' from Poland, someplace, draftees, young kids most of them. I made them squat and empty their pockets. They had 'kennkarten' and a few pfennig and I looked at this stuff and said, 'What am I going to do with this shit?' I told them in German, 'Put it away' and then my buddy Wrobleski from Pennsylvania was standing there with an M-1 and a bayonet and he looked at them and he looked at me and he says, 'If you want me to kill them, I'll kill them. Just tell me.' I said, 'Don't kill them.' And I told them to get up and form a file and I marched them down to the beach and turned them over to one of the LCVPs that were leaving the beach. Later, there were regular German speaking troops. They had one guy who was wounded. His leg was twisted 180 degrees. He was in great pain and he was yelling 'Mother, Mother!' Their noncom told two of them to get a door from a house that was shot to pieces. They put him on a door and I gave this noncom my canteen to give this guy water and then told him to get the hell on the beach and get on an LCVP. At that point there was an infantryman from the 116th and he was in a rage. He said to me, 'These son of a bitches shot my buddies and I'm going to shoot them.' He cocked his M-1 and I thought, oh my God. And I told this German noncom 'Hau ab,' and I told this GI, 'Listen, buddy, hold it.' And I separated them. I think I prevented a war crime right there. I told the German, in German, to get the hell out of there, march down, get on an LCVP.

'There were quite a few from our platoon. We assembled and we took over an abandoned German bunker about 500 or 1000 feet away from the Vierville exit. We put our stuff in there. We got working radios and set up. Before we did that, Newman and I were on the bottom of the hill, maybe 500 feet further east, toward the British sector. By that time we had not eaten for 48 hours. Then Newman found a can of British field rations. It had a fuse and would heat itself up by a burning fuse going through the centre of this can. He didn't know how to do this, well, I did it, I pulled the cord and I burned the whole thing up. The whole thing was burned, I didn't do it right. We ate the burned food. Newman was cursing me up and down for screwing it up. But that was the first food we had. It wasn't really food, it was just burned crap. And that was shortly before we found the rest of the outfit and got into this bunker and set ourselves up.

'Also, just about at that time, there was a German sniper who kept pinging away right above our heads. After awhile, we wouldn't hear him for awhile, but then he would ping again. Somebody with a Jeep brought up an ack-ack wagon, a trailer, with 50s. He used these 50s to rake the hill there. He raked the location where that sniper was and we were yelling with joy, finally somebody's doing something here. I remember we were applauding this guy, yelling, 'Great! Wonderful! Give 'em hell!' I don't know whether he actually killed the sniper, but this was great. Apparently they had an artillery observer somewhere because a destroyer came at high speed and he fired all his guns and in 10 minutes that German artillery was silent. Apparently somebody had spotted it and was giving fire directions to this destroyer. Also on the second day, the Indianhead Division started to move through the eastern exit. From then on, that was end for the krauts there on the beach.

'There was a corpse right on the beach, on the seawall not far from the destroyed tank. This corpse was that of an officer and he had the stars. I couldn't believe my eyes, this was a Brigadier General. I passed this corpse several times and the last time I passed it, some son of a bitch had stolen the stars. I was outraged. If I had seen this, I would've shot the guy. Some bastard had pilfered the corpse. Also at the bluff that morning, on the 7th, I saw two paratroopers from the 101st and they were sitting against the rocks there where we had spent the night. They were in very bad shape and they needed water. At that time the snipers were still pretty strong. Some guy from another outfit, a sergeant, ran to the beach to try to get water for them. They were shooting at him like a turkey shoot and he zig zagged. You could see the dust kick up at his feet. He came back with water. They were unable to pick him off. They had the whole beach under observation and under fire so anything that moved on the beach they were able to shoot at. I must say that nothing much moved through that exit until later.

'There was a big pile of gravel right at that exit right next to some unfinished bunker that the Germans had left. A guy lay there pointing his rifle toward the beach road. I crawled up next to him and I noticed that this guy was dead. I stayed but I didn't see any Germans. In the course of the second day things were getting more and more civilized and the 2nd Division came in. Things quieted down. There were just snipers left. There were attempts to start taking up the bodies. Bodies were stacked one on top of each other, just the shoes sticking out. I still wondered who that Brigadier General was and I hoped he had been properly identified. One thing I noticed, everybody on the beach in the first day and even the second day, the fear was such that everybody looked the same to me. They had yellow faces. I guess this was from the adrenaline. I guess fear did that."

Technical Sergeant Fritz Weinshank, 293rd Joint Assault Signal Company.

'Dear Mable,

It is mid-afternoon here in France several weeks after D-Day. Shells from heavy artillery are humming overhead and the sounds of shells bursting are coming from all directions in the not-so-far-off distance. The regiment I'm with forms part of the front line.

I entered France on D-Day with the 'Fighting First Division.' This Division has well-trained, courageous and experienced men.

Our officers are of the highest order, men of great courage and experience who are war-wise and have seen a lot of battle.

The First Division was the first to enter France in World War I and first to enter France in this war; they were the assault troops in the American sector on D-Day. There are not many close-up photographs of the First Division on D-Day because the beach was too hot for photography in those early morning hours. Picture-taking was better in the days that followed.

When my part of the Division landed, there were impressions made on my mind that will never leave it. Just before landing we could see heavy artillery shells bursting all up and down the beach at the water's edge under well directed fire. As I stood in line waiting to get off the LCI to a smaller craft to go into shore, I was looking toward land and saw a large shell fall right on a landing craft full of men. I had been praying quite a bit through the night as we approached the French coast but now I began praying more earnestly than ever. Danger was everywhere; death was not far off. I knew that God alone is the maker and preserver of life, who loves to hear and answer prayer. We finally landed and our assault craft was miraculously spared, for we landed with no shells hitting our boat.

Ernie Pyle came ashore the morning after the assault and after seeing the results of what took place the day before he wrote, 'Now that it's all over, it seems to me a pure miracle we ever took the beach at all.'

The enemy had a long time to fix up the beach. The beach was covered with large pebbles to prevent tank movements and mines were everywhere. The enemy was well dug in and had set up well prepared positions for machine guns and had well chosen places for sniping.

Everything was to their advantage and to our disadvantage, except one thing, the righteous cause for which we are fighting - liberation and freedom.

For the moment our advantage was in the abstract and theirs was in the concrete.

The beach was spotted with dead and wounded men. I passed one man whose foot had been blown completely off. Another soldier lying close by was suffering from several injuries; his foot was ripped and distorted until it didn't look much like a foot. Another I passed was lying very still, flat on his back, covered in blood. Bodies of injured men all around. Sad and horrible sights were plentiful.

In a recent write-up it is said of one of the colonels of the First Division that led his regiment in on the beach during the early morning, 'This blue-eyed soldier had stood on the beach where thousands of men were pinned down by enemy fire and in a quiet drawl said, 'Gentlemen, we are being killed here on the beaches; let's move inland and be killed there.'

In from the beach were high hills which we had to climb. We crawled most of the way up. As we filed by those awful scenes going up the hill and moving inland, I prayed hard for those suffering men, scattered here and there and seemingly everywhere.

We filed over the hill as shells were falling on the beach back of us, meaning death for others who were still coming in. Later, one of the soldiers told me that on this occasion he saw a shell land right on top of a wounded man and blow him to bits. Before going over the top of the hill we crouched for awhile close to the ground just below the top. While lying there I did most of my praying. The shells were falling all around and how I knew that God alone was able to keep them away from us. I shall never forget those moments. I am sure that during that time I was drawn very close to God.

Later, about ten of us were crossing along the edge of a field when we heard sniper bullets whiz by. We all fell to the ground. As we lay there hugging the earth, that we might escape shrapnel from shell fire and bullets from sniper's guns, the birds were singing beautifully in the trees close by. As I lay there listening I thought of the awfulness of it all; the birds were singing and we Human Beings were trying to kill each other.

We are the greatest of God's creation, made in the image of God and here human blood was being spilt everywhere.

About three minutes later and only about forty yards away we filed by one of our own boys lying by the side of the hedge, crouched over with a hole in the back of his head. His eyes were open but he was dead, hit by a sniper. We didn't have time to stop, we were pushing on inland making a new front as we went. Someone behind and hours later would move him.

On the afternoon of the second day we were quite a way inland and two of my assistants and I were out trying to locate bodies of dead soldiers. We always take care of the American dead first and then the enemy dead. This was the second day and we were still fighting our way; inland, moving fast. Since we did not have any vehicles yet to send bodies back, all we could do on the move was to put the bodies in mattress covers and leave them in a marked place to be taken care of later by the rear echelons. Our business was to keep fighting on inland and pushing the enemy back. On the roadside my assistants and I saw a dead German officer. He was a tall fellow; must have been about six feet four. We turned him over and stretched him out the best we could. I looked at his face and was surprised to see how young he looked. No doubt he was in his twenties but he had the face of a boy. I thought: surely, this fellow was too young to die. It almost seemed that he had asked for it. I became conscious of an awful evil force behind it all to cause a young fellow like this to seemingly hunger and delight to kill and be killed. We slid his body into a mattress cover and left him by the side of the road.

Most of this section of France we are moving through is farming area with fields and hedges and orchards. We see cows and chickens and ducks and pigs and all that goes with farming.

On one occasion we were near some farm houses and some large shells began to fall, so several of us near a stone barn dashed into it to get out of the way of shrapnel.

Just inside was a mother hen covering her little chicks. When we hurried in she became frightened and fluffing her feathers rose up to protect her young.

I looked at her and silently said, 'No, mother hen, we are not trying to hurt you and your little family, we are trying to hurt each other.'

Nobody can love God better than when he is looking death square in the face and talks to God and then sees God come to the rescue. As I look back through hectic days just gone by to that hellish beach I agree with Ernie Pyle, that it was a pure miracle we even took the beach at all. Yes, there were a lot of miracles on the beach that day. God was on the beach D-Day; I know He was because I was talking with Him.

Former Miami minister Chaplain John G. Burkhalter who penned this letter to his wife Mabel shortly after the invasion.

'When we first went into 'Omaha' it was dark. A little boat came alongside and someone said, 'Fellows, I've been here all night and I've been destroying mines, pulling them out of the way and clearing the harbour. Now, don't get out from between these two orange buoys floating in the water, stay within 'em because if you get out of it, you're going to hit a mine that's going to blow you up.' It wasn't daylight yet. We just went along real slow. I dropped a ramp part of the way down so we could disembark our DD tanks and we got up pretty close to the beach. It was nearly H hour. We were supposed to go in with the troops at 6 o'clock and we went in at 5 o'clock. Big shells began to land around us. Shrapnel hit the side of our landing barge but we kept going because we had to give our men and the tanks the best possible chance of getting to the beach. It was so rough that we were scared none of them would make it. There were big barricades driven down into the sand. If you hit one of these, it would tear the bottom out of your landing barge. That 125 foot landing barge of mine, it didn't draw but just a couple of feet of water, even with six tanks on it. We went on in the beach as close as we dared; probably only a couple of hundred yards from it. That's when we let our tanks off. They steered these DDs in and we turned around and went back out into deeper water. Two of the tanks didn't make it. The water was so rough. We picked the bodies up and stacked them up on deck. (We would have about eight bodies that we carried around for several days because it was so 'hot' that we couldn't get into the beach). They were real nice people on those tanks.

'Daylight was breaking and Lord, Lo and Behold, I have never seen so many ships in one bunch in all my life. It was such a fantastic thing to know that that many ships coming from all different parts of the English Channel could gather together during the dark hours and all meet at the same time at the same place!

It was just indescribable! Everywhere you looked you'd see a ship. Some would be different shapes; all different sizes - everything from a little ole' 36 foot landing barge on up to the big destroyers and stuff like that. The ole' *Texas* had been shelling the beach and I kept imagining what the Germans thought about it when daylight broke and they could see the ships that were fixing to get straddle of their damn necks. The Texas and other war ships were firing into the beach trying to knock those gun emplacements out and they did a pretty efficient job of it, but it was still awful hot.

'After putting the tanks off we went up alongside a big luxury liner painted grey and we loaded approximately 350 GIs on my landing barge. Then we broke away and carried those troops into the beach. When we got close it was the first time we were able to see the beach. Three Spitfires flew over and in just a blink of an eye, German flak went up and picked one out of the air, two out of the air, three out of the air and they'd just go down in flames. They were ungodly accurate. Ships were piled up and shot to pieces. It was just absolutely unbelievable that this could happen just an hour or so from the time we put our tanks off. The troops came off the ships pretty fast. Some were on fire and some were torn all to pieces from those big high explosive shells. You would look at it and see it, but your brain couldn't grasp the multitude of ships that were already on fire and sinking. Some of them had hit mines that blew the bottom out and they would just sit right there and go down. Then you would have to go around them to get in. Gunfire was really accurate. Explosive shells were just deadly. They would just tear up whatever they hit. Our landing barges were so thick that these big breakers would come rolling into the beach and pick up those LCVP troop carriers and just lift them up into the air and then when they dropped, they would split wide open and the men just had to swim away from them. If they were in shallow water most just walked away. Everywhere you looked, there were dead men. It was real depressing. We didn't realize that that many men were killed on that beach. One great big machine gun nest had been dug in back in the side of this big hill. The old Texas went in and lobbed some 16 inch shells in there and they just caved in all the side of that big hill, the guns, Germans and everything at the same time.

'We were getting deadly fire on White Beach at the very end. There was a big hill at the back of it and they had a big gun emplacement down there. They would have an inch of steel, then 12 or 14 inches of concrete and with more steel in it. The vents in it were all zig-zagged. They were pretty shrewd people, I'll tell you. The battleships would fire at that gun and you'd just see a big red flash of fire and black smoke boil up in the air. They kept shooting and this gun kept firing back and we couldn't understand why they couldn't knock it out with those 16-inch shells. They weighed approximately 2,000lbs from what I understood. That's a lot of weight. You could follow the trail of the projectile from the muzzle of the gun until it hit the beach and it was a pretty fascinating thing to see. Everyone was just dumbfounded because we were knee deep in death and expecting it to jump on us just any time. It was so uncomfortable to feel that way.

'When we started back out, we picked up some dead men and Dean Chappelier walks up to me and said: 'Hey, Tex, do you recognize those people?'

'No I don't Dean.'

'Those are the ones we trained with at Slapton Sands.'

'Apparently, their tank sunk before it got into shallow water. That's the bodies that we carried around for several days before we could get a chance to put them ashore. People were very conscious of these men that were dead. I guess for the grace of God, it wasn't one of us because no man received a wound on my landing barge through any of the invasions I was ever in. It turned out the same way on D-Day.

'By 8 o'clock I guess we had already carried our tanks in and we carried a couple of loads of infantrymen into the beach. We would let them off and some of them I guess were just unlucky. It was their time because a big shell would hit them and just burst them wide open and then they would hit mines that would tear them up too. Sometimes the water was so shallow that we would hit a sand bar from the wave action on the beach because it was terribly rough. We would have to let our men off a hundred yards of so from the beach because we couldn't get over the sand bar and they would struggle into the water. You could see the machine gun bullets hitting in the water all around them. Sometimes it would be low to the left or right and they would correct that firing until they were just dumping every damn shell right in on our soldiers. They dropped their guns and just fell into the water and then the wave action from the rough water would wash those bodies up on the beach. Some of them would be half covered up with sand. It was just unbelievable. The carnage on the beach was just awful. It looked worse than a garbage dump with old wrecked cars except that they were boats. Some of the tanks had the turrets slapped off of them and the shells were so powerful they would hit and just tear them up. It was so amazing to see something that could go through three inches of solid steel and it would burn a hole right through them.

'The shell fire was so intense that our men would hit the beach from those landing barges and they would only go up to where they would find shelter and protection under a little sand hill. They were scared to move because they knew they would die if they did and everybody was trying to get them to get up to move on in. But it just took so much more grit than a person would ever realize to get up under imminent fire that way and go onto the beach. But they would have been safer if they had done that. But then, fear would overrule lots of them and I was pretty well full of fear myself. This was my fourth invasion. I'd seen people killed before, but it never did get to me like Normandy did. You just had to go in and try and some would make it and some would just drop right there. They didn't make it.

'Nobody seemed to have any mercy and nobody gave any ground. That was the key to the whole thing. Nobody gave up; just scared to death that they would still go on and continue to try and work their way back in. Encouragement from the officers helped. They would just cuss them out and tell them get the hell on into the beach. They didn't mean to be cruel. They needed to move them in, because fear had such an ungodly hold on them that they just couldn't seem to get up on their own initiative and walk into a deadly fire that they knew was going to take their life away from them. That's the way it was all that first day.

'On the beach up just a little ways was a big tank trap 15 or 20 feet deep and real wide and I guess the Germans thought that our tanks would run off into them before they discovered it was there. I think a few of them did. But then it didn't take our ole' CBs with those big giant bulldozers just a damn short while to go and cover that up. Even though it was late in the afternoon before they finally got most of it covered up where a tank could travel over it. It was a full time job. Those jeeps, half tracks with 20mm pods on them. Tanks and big stakes trucks and bodies just completely littered the whole beach. You could hardly take a step without stepping on a body. I heard somebody say that we lost 7,000 men.

'When darkness finally came we were still getting a lot of heavy artillery and stuff from the Germans and we couldn't figure out where it was coming from. We knew that they had a hidden emplacement somewhere and back inland, they had pill boxes and they was hexagon shaped and on each pill box side that was flat, they had a picture of the beach, how many yards and feet and everything it was. If they elevated this mortar so high, to the left or right, they could tell just exactly where it would hit on that beach down there. They were probably a quarter of mile back inland. But they could still drop mortars on us with ungodly accuracy and we couldn't figure that out until later when we found the pillboxes and the GI Joe had already destroyed them by throwing a hand grenade in them. They were made with natural green vegetation woven through chicken wire and half of it was secured. They had hinges on one side of it where they would get in it and they would raise that up and let a few rounds go and pull it over them and you couldn't see it if you was ten feet from them they were so cleverly hidden.

'Sometime the first day, they knocked this big gun emplacement out on White Beach. That gave us such a terrific release but some gun that was hidden somewhere just kept tearing us up every time we would hit the beach. On the second day, early in the morning, I was standing up on the conning tower with the binoculars and looking at the beach and one LCT would go in, then two and then three and then they would open fire; never on a single one. So we learned to go in just one at a time and soon we did empty up and pull off. I saw LCI 90 go into the beach and there was a big explosion on the starboard side at the engine room right at the water level. It tore out the other side and the LCI sunk right there. Ninety-one hit the beach loaded with troops and infantrymen and the same gun turned loose another round or two. They sunk 90, 91 and 92, just jammed up right side by side on the beach. As they would run down the gangway, the machine guns would just cut them down like you would shoot blackbirds out in the rice field that were destroying your crops.

'In the morning of the second day, we were still getting torn up pretty bad, all through the night, all through the day. They would just lob those shells in there and they all seemed to come from one place. So I took the binoculars and got up on the conning tower and watched the shells hitting the beach. They seemed to be hitting almost in the same place all the time so I got to looking at the hedgerows all up and down those bluffs. Finally I saw the trees move suddenly and just seconds later, a big HE shell hit the beach. Then another. But they wouldn't fire constantly; just at intervals. I called up my skipper: 'Mr. McGee, we got a big gun emplacement over where that hedgerow comes down to the low water and another hedgerow meets it. Let me have the glasses and you look at the beach and I'll tell you when a shell is going to hit.' I saw the vegetation move and just seconds later, this big HE shell hit right in the middle of the little landing barges, tearing them up. I'd say 'Now!' By that time the shell hit the beach.

'Dang if you're not right, Joe; it must be the one. Let's crank the radio up.'

'We called a big destroyer and told them what we had found and where it was located. It came barrelling in and popped port side to the beach and turned loose about eight rounds of 5-inch projectiles. They just completely tore that place all to pieces. After that our ships began to go in without being under enemy fire. They congratulated me on finding it. If I hadn't been looking for it, I'd never have found it. I said, 'Well it had to be coming from somewhere.'

'On the second day there was less enemy fire coming down to the beach but we were still losing a lot of ships by hitting mines. Then this big storm got worse and it took landing barges and broke anchor cables on LCTs, LCIs, LSTs and LCMs and smaller boats. The wind was so strong that it would just pile them up on the beach. They would just bounce up and down until finally they were hard aground. The longer they sat there, the more the Germans tore them up. They just kept shooting them. My friend Harold Shook was on LCT 703. I saw his boat on the beach. When I went to look at it several days later, there were hundreds of holes in the side where machine gun fire had penetrated. It was just thin metal and the crew had gotten off. Harold Shook was safe, thank God. He was down the beach a ways, but I was just scared to death I was gonna find the man dead.

'On the third day we kept hauling great big heavy artillery and stuff off of ships to catch up with the demand. They had special booms that they could let them over the side to us. Then the CBs put a big ramp out in the water and anchored it down and our LSTs would go up on it and dock right on it several hundred yards out in the Channel. They would dump off the tanks and they would run over these big pontoons until they got on solid ground. That was a big saver. Then they brought 'Mulberry' in from England. They had big gun emplacements but I don't think that they were very effective because it was so far out in the water and they were sunk just a little bit too deep. When the water rose and fall one foot every ten minutes, from low tide to high tide, it was 42 feet. When you dump a load of tanks, if you didn't get out damned quick, then you are grounded and you stay there for 12 hours until the water comes back in and you pull yourself off, until we learned to cope with it.

'On the fourth day the beach was quiet and it was relatively safe, with the exception of stepping on a mine and stuff and we would walk around. The Germans laying there were black. They'd been dead several days, I suppose. I found a potato masher (a hand grenade). It had a swastika on it, made in 1940. I found a stainless steel fork that had fallen out of that German soldier's mess kit and I picked that up. Dog tags were laying there. He didn't have any more use for it and I didn't feel like I was stealing or anything so I took that, too.

'The second day we took three little Piper Cubs for observation planes into the beach. We hit the beach seven times and every time the MPs kept running us off. He would tell us it was still full of mines and we were lucky we weren't blown up. Finally, we told them that we had to get the damn planes off, mines or no mines. All the crew got together, picked them up and set them up on the beach. The pilot checked all the engines and everything. When he started flying reconnaissance, telling them where to fire, that's when they really cleaned up our beachhead. He found all the gun emplacements back inland and would tell them what number on the map to fire on and they would do it. Then he'd tell them left to right, up or down and that's the way that they finished cleaning out all the gun emplacements that were off the beachhead. It was pretty well full of them, too.

'After we dumped our initial load, we went back out alongside the *Samuel Chase*. A little LCVP with troops came up alongside of us. We waited on them to send personnel to take care of. They never did, so they finally let a big pallet down by the winch that you could set these stretchers on. I jumped into LCVP to unload one of the badly injured men and he said, 'Is my gun around here?'

'Yeah.'

'He told me that he didn't want to use the rifle.

'What do you want me to do with it?'

'Put it between my eyes and pull the trigger.'

'It just seemed to make me sick because his legs were torn all to pieces. His heels were under his head and while I was fussing with him, I was taking his feet out from under him and it was just like a - Oh, God, I don't know how to explain. His bones were all crushed. I got him on the stretcher while I was fussing and cussing at him. I didn't know anything else to do. I was so heartsick from it all. I got him in this basket - it had an individual place for each leg instead of just a plain open litter basket - and carried him over and put him on this pallet so they could lift him up to a hospital ship. Probably about 15 or 20 minutes later they let him back down to us. He was dead. He was one of the bodies that we had carried around.

'I don't know how many people we pulled out of those LCTs were in that shape. I don't imagine very many even lived because there were bullet holes punched into the sides of the boat and a man wouldn't have much of a chance being riddled in a small confined place by a darn machine gun blazing away at them.

'Just as I got through unloading this soldier and got this boat cleared out and before another one come in, Melvin Blume, my cook, said, 'Joe, I got dinner ready.'

'Okay.'

'I hadn't eaten in a couple of days. I went into the galley and he handed me a piece of cooked liver on a plate with a spoonful of green peas in it and the peas were just floating around in the blood from this half-cooked liver. I guess I must have gone ape for a few seconds. After I threw the plate in the garbage can I got a .45 Tommy gun, kicked the safety off and jammed it under his throat. I told him that if he ever stuck something like that in front of me again, I'd shoot his damn head off. Later, I apologized and he said he didn't realize what he was doing. It is normal enough that under these conditions that two people could make a mistake but I didn't hold it against him. I just took it in my stride because neither the skipper or the crew had ever been in action and they had to depend on me quite a bit. Working on a tow boat and all I could handle one of the landing barges under my own power and I often did that helping my officers out but you just stay up day and night and it wears you out. Your patience wears thin and you have to have a lot of tolerance.

'We went into the beach and dumped our troops off. I had extensive experience landing these barges but some of these young men didn't know much about them. Some hit the first sandbar and dumped their troops off. Between that first sandbar and the beach, the water dropped down to eight feet deep. As far as I know, on one barge all of them except five drowned.

'I told the skipper, Mr. McGee, to throw our little boat overboard and let's pick some of them up.

'Joe, you can row a boat better than any of us. Will you do it?'

'Yes. I don't give a damn who does it, just as long as somebody does.'

'The first man I got to, I didn't see his face. He had his big pack on his back. They'd all thrown their rifles away. The foam was over his face; just big bubbles. He was so near dead from drowning that I had to roll him into the boat manually and I put him right into the bow. He asked me not to throw his pack away. Like a jerk, I picked it up out of the water. It was so heavy. I put it in the little boat and then Melvin Blume and I picked another two up. Now that made five people in that little old boat that was built for one to pick up mail. You can't tell me there isn't a God because there's no way in the world anything like this could happen that somebody wasn't on your side. I rode through this high-breaking surf, waves seven and eight feet high. When I got to the beach, a Major Duncan was there. He was beach captain. His men ran out and grabbed the bow-line and pulled us into the beach. They unloaded the men and put them in an ambulance and carried them off because I guess they lived. I don't know. I had no other contact with them.

'The sound from the surf was just terrific, rolling in and Major Duncan said, 'Son, I wish you wouldn't try to go back through that.'

'Why, Major?'

'Because nobody can row through that surf, even one time and get by with it.'

'Well, I got all the help I need, Major.'

'I don't see anybody there but you, Joe.'

'The Man is helping me, you don't see Him. He's just above me and no one can see Him but He tells me every move to make. So I have no fear, Major, I've got to back. They need me on my landing barge.'

'So he got the troops around and they picked this little boat up and carried Melvin Blume and I in it. They wouldn't even let us get out. They carried us out in the water up to our waist and gave us a hard shove. I rode through the surf and just as I got in the clear, I saw two heads sticking up. They were together. I said, 'What do you have under you?'

'A dead jeep.' He said he was a captain. 'Could you find my typewriter?'

'Man, the beach is running about 10 or 12 knots an hour. You can't stand up against it and you want me to go and look for something like that?'

'Well, it's in a case, zipped up, it won't leak.'

'Men are dying out there by the hundreds and you expect me to waste my time looking for a typewriter?'

'No, I guess not.'

'But I told I would row right between 'em and I told one of them when they got in to pass the signal to the other one and both of them put a leg over the sides of the boat at the same time so they wouldn't tip me over. So they did. I turned around and rode them back into the beach through the breakers and everything. I still don't know how I done it unless God was with me. He had to be. I carried them back.

'That major was just storming, back and forth and he said he wasn't going to let me go out through that again because no one could possibly make that four times, let alone three. But I talked him into it. They unloaded the two men. They could get around on their own power because they hadn't swallowed any water and they went ahead and got out of the boat. Then, when I told the major that I would wave at him when I got in the open, he said, 'You'll never make it, sailor.'

'Well, I've got to try haven't I?'

'Yes. You're hard-headed as hell, too. I ought not to let you go.'

'Sir, you're in the Army, I'm in the Navy. You have no command over me.'

'Well, that's true, too. All right, get the hell away from the beach, then. I'm going to watch you and I'm going to expect that wave, but I know I'll never see it. Four times? It's impossible to do what you just did.'

'They carried me out in water pretty deep and I started rowing the boat and I rowed through the breakers and when I got in the open, Major Duffie was still standing there and shading his eyes. When I got in the open, I waved my hand from left to right and he held his hand up and he put his palm towards me to motion to go on. He just shook his head and turned around and walked off. But, I had all the help in the world that I needed and I know that God had to be with me because another incident like this happened one time and I got the premonition that it was my day to die. I accepted the fact because too many had died for me to be spared. While unloading the landing barges I asked God if he would spare me and not take my life and I would never let a day pass that I wouldn't thank him. After I'd made this promise to Him I felt free. Yet, I was surrounded by death. So I guess God does answer prayers because he certainly did answer mine that morning at Normandy beachhead.

'Unknowing to me, for rescuing those five soldiers, my skipper had put in a letter for me to get a Bronze Star. I did get it when I got back to England. Like all those sailors and officers out there, well, I was just petrified from fear and my commander, Pruett, said, 'Joe, what the heck's the matter with you, boy?'

'Commander Pruett, I've been in four invasions and this has scared me more than any invasion I was ever in.' And then the whole crowd just burst out and laughed and that broke the spell and I limbered up after that. But that's what it took to break it. I saved the lives of five fellow men and that's all that The Bronze Star has ever meant to me.

'We were dried out on Red Beach. There was a big shell crater with two bodies in it. Two English sailors come walking along the beach and started probing at the bodies with their guns. One of them reached down and opened up one of the soldier's packs and they started to rob him. I kind of went nuts there for a second. I grabbed a machine gun and kicked the safety off and just as I started to pull the trigger. Well, each one of my officers hit me from each side. That's all that saved those people because if there's anything I could never stand, it's them robbing a dead body who had given his life to help save England and then they come around and do that to a body. I just couldn't understand those kind of people.

'After about a week, trucks, jeeps, tanks, stake trucks and everything in the world had run up and down that beach. Some were loaded with ammunition to take to the front line. One soldier was walking along the beach when all of a sudden, he started up in the air and then there was the sound of an explosion. It just blew that soldier all to pieces. I just can't understand how something like that could happen when you step on a mine that blows you up after just hundreds of thousands of tons of machinery and stuff had run over it and it didn't explode. It didn't make sense. The world should know that we went through pure, unadulterated hell. Of the three invasions I was in; none of them was as bloody as Normandy. We lost a lot of men. One man was too much.'

Joseph Henry Esclavon.

On the 1st divisional front the 18th Infantry Regiment blocked an attempt by two companies from the 916th and 726th Grenadiers to break out of WN63 and Colleville, both of which were subsequently taken by the 16th Infantry Regiment which also moved on Port-en-Bessin. The main advance was made by the 18th Infantry Regiment, with the 3rd battalion of the 26th Infantry Regiment attached, south and south eastwards. The heaviest opposition was encountered at Formigny where troops of the 2nd battalion 915th Grenadiers had reinforced the HQ troops of 2nd Battalion, 916th Grenadiers. Attempts by 3/26 and B/18 with support from the tanks of B/745 were held off and the town did not fall until the morning of June 8. The threat of an armoured counter attack kept the 18th Infantry Regiment on the defensive for the rest of June 8. The 26th Infantry Regiment's three battalions, having been attached to the 16th, 18th and 115th Regiments the previous day, spent June 8 reassembling before pushing eastwards, forcing the 1st battalion of the German 726th Grenadiers to spend the night extricating itself from the pocket thus forming between Bayeux and Port-en-Bessin. By the morning of June 9 the 1st Division had established contact with the British XXX Corps, thus linking 'Omaha' with 'Gold' Beach.

On the 29th divisional front two battalions of the 116th Infantry Regiment cleared the last defenders from the bluffs while the remaining 116th battalion joined the Rangers in their move west along the coast. This force relieved the 2nd Ranger companies who were holding Pointe-du-Hoc on June 8 and subsequently forced the German 914th Grenadiers and the 439th Ost-Battalion to withdraw from the Grandcamp area which lay further to the west. Early on June 7 WN-69 defending St. Laurent was abandoned and the 115th Infantry Regiment was therefore able to push inland to the south west, reaching the Formigny area on the June 7 and the original D-Day phase line the following day. The third regiment of 29th Division; the 175th, started landing on June 7. By the morning of June 9 this regiment had taken Isigny and on the evening of the following day forward patrols established contact with the 101st Airborne Division, thus linking 'Omaha' with 'Utah' Beach. In the meantime, the original defender at 'Omaha', the 352nd Division, was being steadily reduced. By the morning of June 9 the division was reported as having been '... reduced to 'small groups'...' while the 726th Grenadier Regiment had '... practically disappeared.' By June 11 the effectiveness of the 352nd was regarded as 'very slight' and by June 14 the German corps command was reporting the 352nd as completely used up and needing to be removed from the line.

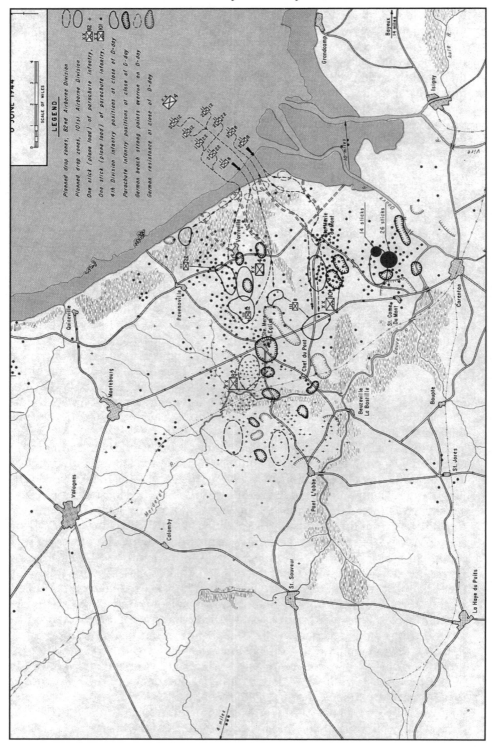

Chapter 2

'Utah'

As the landing craft turned to the westward and plunged into the head sea, George Mabry was so excited and so passionately interested in the military scene that he never thought about getting wet and stood in the bows of the craft looking over the ramp. He was in a free boat - a boat which was not attached to any particular wave of the assault, but could make its own landing at whatever stage seemed best. It started behind the second wave, but soon passed through it and began to catch up with the first.

Mabry was twenty-four and he had lived all his youth in Sumter County, South Carolina, where his father, who had once been a celebrated baseball star, was a farmer on a fairly big scale. The farm grew cotton, the farm workers were descendants of slaves and George's pastimes when he was a boy were fishing in the rivers and hunting in the woods around his home. George's greatest sorrow in his youth was being small. He overcame that disadvantage by making himself go one better than the other boys, walk further, swim longer, climb higher trees. In England, Mabry's battalion was stationed at Seaton, a small old-fashioned resort on the south coast of Devonshire. When an Englishman heard George speak of his boyhood, it seemed unexpectedly familiar and he felt that they must have met before; and then he realized that he was thinking of his own boyhood recollection of Mark Twain.

The shore was still far out of sight, but already Mabry could see part of the concourse of ships: ahead, the battleship *Nevada* and a line of British and American cruisers lying at anchor; astern the command ship Bayfield, the transports and tank landing craft. As the dawn light increased, ships more and more distant emerged from the cover of night: destroyers, minesweepers, the ancient British monitor *Erebus, Quincy* and *Tuscaloosa*, incredible uncountable numbers of ships from horizon to horizon. They lay still and silent and unreal, though already the sound of distant guns was rolling in from the north-west, where American destroyers, still out of Mabry's sight, were under fire from the coast and the British cruiser *Black Prince* was fighting a duel with a German battery which had shelled some minesweepers. [23]

The column of boats - a score of them ahead of Mabry's and a hundred more astern - sailed on towards the line of heavy ships, steering for a gap in the line

---

23   The battery, at Morsalines, consisted of six 155 guns in open emplacements and two fire-control posts. The original battery was heavily damaged during an air raid in May 1944 and new positions were still under construction on D-Day when it was shelled by the 5¼-inch guns of the cruiser HMS *Black Prince. The* battery was captured during the American advance on Cherbourg. *Hitler's Atlantic Wall* by Anthony Saunders (Sutton Publishing 2001).

to the south of Nevada; and as they approached the gap, the hands of clocks moved on to the minute for which the ships were waiting: 5.40. Mabry saw the muzzle flashes and the smoke and then the splitting crash of the first salvoes of the bombardment came across the water like a wall of sound. From then, for forty-seven minutes, there was never a pause in the roar of naval gunfire.

The boats crept in beyond the warships, underneath the shells. Before six o'clock, Mabry could see the shore; or if not the shore, the smoke and the dust of shell-bursts which sprouted from it. He peered at the coast-line he knew so well from its maps and photographs, but so far there were no landmarks to be seen. He saw the bombers come down through the low grey clouds, squadrons and squadrons of them and the anti-aircraft fire go up to challenge them. The firing looked to him so fierce and thick that he could hardly believe an aircraft could fly through It. Ahead, he saw a bomber explode in an orange flame; the sound of the explosion drowned in the sea of noise. The shore erupted again and again, the bombs being added to the shells.

In the last minutes, Mabry glanced back at the men in the boat with him. The Colonel's bodyguard, a very small man-smaller than Mabry - whom everyone in the battalion knew as Smoky David, was being sick in his helmet. Some others were grinning, watching him out of the corners of their eyes; but several looked green themselves. Looking at all their familiar faces, each with a hint of serious anticipation or else of exaggerated calm, Mabry had the sense of solid companionship; and beside that feeling of esprit de corps, he was aware also of himself, an individual, the real George Mabry beneath the grotesque helmet and the uniform and equipment and badges of rank; aware of home, the farm, the cotton fields in the sun, the hunting and fishing, his father and mother and wife, all the people and things which had made him the person he was. He wondered at seeing George Mabry as a witness of such great events and like the bowmen of Agincourt he knew he would remember this day and this hour for the rest of his life, whether life was short or long. There was no time then for these thoughts to be put into words, but he knew they were there, in the back of his mind. Something like them was in the minds of most men who landed that morning in Normandy. If Mabry had spoken at all, in those few seconds before the boat's engine slowed down and the bottom grated gently on the sand, he might only have said that this would be something to tell the folks back home in Carolina.

Once on the beach, he only paused to see his companions close behind him with expressions of incredulous relief on their faces and then he set off for the dune line. Even on the beach, he could not run. His sodden clothes were heavy and his legs were cramped and numb from the coldness of the two hours' journey in the boat.

There was a man lying on the sand. He went to him: a corporal he knew, wounded in both legs. He bent down to him and said he would drag him up to cover in the dunes. 'No, I'm all right,' the corporal said. 'Keep going, captain:' (But he died of his wounds, or was drowned when the tide rose.) A man close in front of Mabry was blown out of existence by a direct hit. Something small struck Mabry in the stomach. It was a thumb.

The whole thing had not been at all the sort of combat which Mabry had always imagined. From a military point of view, he had made rather a mess of it. But even though it had happened by mistake, he had fulfilled an ambition: he was certainly out in front.

Dawn Of D-Day by David Howarth.[24] **Captain George Mabry, S-3 (operations officer), 8th Infantry was the first seaborne officer to report to General Maxwell D. Taylor commanding the 101st Airborne Division when at 11.05 they met in the sand dunes of 'Utah' beach. 25**

Five Wiederstandnester (WN 4, 5, 7, 8 and 10) and one Stützpunkt (St.9, with two casements for 88mm guns facing north and south) guarded three exits between la Grande Dune (WN 5) and les Dunes-de-Varreville (WN 10, guarding Exit 4). The exit at la Grande Dune (Exit 2) was protected by two (WN 4 and 5), while Exit 3 had one with another at la Madeleine (WN 7) about halfway between the two exits. When the naval bombardment began these defences defended by the 1st Battalion 919th Grenadier Regiment, 709th Infantry Division were shelled by the cruisers HMS *Hawkins* and HMS *Enterprise*, armed with seven 7½-inch and six 6-inch guns respectively and the Dutch gunboat HNMS *Soemba* with its three 5.9 inch guns. An hour later 209 Marauders and Havocs dropped 4,404 250lb bombs on them. (These were used to avoid excessive cratering of the beach that would hinder the troops as they came ashore). As at 'Omaha', specially equipped landing craft then fired salvoes of rockets at the defences as the assault waves moved towards the beaches.

'Here was a truly lunatic sight. I wondered if I were hallucinating as a result of the bombardment. Amphibious tanks! This must be the Allies' secret weapon. It looks as though God and the world have forsaken us. What's happened to our airmen?

Leutnant Arthur Jahnke the bespectacled 23-year old commander of Widerstandsnest 5 at La Grande Dune near Ste-Germain-de-Varreville, held by the 1st Platoon, 3rd Company, 919th Grenadier Regiment of the 709th Division. The young officer had been posted to France after being wounded on the Eastern Front where his leadership had earned him the Ritterkreuz. During an earlier visit to WN 5 Rommel had said to Jahnke, 'Let me see your hands' and only when the Leutnant took off his gloves to reveal bloody calluses scored by barbed wire did he nod with satisfaction. 'Well done'. 'The blood on an officer's hands from fortification work is worth every bit as much as that shed in battle.' Rommel often issued gifts of mouth organs and accordions to units which had performed their tasks well.

'The location of the landing north of the Carentan estuary could be fixed exactly. This was in the sector of the 919th Infantry Regiment... Widerstandsnest

---

24   The Companion Book Club 1959.
25   General Taylor and the 101st Airborne Division entered Carentan on 12 June. On 13 June a German counter-attack was mounted by the 17.SS-Panzergrenadier-Division and Fallschirrnjager-Regiment 6. With little in the way of anti-tank weapons, the 101st was reinforced by a combat command of the 2nd Armoured Division and together they held Carentan during the ensuing weeks while the American divisions from 'Utah' Beach occupied the peninsula and port of Cherbourg to the north. The battle for Carentan ended the 101st's part of the serious fighting in Normandy as they were withdrawn to England following the capture of Cherbourg and before the Allied breakout from the beach-head. In the campaign, 101st casualties totalled 3,800 men, approximately one-third of the men who reached Normandy.

5 was the first to be in immediate contact with the enemy... the garrison of which got buried and had to be dug out by the Americans... The minutes dragged by. Nerves were tense. One individual report followed another; they confirmed or contradicted each other. Army or Army Group HQ were constantly telephoning. But all the Corps staff could do was to wait, wait, wait until the confused overall picture had been clarified, until the main centres of the dropping and landing zones had become apparent, until we had heard from strongpoints either encircled by the enemy or by-passed by him, or until reconnaissance thrusts had brought in important statements by prisoners. What complicated matters, was that all reports came from the Army exclusively. Support from our own air force was non-existent from the very first minute. That was why the facts as they became apparent did not add up to a fixed overall picture.'

Report by LXXXIV Corps HQ at St Lô. B-26 Marauders and the naval bombardment had put the battery out of action. Weaponry included two 50mm guns, a former French Renault R67 tank turret with 3.7cm gun concentrated into a bunker, machine guns covering the beach and landwards approaches and barbed wire and minefields. On either flank were four Goliath remote-controlled tracked demolition vehicles carrying 60kg (132lb) of TNT and were directed towards their targets by an operator through signals transmitted along cable links. These too were put out of action by the bombing and naval gunfire.

'My position was in the right rear of the boat and I could hear the bullets splitting the air over our heads and I looked back and all I could see was two hands on the wheel and a hand on each .50-caliber machine gun, which the Navy guys were firing. I said to my platoon leader, Lieutenant Rebarcheck, 'These guys aren't even looking where they are going or shooting.' About that time the coxswain stood up and looked at the beach and then ducked back down. The machine gunners were doing the same and we just prayed they would get us on the beach.

'The boat hit a sandbar and the coxswain said it was time for the infantry to go, that he was getting out of there. Lieutenant Rebarcheck responded, 'You are not going to drown these men. Give her another try.' The coxswain backed off the bar, went nine feet to the left, tried to go in and hit the bar again. Rebarcheck said, 'OK, let's go,' but then the ramp got stuck. 'The hell with this,' Rebarcheck called out. He jumped over the side; his men followed.

'I jumped out in waist-deep water. We had 200 feet to go to shore and you couldn't run, you could just kind of push forward. We finally made it to the edge of the water and then we had 200 yards of open beach to cross, through the obstacles. But fortunately most of the Germans were not able to fight, they were all shook up from the bombing and the shelling and the rockets and most of them just wanted to surrender.'

Sergeant Malvin Pike, Company 'E', in the second wave of 32 Higgins boats carrying the 1st Battalion, 8th Infantry, plus combat engineers and naval demolition teams, which luckily, landed at exit 2 opposite WN 5 (listed by First Army as 'Target 60' [26]). A direct hit from an American 75mm tank gun

destroyed the Renault turret and shattered Lance Corporal Friedrich's leg. There was only some small-arms fire from riflemen in the sand dune 10-20 feet high just behind the four-foot concrete seawall. Leutnant Jahnke was captured and as he was marched off he was wounded by a late shell from the German battery inland, which had been supporting his position.

'The alert came at 1 am. My platoon was stationed at Wiederstandnest 62. Half of us were under 18, the others were older troops injured on the Eastern Front and not yet fully fit. We had two concrete gun emplacements linked by trenches. I was alone in an earth and wood machine-gun nest, waiting to fire. The alarm call into the bunker woke us from a deep sleep. A comrade stood in the entrance and continued to shout the alarm, to dispel any doubt and urged us to hurry. We had so often been shaken to our feet by this call in the past few weeks that we no longer took the alarms seriously and some of the men rolled over in their bunks and attempted to sleep. An NCO appeared in the entranceway behind our comrade and brought us to our feet with the words 'Guys, this time it's for real. They're coming!

'We were told to man our positions. Then at 5 am, with the dawn, I spotted the approaching Allied fleet. The horizon was black with ships. It was unbelievable. Some people still thought the real landing would come at the Pas-de-Calais, but I knew that this number of ships could only have been amassed for the genuine invasion.

'I was shocked that the attack was at last coming, but I was also angry with the Allies, angry that they were sending such a huge force against us. Soon the Allied bombardment began. It was incredible - the earth shook. It caused us, as we say in Germany, to lose all sight and hearing. We could not talk and no orders could be given. So I did what my mother had told me to do in one of her letters, I prayed a lot and very loudly.

'The heavy naval guns fired salvo after salvo into our positions. In the beginnings, the ships lay at twenty kilometres, but the range slowly decreased. With unbelieving eyes we could recognize individual landing craft. The hail of shells falling upon us grew heavier, sending fountains of sand and debris into the air. The mined obstacles in the water were partly destroyed.

'The morning dawn over the approaching landing fleet exhibited for us approaching doom. Bombs and heavy-calibre shells continued to slam into the earth, tossing tangles of barbed wire, obstacles and dirt into the air. The fight for survival began. The explosions of naval gunfire became mixed with rapid-fire weapons. I attempted to seek shelter under my machine-gun position.

'Our weapons were preset on defensive fire zones; thus we could only wait. It appeared that the enemy would land in the approximate centre of the beach. We had planned that he should land at high tide to drive the boats over the open beach, but this was low tide. The waterline was three hundred metres distant. When the landing craft arrived, the tide was out and the Americans

26 WN 5 was one of four main German strong points which had been chosen for the assault. The others listed by First Army were: WN 7 (Target 62) at La Madeleine; WN 8 (Target 66) astride Exit 3; Stützpunkt 9 (Target 70) and WN 10 (Target 74) at Les Dunes-de-Varreville. *D-Day Then and Now Vol.2* (After the Battle 1995).

had a lot of beach to cross. As they swarmed towards me I opened fire. The Americans fell and many never stood up again. I don't know how many I killed. I just wanted to defend myself, to survive.

'Surprisingly, we had not suffered heavy casualties. We used every available minute to contact one another throughout the rain of shells and although we saw no possibility to escape from this chaos, we clung desperately to every minute won.

'Suddenly the rain of shells ceased, but only for a very short time. Again it came. Slowly the wall of explosions approached, metre by metre, worse than before - a deafening torrent - cracking, screaming, whistling and sizzling, destroying everything in its path. There was no escape and I crouched helplessly behind my weapon. I prayed for survival and my fear passed. Suddenly it was silent again.

'There were six of us in the position and still no one was wounded. A comrade stumbled out of the smoke and dust into my position and screamed, Franz, watch out! They're coming!'

'At noon, some Americans broke into our area. They caught me by surprise, running along our trench system and shot me in the hand. It wasn't a bad wound, but it was a good excuse for me to be evacuated back to Germany.'

18-year old Franz Gockel, 726th Infantry Regiment, 352nd Division. He was sent first to the village of Colleville and then to Paris. After he recovered from his wound he was again in action until captured by the Americans in the Vosages in November 1944.

'We were briefed by various officers. We were to land on the coast of Normandy at 5 am. We were to be the first troops to hit the beach. Beyond the head of the beach we were to look for a road and then fight our way inland. The road served as a dike next to low-lying fields that were flooded up to a depth of three feet. We were shown a detailed map which displayed the type of terrain and the location of some of the German fortifications. Once inland we would link with units of paratroopers and glider troops at some point between the beach and Ste-Mère-Église. An officer stated that some of the German troops would be members of the SS. We were not to take them prisoners but must kill them. They would be identified by their uniforms.... They might be carrying a bomb and surrender in order to get close enough to explode it near an officer or a group of men. Even if they did submit to capture there would be no hope of getting information from them.'

John (Jack) Capell, Wireman HQ 8th Infantry Regiment.

'Fighter Cover for UTAH beach. 1.40 hrs.

'Patrolling at 0520 hrs - Navy shelling west coast Defences - first landing made at 0620 hrs - Nearly shot down by Thunderbolt - Spitfire in front actually was - another Spit hit by naval shell & blew up - General Brock's 'benefit'.

...Fighter Cover for 'Omaha' Beach. Hun bomber attacked invasion fleet. Tremendous return fire from ships - one bomber destroyed.'

Log book entries, Flight Lieutenant Tony Cooper, Spitfire VB pilot, 64 Squadron.

'At about 01:00 the landing craft was lowered and the demolition crews came aboard. We took them within about 200 yards of the beach and they attached demolition charges to the underwater obstacles, which to me looked like pieces of old railroad track. They were everywhere. I was the second LCVP in the sixth wave into 'Utah' Beach. An LCI was blown up next to us. Troops were jumping out trying to survive, so we went over and we picked up 25 to 40 that I guess eventually would have drowned and then we returned back to the *Bayfield.* We were told that we were one of twelve barges that were going to be sent to other ships to pick up troops, guns, small cannons, jeeps and whatever. We didn't know what we were going to get. About 02:15 I was sent over to the Barnett and was told to go to the stern on the port side. They loaded 15 soldiers, lieutenants and a jeep with a machine gun mounted on it and a little trailer with a whole bunch of ammunition. We went to the rendezvous area and they were shouting back and forth but you couldn't hear anything. Even though it was pitch dark it was like being in any big city downtown with all the lights turned on.

'The good Lord just sent me to the right spot at the right time. It was the biggest 'Fourth of July' that I'd ever seen. There were thousands of tracer bullets. There was everything happening. We didn't have to worry about taking a bath. There were big salvos falling in the water all around us. Those 88s hit the water around us or right beside our barge and great fountains of water would go up in the air and come back down. Thank God that I had a good bilge pump. The water would almost drown you. It was just like looking death square in the face; like somebody pointing a gun at you and you just hope that the bullet didn't come out of the gun barrel. One shell explosion came right down close to the boat while we were on the beach with the ramp down. I had a pair of Ray Ban sunglasses that my wife had sent me. I was so proud of them. You could put them on in dark and still see. This explosion came and just cleared out everything that I had in my pockets - a couple of fountain pens, a pencil and a pad, a pack of cigarettes and a cigarette lighter. It even took my shoes off. I guess it lifted me up in the air, but I came right back down and I kind of was in the same place. My helmet was gone, my life jacket was only hanging on over one arm and I had that thing tied on pretty good. It was just terrible to see your buddies and people you didn't know standing on the beach and all these shells exploding and all of a sudden everything just vanishing. It kind of tore me up.

'I started back to the *Bayfield,* but the beach master told us, 'Now boys, I want ya'll to stand by here. I'm going to need you to take these wounded troops back to the hospital ship.' The *Bayfield* was an auxiliary hospital ship so we loaded the wounded and started back. Some were pretty bad. At one time, the beach was so congested and so full of torn up vehicles and dead soldiers and blown up tanks that we had to wait for the beach master to clear out a way for us to get up there to pick up what few survivors that we could get to. I guess we made at least ten trips that first morning into the beach, picking up wounded, picking up survivors, just doing a general mop up and bringing them back out. I never thought that I would ever live to tell about it.

'We got back to the ship and we were re-assigned as a dispatch boat to carry messages to cruisers and battleships in the task force. They would give us an order to go out to, say a cruiser and they would give us the number of the ship. It was fantastic. We kept on doing our thing and the next day we continued to go to different ships. When we needed something to eat we'd just come over near the ship and holler. They lowered a bag or a box of food over the side and just told us to eat what we could and keep on going. Some of the boys in the first deck division would throw food at us and we'd try to grab it and a lot of times we'd miss it. So what went into the drink, I guess the fish got. It was sure good to get back aboard the good ol' *Bayfield* and go to the galley and get some good food. And we had good cooks.

'Then I was assigned to go back over to the Barnett to pick up a couple of more jeeps and take them into the beach. We got them in and everything seemed to die down a little bit and then a storm came. One minute we were 25 feet down and the next minute we were up above the deck of the ship. But we rode this storm out in little ol' LCVP three and then we ran out of diesel fuel and started drifting. Thank goodness we came upon a Dutch oiler. They said, 'We'll give you some fuel. You all look like you're kind of hungry. We've got breakfast going here.' It was the first that I can ever remember having, other than the K rations and C rations that we were eating for about 20 some odd days.

'We got back to the *Bayfield* and they said, 'Well as you're already in the water and all the other boats have been assigned to different details (and I wasn't because we'd been getting refuelled and getting breakfast) they said, 'We're going to put you on smoke pot detail for about a week; every afternoon around 5:30 to 6:00. We had this big aircraft motor that was mounted on a barge and it was the British who took care of it. The Germans would come over and drop bombs and try to blast us out. One afternoon after putting the smoke pots out and we were under attack I returned to the ship and was going to tie up alongside when the officer of the deck hollered down to me and he said, 'Ahoy, down there in boat three, would you mind going over to that barge and finding out why the airplane motor is not blowing the smoke over here?' I said, 'Well, fine. Aye aye.' I took off, saw what the problem was and came back. I said 'Ahoy on deck! Officer of the deck! Evidently the operator, because of the roughness of the sea, fell into the propeller and it cut his head off.' Now get this, the officer of the deck hollers down to me and says, 'Did it kill him?'

'I guess he was so flustered that it was the first thing that came into his mind.'

Larry Orr, USS *Bayfield*, Coxswain of Boat Three. (The APA 5 USS *Barnett* was part of the Assault Group Red ('Uncle Red Beach') together with APA 33 *Bayfield*). 'After Normandy, we made the invasion of Southern France and then we returned to the States and were outfitted with radar and sonar which we didn't have and then we were sent to the Pacific. I landed the Marines at Iwo Jima and at Okinawa. At Iwo Jima I just happened to be on the beach area of Mount Surabachi, which went directly down into the ocean and was letting Marines off when I saw them putting the US flag up. By the time we unloaded our barge, put the ramp up, backed off and started to go back to the ship, I looked around and that flag was gone. I mean zoombo!' The invasion of Normandy was the biggest. I've never seen such firepower in all my life. I just happened to be in the right place at the right time.'

'I was a 19 year old sergeant and a member of an Army Navy demolition team that trained together in England for several weeks for that eventful day. Our team consisted of six or seven combat Engineers (my half-squad contingency) and about the same number of navy underwater demolition specialists. Our training with the navy included underwater demolition methods as well and fortunately, it was never necessary to put those methods to a test as I was not a swimmer, but I never admitted it to anyone. We were under the command of Lieutenant E. P. Clayton, a navy deep-sea diver who gained some prominence in 1939 in his salvage activities involving the sinking of the ss *Squalis*. The teams were called Naval Combat Demolition Units (NCDUs) and the assignment of each unit was to clear its designated fifty-yard beach sector of all German beach obstacles as these would impede and even damage, subsequent landing craft when the tide came in. That is why we had to land at an early morning hour, when the tide was low and the obstacles were readily visible.

'D-Day began with us aboard an LST in a rendezvous location somewhere in the Channel not far from the English coastline. We were too nervous to know or care from where we were leaving and more interested in where we were going and what the reception would be like. Hundreds of other troop carriers and warships were doing likewise (although I could not see any of them in the darkness of night) - all in readiness to do battle with the Germans. Everything seemed to be riding on the weather and the element of surprise. We had already been keyed up for the June 5 assault and now we had another day of adrenalin rush to deal with. The postponement gave us more time to reflect on the unknown that they lay ahead and to engage our thoughts in some private meditation. We knew we were on a dangerous mission, that some of us would not survive even the initial assault landing, so there was not much in the way of banter and bravado taking place aboard ship.

'We finally got the clear notice and our LST moved to a new rendezvous position the night of June 5. Around midnight, many planes could be heard flying overhead in the direction of Normandy. We knew that airborne troops would soon be making advance assaults to establish an inland foothold and that it would help make our job easier in establishing beachheads. From our position on the LST we could hear the sounds of bombing and anti-aircraft coming from the coast. And over the next hour or so, the intensity increased and the coastline was being lighted by all this activity. In the meantime, many more transports planes had been flying overhead, carrying still more paratroopers. As we heard and saw later, many of them died in their courageous efforts to establish a rear flank.

'Sometime around 02:00 we were given our orders to debark from the LST. Our landing craft was lowered into the water and we went over the side with full combat gear, including individual satchels of various explosives, detonators and fuses which we had prepared and waterproofed at the end of training. Part of the waterproofing included the novel use of latex condoms fitted over pull-type manual fuses and then taped at the open end with rubber friction tape. The fuses were thus waterproofed and they could still be pulled to activate them.

'The Channel was still quite choppy and climbing down a 'scramble net' into a bobbing small craft was frightful in itself and the jump off the net had to be timed so that the craft was not jolting upward at the instant one decided to drop to the deck, or one might wind up with broken bones.

'Our outer clothing, in addition to woollen undergarments, included military cotton fatigues, specially treated with a wax-like, waterproof coating. But, as we realized later, it was of no value once seawater penetrated inside through various openings and remained trapped there even after we reached shore. It was intended to provide protection in case the Germans resorted to gas attacks, particularly with mustard gas, which causes skin burns. A gas mask was a required part of our equipment that offered primary protection from a gas attack because if the lungs were attacked, there was little hope for survival.

'Our craft, piloted by a navy helmsman, headed for our final rendezvous location. There we teamed up with other landing craft from the LST to form a wide circle that maintained a throttled-down rotation, awaiting the arrival of dawn and 'H-Hour'. The wait seemed to last forever. The combined effects of bobbing craft, drenching salt water spray and sickening diesel fumes made most of us wish to be on the beach as soon as possible. I thought that if I had to die, I preferred it to happen on terra firma.

'At the break of dawn, every ship in the Channel opened up with awesome firepower which was directed, along with increased aerial bombing, at the beaches and German shore batteries. The light flashes from the naval guns outlined the silhouettes of many ships that had not been visible because of the pre-dawn and early morning mist. It was a reassuring sight and a boost to our morale, to know that we, in our little crafts, had all that support for our landing. The longer the bombardment went on, the more hopeful we were that our chances for survival would be improved.

'The signal was finally given for our circle of landing craft to fan out and head for our designated beach sectors. On our way in, we passed some landing crafts that may have encountered mines or had been hit by German artillery. Floating dead bodies of GIs suddenly gave me a first-hand glimpse of what war is like. Now, I thought, maybe the odds were not as promising.

'Our helmsman was reluctant to bring his craft near the shoreline, saying it would get hung up on the bottom. These boats were designed for shallow drafts and he certainly could have advanced farther toward the beach, but without a countermanding order from Lieutenant Clayton, that was where we had to jump off. I felt certain that the helmsman was fearful for himself and playing it safe so that he could get out of harm's way regardless of the added danger his action posed for us. That memory has stayed with me all these years. My suspicions were confirmed when we jumped off the ramp and found ourselves in water up to our chests or necks, depending on an individual's height. Making the slow advance to shore with all our gear seemed like an eternity; fortunately, there was no indication of small arms fire coming from the Germans at the time, but there was sporadic enemy artillery fire along the beach. The time of our landing was about 06:30, which was planned to give us enough time to destroy all the obstacles before the tide came in. We had to place our demolition charges on the backside of the obstacles so that the explosions would hurl the fragments seaward. This would protect personnel already on the beach, but it also meant for some delays in the demolition progress when subsequent waves of landing craft were arriving. It all worked out fairly smoothly. The job was finished around mid-morning, but there was pain associated with it, due to the loss of a member of my squad, Leo Indelicato, who was killed by artillery fire during that task.

'Later in the morning, a fellow squad leader, Leon 'Toby' Tobin, came over to my sector. He had landed with Baker Company a few sectors to my left. We compared notes and casualties. My assistant squad leader, Corporal Alfred Kurzawski, had been killed, along with a private - and one other who had been wounded and evacuated back to a hospital ship and eventually back to England. It meant that I had lost four fellow New Yorkers from a roster of thirteen - about average for D-Day, as it turned out. Toby showed me the close call he experienced. He shook his water canteen and there was a rattle from a large steel bearing inside. The bearing was from a special German land mine that would spring up in the air, after being stepped on and explode numerous bearings in all directions. He did not know the bearing had penetrated the canteen because of the water that was in it all the time. But, as the water ran out the puncture hole, he felt wetness in that area and also became aware of the rattling noise. Somehow, that type of mine became known as the Bouncing Betty.

'At one point when Toby and I were facing the seawall, we heard an explosion very close by and from the corner of my eye I saw two soldiers blown out of their entrenchment at the base of the wall. They may have struck a mine, but, instinctively, I turned to look seaward and noticed a small naval craft a hundred yards or so offshore with a couple of men hovering over a mounted rocket launcher. I wondered if they were experimenting with it or knew what they were doing. I had never seen or heard of such a device before. That little boat was bobbing up and down and I wondered, also, how they knew when to fire the rockets so as to hit an enemy target - or, by chance, some poor American GIs who never expected to be killed by their own side. To this day, I still wonder what really caused their death.

'Around 01:00 we said goodbye to our navy counterparts when our unit was no longer needed. They had to get on a landing craft as a first step in returning to England and we engineers had to move inland and regroup with our Company 'B'. At that moment, we were very quite envious of our navy friends and wishing we too could be on that craft; this could be the last day of war for them but only the beginning for us. We moved off the beach and were joined by the remainder of my squad and we were instructed to take up rear guard position in a field 300 yards from the beach. It was good to be together again and still alive, although I had lost my personal items in a backpack which I undoubtedly left on the landing craft after the helmsman had said he was not going any closer to the beach. In addition to shaving kit, K rations and other personal items, the backpack also contained a complete change of clothes which I sorely needed because I had developed hives from my saltwater drenched clothes and the impregnated fatigues were adding to that problem. The fatigues were the first things to go in order to dry out the rest of me, but the night was a chilly one and I had to make the best of it.

'We did not know what was happening to our buddies in A and C Companies who were in the 'Omaha' Beach assault. But, as events later revealed, it was a hellish nightmare producing vivid memories for the survivors and which persist to the present for those still alive. Approximately one-third of our battalion men, who were mostly from the western half of New York were either killed, wounded or missing in action. But we had good replacements who became proud members of the Famous 299th Engineer Combat Battalion and served well along with us in the other campaigns (notably Northern France, Bastogne, Ardennes and the Rhineland) all leading up to V-E Day in Germany.

Sergeant Eugene D. Shales, 3rd Platoon, Company 'B', 299th Combat Engineer Battalion.

'I was aboard the LCT 663 at 0001 hours somewhere in the convoy with other LCTs of Flotilla 16 heading across the English Channel. The weather was heavy, wet and windy. The Channel was very rough, not ideal conditions for flat-bottomed landing craft. Many soldiers were seasick. My assignment was Quartermaster on duty on the conning tower. Next to the ship's Skipper, I was the one charged with relaying orders from the Skipper to the other members of the crew at their battle stations. We were wearing impregnated clothes over our dungarees. These clothes covered all of our bodies from the neck down. And they were hot as hell, itchy and the odour was unbearable. Our gas masks were at hand and we wore the standard helmets and boots.

'As daybreak neared, the LCT crew assumed their assigned battle stations. I don't believe anyone aboard slept this night. Our passengers were combat engineers and infantrymen. Our cargo - the vehicles, trailers, explosives and other gear that belonged to these soldiers. There was a lot of talk and speculation aboard. Some of the soldiers came out of the North African campaign and one of them told us he had a feeling he would not make it this time. I often wondered about him. As daybreak approached, stillness fell and in soft voices you could hear different groups discussing what they thought the dawn would bring and how they would fare in all of this. All night long airplanes and gliders passed overhead. And all around you could see ships of all sizes and shapes. When day broke all around us and above us, it was a sight you would have to behold to believe. A ball of flames everywhere. Fighter planes, cargo planes, gliders and bombers. And on the water, there were ships as far as the eyes could see. There were battleships, cruisers, destroyers, landing craft and cargo ships. The water was rough for landing craft and some soldiers were seasick.

'Then all hell broke loose as the battleships, cruisers, destroyers and other ships opened up and shelled the shoreline. The concussions of these guns seemed to want to pull your clothes off. There was activity all around. We headed to the beach in columns. The LCT 777, one of the LCTs in our Flotilla, was ahead of us as we headed for the beach. There was a terrific explosion and the LCT 777 seemed to break in half. We learned later she had hit a mine. The skipper altered course slightly to avoid running over survivors who were in the water. It was heartbreaking not to be able to stop and render assistance to the men who were so desperately in need of help. And to make matters worse, some of these men were our friends.

'As we got closer to the beach, we could see the sand being kicked up by exploding shells. The skipper altered course slightly to starboard and was immediately ordered to return to our original course. There was smoke rising along the beach from burning vehicles. By this time, Ensign Edwards, who was on Flotilla staff and standing next to the Skipper and I on the conning tower, said to me, 'Thomas, it looks like they are playing for keeps.' I said, 'Yes, sir, they are.'

'A few minutes after this Ensign Edwards was killed and the Skipper and I were wounded by an exploding shell. The Skipper and I were able to remain at our stations. As Ensign Edwards was falling, I grabbed hold of him and laid him on the deck and called for a medic. As help was coming up, I helped lower Ensign Edwards to a catwalk near the wheelhouse. I returned to my station next to the Skipper. He had suffered a head wound but was able to continue commanding the LCT 663. We continued to the beach for our initial landing. We beached and dropped our ramp and the combat engineers and infantrymen and their equipment were discharged on French soil. The sounds of shells exploding, the machine guns firing, the airplanes overhead and all the other sounds of war were deafening. At this time Ensign Edwards' body was taken off the LCT 663. The Skipper and I were taken to a hospital ship anchored offshore. We were checked, given booster shots and returned to LCT 663. We continued making shuttles between the ship and the beach.'

August Leo Thomas, born 5 May 1924 in St. Martinville, Louisiana, coxswain on LCT 633.

US Assault Divisions 'Utah' Beach
VII Corps
4th US Division
Major General Raymond O. Barton

8th Infantry	12th Infantry	70th Tank Battalion
22nd Infantry	359th Infantry (attached from 90th Division)	

The German forces responsible for the defence of the beach are elements of the 709th Infantry Division, commanded by Generalleutnant Karl-Wilhelm von Schlieben and the 352nd Infantry Division, commanded by Generalleutnant Dietrich Kraiss. There are fewer bunkers than at 'Omaha' with defence largely being based on flooding the coastal plain behind the beaches.

Objective: To gain a beachhead, leading in time to the capture of the Cotentin Peninsula and of the port of Cherbourg. The landing on the beach, which is about 3 miles, is planned in four waves. The first consists of 20 Higgins boats or LCVPs, each carrying a 30-man assault team from the 8th Infantry Regiment. Ten craft are to land on Tare Green Beach, opposite the strong-point at les Dunes de Varreville. The other ten are intended for Uncle Red Beach, 1,000 yards further south. The entire operation is timed against the touchdown of this first assault wave, which is scheduled to take place at 06:30. Eight LCTs, each carrying four amphibious DD Tanks, are scheduled to land at the same time or as soon thereafter as possible. The second wave consists of another 32 Higgins boats with additional troops of the two assault battalions, some combat engineers and also eight naval demolition teams that are to clear the beach of underwater obstacles. The third wave, timed for H plus 15 minutes, contains eight more Higgins boats with DD tanks. It is followed within 2 minutes by the fourth wave, mainly detachments of the 237th and 299th Combat Engineer Battalions, to clear the beaches between high- and low-water marks. The first wave arrives at the line of departure on time and all 20 craft are dispatched abreast. Support craft to the rear fire machine guns, possibly with the hope of exploding mines. When the LCVPs are 300-400 yards from the beach, the assault company commanders fire special smoke projectors to signal the lifting of naval support craft fire. Almost exactly at H Hour the assault craft lower their ramps and 600 men wade through waist-deep water for the last 100 or more yards to the beach. The actual touchdown on the beach is therefore a few minutes late, but the delay is negligible and has no effect on the phasing of the succeeding waves. Enemy artillery fires a few air bursts at the sea, but otherwise there is no opposition at H Hour. The first troops to reach shore are from the 2nd Battalion, 8th Infantry. Captain Leonard T. Schroeder, leading Company 'F', is the first man from a landing craft to reach the beach. The 1st Battalion lands a few minutes later. Both came ashore considerably south of the designated beaches. The 2nd Battalion should have hit Uncle Red Beach opposite Exit 3. The 1st Battalion was supposed to land directly opposite the strong-point at les Dunes de Varreville. The landings, however, are made astride Exit 2 about 2,000 yards south.

Beach Timetable

0115-0130 The main body of the US 82nd and 101st Airborne Divisions begins landing by parachute and glider inland. They occupy German defenders and begin securing the exits from 'Utah' Beach.

0200 34 British and US minesweepers under Commander M. H. Brown RN begin sweeping the transport area 10 miles offshore, the fire support areas and the approach channels for boats and bombardment ships.

0430 - US 4th Cavalry Squadron land on Iles-Ste-Marcouf, offshore and begin to occupy the islands.

0530 Attack by 276 B-26 Marauder aircraft destroys Blockhouse 5 and all five artillery pieces.

0536 Rear Admiral Morton L. Deyo, commander Task Force 'A' aboard the heavy cruiser USS *Tuscaloosa*, orders the pre-landing shore bombardment to begin earlier than scheduled because German gun batteries have already begun firing at the Allied ships. *Tuscaloosa*, in a fire-support line with *Quincy* and *Nevada* about 11,000 yards offshore, unleashes its nine 8 inch guns of its main battery and then opens up shortly afterward with its eight 5-inch Antiaircraft guns. For 50 minutes following H-Hour, battleship USS *Nevada*, cruiser HMS *Black Prince*, monitor HMS *Erebus* and *Tuscaloosa*, provide abundant and accurate naval gunfire support, especially on the remote and large-calibre batteries inaccessible to the ground troops.

0555 Guiding craft for the landing force is sunk; remaining ships head off course.

0630 After an effective air bombardment, the 8th Regimental Combat Team lands to the south of the intended sector, on a lightly defended beach.

0631 One minute behind schedule the first wave of up to 20 LCVPs each with a 30-man assault team from the 8th Infantry Regiment, 4th Infantry Division, come within 100 yards of the shore. 28 of the 32 33-ton amphibious DD Sherman tanks are landed. Because of a strong current 4th Infantry Division have actually landed 2,000 yards south of their intended target but the beach is less heavily defended than the original. The 4th Infantry Division lands opposite Pouppeville instead of their objective at Ste-Martin-de-Varreville, 1½ miles to the north. Colonel Russell 'Red' Reeder decides that they should wade through the flooded fields behind the beach towards their objective. With water up to their waists and sometimes over their heads they struggle on while the causeways and fields come under fire from the battery at Ste-Marcouf.

0640 Almost all DD (swimming) tanks land successfully. Light opposition is quickly dealt with. The beach defences are mostly cleared by high tide.

By **0730** All resistance by the German 709th Division ends.

0800 Brigadier General Theodore Roosevelt orders in follow-up troops.

0930 Beach exits 1, 2 and 3 are secured.

1000 Six battalions landed, including follow up troops - 12th and 22nd Regimental Combat Teams. The La Madeleine battery and the beach exits are captured. 26 assault waves are landed before noon.

1300 101st and US 4th Infantry Division link up at Pouppeville. It provides a route and the extra force with which to attack and capture Ste-Marie-du-Mont later in the day. US troops gradually fan out to Beuzeville au Plain and Les Forges.

1600 German 7th Army HQ informed of 'Utah' landings.

By **1800** 21,328 men and 1,700 vehicles are ashore.

24.00 The troops who landed on the beaches have reached about six miles inland. An almost textbook landing; by midnight, 23,250 troops are ashore. Casualties, 4th Infantry Division, 197 killed, 60 missing, presumed drowned.

Among the handful of reporters assigned to cover the beaches on D-Day was Charles Collingwood, who carried with him a large, primitive tape recorder. CBS was for the first time allowing recorded reports to be broadcast to listeners back home. Collingwood landed at 'Utah' after the first wave had come ashore.

'We are on the beach today on D-Day. We've just come in. We caught a ride in a small craft loaded with 1,000lbs of TNT. This beach is still under considerable enemy gunfire. These boys are apparently having a pretty rough time here on the beach. It's not very pleasant. It's exposed and it must have been a rugged fight to get it. Further up the beach there's a fire which apparently has just been started by enemy shelling. It's maybe a quarter of a mile up from us. At the moment there's no shelling from our immediate vicinity although when we first landed our little old LCVP about 100 yards from the beach, German 88s were kicking up big clouds of sand as they shelled opposition down there and you can still see some smoke drifting from it.'

Collingwood's taped account from 'Utah' beach aired two days later.

'Approximately 03:45 I was relieved of duty by another officer. I had been on duty from 12:00 to 4:00; he was to take it from 04:00 to 08:00. I went below to try to get some sleep along with the other men that were relieved of their duties. Of course, how could you rest with eight inch guns popping off and such over flights? Maybe I had a premonition but I put whatever money I had in my pocket along with a fountain pen that was a gift to me upon graduation. At about 05:00 I went topside and just stood where the other officer was on duty with the signal man and since I couldn't sleep, just watched what was going on. Approximately 05:40 we were 40 minutes from launch time. Maybe we were 6,000 yards from the beach. The water was so rough; the waves were at least a six foot sea. We received orders by flag and Morse light to form a line abreast, proceed into the beach and not launch the tanks because there was a chance that they would be swamped and sink in the rough seas where the water was too deep for the draft of the tank. I had been an Eagle Scout and I could read these messages before the signalman told me what the message was. The other officer didn't give the command for the LCT to steer left and pull into a line abreast. It was like he froze and so the signalman looked at me, I looked at him and I then re-took command of the boat. I gave the signal that we were obeying the order by dropping the flag, which indicated that we were going to move into a line abreast. A few minutes thereafter, when we were almost a line abreast, we hit what I later learned was a mine, powerful enough to destroy a ship let alone a small boat. I found out later that it literally blew us sky high. I didn't hear the explosion, but when I opened my eyes, the next thing I knew, I was under water. I opened my eyes, looked up and vividly remember paddling as fast as I could to reach the surface. Were it not for my Mae West life jacket, I don't think I would have survived. I recall swimming around not seeing too much, but hearing somebody yell, 'Skipper, Skipper!' It was Abernathy on what remained of our craft. I guess he grabbed me as I floated in his vicinity, pulled me up by the Mae West collar and pulled me onto the overturned boat. All the other men except the signalman (who I met later on a hospital ship and who wasn't even scratched) were killed. The four tanks were lost.

'An LCM that was going into the beach stopped by us. Abernathy jumped onboard with me and we proceeded into the beach with the first wave of the Army units to land. I remember the coxswain dropping his ramp and I watched the soldiers debark. As soon as the last one was off, the coxswain raised the ramp back up and headed back out to the English Channel and safety. I saw many bullets landing around and I guess it was a miracle that none of them hit the LCM or me or anyone else on the boat. I don't remember docking to a destroyer, but I do remember being hauled up hand by hand, people passing me up a ladder on to the deck of the destroyer and someone yelling, 'Take him down below to sick bay!' I couldn't see very well. I had bloodshot eyes I guess because nothing was clear. However, when they put me in some officer's room, I remember them cutting the clothes off me and putting me on kind of a leather couch which was very cold and covering me with a blanket until they could get me down to the surgery clinic. They patched up my face, sewed my nose back in place, patched up my right leg and then bandaged me up and took me back to the room I was first in. We must have gone back to England and docked

at Plymouth or Portsmouth and I was put in an ambulance. I awoke approximately a week later at the 182nd Army General Hospital in Vernon.'
   Sam Grundfast, LCT 607.

'At Dartmouth in the early hours of D-Day, nearly everyone was up and about. Before daylight the drivers checked their engines and ack-ack crews burst off a few test rounds. Most people were seasick so not too much stuff was given to eat. Fortunately, I wasn't bothered that way. But on 5 June when we had received the word to reverse course in view of the postponement of D-Day for 24 hours I had had a bad fall on the slippery, wet deck, which resulted in a badly sprained ankle. I tried to control the swelling as much as possible and kept to my bunk the next 24 hours. I had my ankle heavily wrapped by the combat medic we were fortunate enough to have on board. I was able to get my jump boots on but it was a very loose job at lacing. I was determined to get on that beach and not be left behind. I also had heard stories about people being able to walk out sprains if they could stand the pain. I took a lot of aspirin in my pocket.
   'Landing at H-Hour with the four assault companies of the 8th Infantry were A and C companies, less one platoon each. Their assignment was to blow gaps in barbed wire obstacles and to blow four gaps in the seawall at Green and at Red beaches, to remove mines and support the assault on fortifications inland. The balance of the 237th was Company 'B' of the 299th Engineer Combat Battalion attached, formed a nucleus of the beach obstacle demolition force. Other elements were 11 Navy combat demolition parties numbering 126 officers and men and 8 tank dozers of the 70th Tank Battalion manned by a crew of three engineers and two gunners each. This ad hoc task force was commanded by the commanding officer of the 237th Engineer Battalion. The beach clearing plan provided for four 50-yard wide lanes on both Green and Red beaches. Navy personnel, augmented with combat engineers, were to work seaward to the waterline, wherever that might be. And combat engineers completed the lanes to the concrete seawall. Since I was to control all engineer operations on Green beach, I was embarked on one of the four LCTs scheduled to land at H plus 5 minutes. Major Herschel E. Linn occupied an LCT destined for Red Beach.[27] On board the LCT were four duplex drive tanks, also some automatic anti-aircraft weapons and crews and my weasel, which was my means of transport. The latter piece of equipment was chosen because of its amphibious capabilities and cross-country mobility.
   'As it started to lighten up we became aware of being surrounded by the shadows of other craft all proceeding rather steadily, not fast. We hadn't seen or heard the paratroop carriers earlier but we became aware of bombers overhead which we could not see. Sometime between 0500 and 0600 they unloaded on the shore ahead and we knew Normandy was for real. Lots of thumps and even a sensation of a distant concussion. As the light came on, the features of the craft about us could be distinguished. I've never seen such an aggregation on the move. Our course to Green Beach took us past the battleship

---

27 Linn was commander of the Beach Obstacle Task Force. His LCT was sunk.

Nevada, assigned in a fire support role. About the time we came abreast of this monster, or so it looked from our little LCT, it let loose with all the guns in its forward main batteries. It was awesome, the flash, the sound and the concussion and I thought to myself, there really can't be much of a chance that there's Germans left to offer serious resistance.

'The weather continued overcast with little wind, cool and moderate seas. As we moved forward toward the landing beaches, we could see the line of LCTs about 100 yards ahead. I tried to identify landmarks on the silhouette of dunes, but could not. Later, after landing, I learned that the whole landing force had slipped to the left about 2,000 yards and that some of the pre-planned beach exit roads would not be available until German covering forces were driven from them.

'Our LCT finally touched down and dropped its ramp. First off was my weasel with myself and driver, Sergeant Newsom. We went only a few yards before we were swamped by waves and the vehicle sank. We had to abandon everything except for a radio which Newsom carried and my map case and musette bag. The water was nearly up to our armpits. We moved directly shoreward and never looked back. Thankfully, those DD tank drivers were skilful enough not to run us down as they came down the ramp behind us. When we reached the waterline, I was somewhat surprised that the beach obstacles were very light. Of course, this was because we had landed at an unlikely spot, which was not so heavily prepared. We went directly to the seawall where the majority of the troops appeared to be huddled. Looking to my left I became aware of some live smoke grenades indicating obstacle demolitions were starting at the water's edge. One of the worst blows came on Green beach when a shell had exploded in front of an LCM just as it dropped its ramp. This result in the loss of six members of one of the Army demolition party.

'When we reached the shelter of the seawall I was pretty quick to get off my feet after hobbling through the surf and across the open beach. We tried to get the radio working that Sergeant Newsom had carried in. It would not work. It had been exposed to too much water. We would have to rely on messengers. I found some of the men of Company 'C' of the 237th behind the seawall and in the dune area checking for mines. I learned that Lieutenant Bazette of that company had been killed a short time before while leading an assault on a pillbox behind the wall. He had been the first platoon leader assigned to Company 'F', 49th Engineer Combat Regiment at Camp Carson while I was a commanding officer.

'Sergeant Newsom and I were picking ourselves up to move down the beach to our left so we would be more near the centre of activity when I became aware of a single, upright figure moving towards us on top of the seawall. It turned out to be Brigadier General Theodore Roosevelt, Jr. of the 4th Division, striding along with his walking stick and ignoring the stray small arms fire and fragments from mortar shells and artillery shells. His calm, business-like demeanour was certainly a staying influence on all who saw him. He also rousted out a lot of laggards from the shelter of the wall and got them moving forward to join their units. I believe it was he who told me that Major Linn of the 237th would not be landing that day since his landing craft had been sunk. I therefore became the commander of the 237th and the beach obstacle task force.

'The clearance of obstacles in the planned lanes on the beaches proceeded pretty much according to plan. Hand placed explosives were used primarily. Later, after the tank dozers arrived in the third wave, they were extremely helpful. The initial lanes across the beach were cleared by H+45 minutes. The primary gap in the seawall was blown at H+55 minutes. This opened up the entrance to the primary road known as Exit 2, which crossed the flooded areas behind the beaches. It was in the early morning hours, probably about 8:30, that I witnessed a rather daring act of bravery.

'Diving into the beach area from the south was a single German fighter. He pulled out at about 400 feet flying the entire length of the assault beach with his machine guns clattering. Of course, when those on the beach became aware of his presence, nearly everyone tried to take a shot. He was fortunate and pulled up and away beyond the north end of 'Utah' beach with no apparent damage. Luckily, his strafing was like a wake-up call and apparently caused no damage.

'About 0800 the 3rd Battalion of the 8th Infantry landed on Red Beach and later started to move inland on the causeway at Exit 2. They were supported by tanks of the 70th Tank Battalion and Company 'A' of the 237th. About half a mile into the inundated area, this force ran into trouble. A large concrete caulk had been blown, creating an effective vehicle obstacle. One of the supporting tanks had been stopped and put out of action by anti-tank fire from the opposing shore. Another tank apparently was disabled by a mine.

'I came upon this situation at about 09:30. I was aware that bridge trucks from the 991 Engineer Treadway Bridge Company were to come shore ashore at about 09:30. The vehicles of this company were to be parked in a holding area near the beach exit. I instructed one of the Company 'A' officers to secure a tank dozer and to clear the disabled tanks off the causeway. I then sent a message to Company 'B' requesting a platoon to assist in installation of a treadway bridge. The operation was a little more complicated than it sounds. The road was only about 10 feet wide; the walk-way bridge trucks could only launch their bridge from the rear. It was necessary, therefore, to back the truck up this narrow road to the blown obstacle, almost a half mile.

'The 30-foot steel treadway bridge finally was in place by noon. This then was the first bridge to be built by the Army Engineers in the invasion of France. It had the capacity to carry any tactical loads of the 1st Army.

'By noon the essential clearing of 'Utah' Beach was complete. Gaps had been blown in the seawall and lanes had been cleared and bulldozed through the dune line to vehicle holding areas. The beach obstacle task force was in effect dissolved, its mission complete. Further improvement efforts became the responsibility of the 1st Engineer Special Brigade.

'The 237th continued to improve the road to Ste-Marie-du-Mont, Exit 2, as it was the main supply road for the advanced elements of the 4th Division. At D-Day night, the unit bivouacked with other elements of the 1106th Engineer Combat Group at Point Ebert and we brought forward all equipment and vehicles from the beach area. It had been a long day and it took the last drop of energy to dig the necessary slit trenches for protection from nuisance bombing and long range artillery. My ankle started hurting again. The battalion had suffered about 11% total casualties.

Captain (later Colonel) Robert P. Tabb, XO of the 237th Engineer Battalion, which was recognized by the award of the Presidential Citation for its actions on D-Day. It also was awarded the Croix de Guerre by the government of France for its role in the liberation of France. In addition, there were numerous individual acts of heroism which were recognized by individual awards.

'My regiment, the 12th Infantry, would be the third regiment in my division to land. After the first landing craft headed toward shore 12 miles away I had a wait of some hours. About 5:30 on D-Day morning the battleship *Nevada* opened fire on 'Utah' Beach an hour before the first troops landed. I remember the thunderclap of its broadside. (After the war I learned the British cruiser HMS *Belfast* also opened fire at 5:30 but against 'Gold' and 'Juno' Beaches; as a boy I visited her when she docked in Brooklyn and had my picture taken wearing a British sailor's cap.) Our aircraft were carpet bombing the coast and some landing craft fired volleys of rockets. Our side was putting a lot more fire on that beach than the Germans were returning.

'My regiment's turn came. My rifle company, Company 'K' climbed the rope netting down the side of our ship into an LCI (landing craft, infantry) that held only us. We landed on 'Utah' about 10:30; walked down the twin gangplanks at the bow; hardly got our boots wet. The beach had already been swept of mines and obstacles. The Germans had been driven from the beach and the seawall had been breached to let vehicles reach the causeway exits from the beach. German artillery was firing on 'Utah' from inland batteries and our ships were answering this fire. Battleship shells flew overhead like freight trains and I actually saw the shells. Within a week the Germans would teach us two new noises: the '88' and 'screaming meemies' (Nebelwerfer). The 88's shell flew so fast that we never heard it coming. 'Screaming meemies' were rockets fired in clusters of six or twelve, a second and a half apart. You could hear them screaming or moaning in flight and the rocket cluster landed in a 'shot pattern'. Crossroads were a favourite target and I had a boot-heel blown off by one later. We also quickly learned to tell other German weapons by their sounds. Their light machine gun fired much faster than any of ours, their burp gun (machine pistol) was unmistakable and their mortar rounds (heavy or light) made a distinctive 'crump'.

'There was not enough room on the few causeways from the beach for our full division to advance. So after climbing the seawall and crossing the mined dunes behind it, we waded knee deep or waist-deep or neck-deep across a good mile of marshland or pasture that Rommel had ordered to be flooded (by shutting drainage gates). Buddies with toggle ropes paired up. One buddy would hold the toggle while the other wrapped the noose around his chest. If either stepped into an underwater ditch his flotation gear would keep him afloat while his buddy pulled him to the next patch of higher ground. Other men roped themselves together like mountain climbers. Some men lightened their loads as soon as they hit the beach by throwing away gasmasks and other 'deadweight', but I kept my toggle rope, gasmask, everything.

'We got soaked to our necks and by afternoon the sun was out and it was hot. The one blessing was that this water was fresh water. We would not bathe for weeks and saltwater would have been a torment on our skin and in our clothes. After 3 hours in the flooded lowland we reached dry ground. Here we encountered our first hedgerows, an obstacle for which training in England had not prepared us and which the brass had not taken into account in drawing up timetables for objectives. Our first objective was the village of Ste-Martin-de-Varreville with its church steeple. As soon as we saw civilians in any village in Normandy we asked them in French, 'Where are the krauts? (*Où sont les boches?*)' If they said 'No Germans here,' we asked 'Do you have any eggs? (*Avez-vous des oeufs?*)' Compared with the powdered eggs in our rations, fresh eggs were a delicacy. Gliders flew in that afternoon and drew German fire. Some gliders cracked up in the little checkerboard fields surrounded by hedgerows and spiked with stakes. We spent the late afternoon of D-Day digging foxholes along hedgerows outside a hamlet named Beuzeville au Plain five miles from 'Utah'. We heard small arms fire that night and saw some tracers. But we lay low, did not smoke, barely talked and hoped not to draw sniper fire. It sounds odd, yet nobody in my squad fired his weapon on D-Day or saw a German soldier, though snipers took pot shots at us.

'June 7 changed all that. My regiment advanced two miles northwest toward the town of Azeville driving the Germans back until we were stopped by artillery and machine gun fire from the fortification at the east end of town. On June 8 my regiment attacked a strongpoint at Émondeville. Strong points were fortified positions protected by mortars, machine guns and riflemen, without the casemated gun emplacements of fortresses such as Azeville and Crisbecq. That day my regiment lost 300 men, almost a tenth of its strength. This was a forewarning of the heavy casualties my division would take in the war. No other American division in Europe suffered as many. On June 9 my regiment captured a German strongpoint at Joganville. On June 10 we almost reached the highway east of Montebourg going toward Quinéville near the coast. We were nearly a mile farther north than the regiments east and west of us. On the morning of June 11, my regiment reached its objective, the heights of Les Fieffes Dancel northeast of Montebourg, but was then ordered to withdraw because we were in danger of being cut off. That same day my regimental commander, Colonel Russell 'Red' Reeder, lost a foot near Montebourg. He was a favourite both with fellow officers and enlisted men, a great athlete and a cheerful soul all his life and later the author of many books. We captured Montebourg on June 19 and Cherbourg a week later. I saw Mongolian prisoners of war with heads like basketballs.'

Sergeant Jim McKee, Rifle Company 'K', 3rd Battalion, 12th Regiment, 4th Division. The assistant commander of my division was Teddy Roosevelt Jr., son of 'the Rough Rider' president and a cousin of FDR. Teddy was beloved by us enlisted men for his habit of turning the tables on the Army. He would sometimes take officers to task in our hearing and at other times would ask us enlisted men for our opinions. Teddy was no snob in spite of his illustrious background. What a welcome relief from all the martinets and spit-and-polish phonies in the Army! Our corps commander once chewed Teddy out for not wearing his helmet. But as soon as the CC departed Teddy cheerfully resumed disobeying his order. Unlike generals who never heard a shot fired in anger, Teddy led his troops into battle rather than following them. He was the first man ashore at 'Utah' Beach just as his dad had been

the first man up San Juan Hill. Patton was 'grounded' in England for the better part of the Normandy campaign. He must have envied Teddy that summer for his bravery under fire and his soldier's death.' Montebourg was reduced to rubble in the fighting which raged for several days as the 243rd Division held on tenaciously in the ruins. The US 22nd Infantry finally took the town on 19 June and found it deserted. General Von Schlieben, who had his HQ in Valognes, had feared encirclement and withdrawn his forces to defend Cherbourg. Valognes fell soon after without a fight.

'For the next half-hour the low-lying coast of France seemed to leap into the air in a sheet of jagged flame and thunder, nor did it settle back until the last bomb bays were emptied by those welcome harbingers of courage to sailor men.

'Meanwhile we headed for the starting line to check the positions of the control ships. Just before we jockeyed into position, a terrific explosion a few hundred yards to starboard rocked our LCI. It was the LCT 707. She had hit a mine full and bye, turning her completely over. Then all seemed to cut loose. German shore batteries recovering from the shock of surprise were returning the slugging salvos of the naval fire-support ships, raising great gouts of water as they plumbed for the correct range.

'Then we all spied it. A red glow lighted the western horizon. Silhouetted by this light was the unmistakable outline of low-lying land. It flashed through my mind that this indelible picture was identical with the silhouettes pasted on the walls of the 'Bigot' room, where we studied the intelligence reports describing 'Utah' beach.

'The USS *Bayfield*, flying our Admiral's two-star flag had anchored and swung to the gentle breeze. Already her LCAs were lowered away... The Bayfield marked the transport area. That would be thirteen miles from the beach and in mine-swept waters leading to the boat lanes. At the head of the boat lanes and about four miles seaward from the beach would be the control vessels which would start the assault waves on the scheduled race for glory and victory - or defeat and indescribable slaughter.

'As the ramp lowered, I was shoved forward up to my knapsack in cold, oily water. German 88s were pounding the beachhead. Two US tanks were drawn up at the high-water line pumping them back into the Jerries. I tried to run to get into the lee of these tanks. I realize now why the infantry likes to have tanks along in a skirmish. They offer a world of security to a man in open terrain who may have a terribly empty sensation in his guts. But my attempt to run was only momentary. Three feet of water is a real deterrent to rapid locomotion of the legs. As I stumbled into a runnel, Kare picked me up. A little soldier following grabbed my other arm. Just for a moment he hung on. Then he dropped, blood spurting from a jagged hole torn by a sniper's bullet.

'An army officer wearing the single star of a Brigadier jumped into my 'headquarters' to duck the blast of an 88.

'Sonsabuzzards,' he muttered, as we untangled sufficiently to look at each other. 'I'm Teddy Roosevelt. You're Arnold of the Navy. I remember you at the briefing at Plymouth. If you have any authority here, I wish you would stop bringing in my troops down on Red beach. They're being slaughtered. Navy ought to know better than send them into that sector where the darn' Krauts have them bracketed.'

'I had in mind to explain to him that N.O.I.C. 'Utah' was not supposed to function until the assault phase was over. Looking at his grim eyes, however, I decided against this procedure.

'Seems to me, General, there was something in the Plan about your soldiers neutralizing this Kraut artillery. But wait a moment' - I could almost feel the blast he was about to erupt - 'I'll shift the unloading from the Red sector over to the Green beach area.'

'How?' he demanded.

'By the simple expedient of alerting the Navy beach battalion on Red beach to send the incoming craft over to the Green beach area. I'll station a ship off a couple of hundred yards and divert them. Somebody's going to raise hell because it isn't according to the book, but I have to agree there's no use landing dead men down in that suicide area. Meantime, General, suppose you alert your outfit to change the staging area, or post guides to direct the incoming troops to wherever you want them stage after they land.'

'Before he could argue, we were on our way to execute the idea. It was remarkably successful, too, until German spotters finally notified their batteries to shift their fire over to Green Beach. That was some three hours later.'

Commodore James C. Arnold USNR, NOIC (Naval Officer In Charge of the beachhead). 57-year old Brigadier General Theodore Roosevelt Jr., son of US 26th President, 'Teddy' Roosevelt, a veteran of WW1 and three assault landings in WW2 already, had finally convinced Major General Raymond O. Barton, 4th Infantry Division Commander, that he should take part in the landings. Roosevelt, whose enthusiasm and powerful voice - a bellow only a few decibels higher than a moose call' - were well known to the troops, went ashore in the first wave, carrying only a cane and a .45 calibre pistol, set an example of coolness under fire and realising that the lead regiment had landed in the wrong place, said, 'We'll start the war right here'. The only problem that had faced the General was how to re-direct traffic away from the Red beach sector. His leadership contributed directly to the 4th Division's success and earned him the award of the Medal of Honor. Roosevelt remained the 4th Division's assistant division commander until he died of a heart attack on 12 July 1944, the day he was due to take command of his own division. Awarded the Medal of Honor, he lies buried at Ste-Laurent, beside the grave of his reinterred brother Quentin, killed in 1918. This cemetery contains 9,286 burials, 307 of whom are unknown. Medal of Honor recipients' headstones are lettered in gold. Thirty other pairs of brothers lie side by side as do a father and son; Colonel Ollie Reed and Ollie Reed Junior. Two other Medals of Honor recipients of the Normandy campaign are buried at 'Omaha'; Tech Sergeant Frank Peregory of the 116th Infantry Division, whose story is told where it happened at Grandcamp Maisy on 8 June and 1st Lieutenant Jimmie W. Monteith, Jr. of the 16th Infantry, 1st Division whose act of conspicuous gallantry took place on 6 June on 'Omaha'. Monteith landed with the initial assault waves under heavy fire. Without regard for his personal safety he continually moved up and down the beach reorganizing men for further assaults, which he then led. He then went back to lead two tanks on

foot through a minefield and then rejoined his company. He continued to attempt to strengthen links in his defensive chain under heavy fire until he and his unit were completely surrounded and he was killed by enemy fire.

'He was a little bit shorter than I. He had red hair and blue eyes and a beautiful smile. He was a perfect gentleman all the time and immaculate in dress and everything and he tended to keep me that way too. I never saw him die. He got killed as he was coming down the ramp on his LCI. His whole squad got wounded. I rushed my squad up the beach - probably the biggest thing I ever did in my life - and we went right up the hill into the trenches and we chased the Germans. We captured four and sent them back. Then we got behind the pill box. Those we didn't kill escaped because they were running from us.

'I would rather have come back without my arms and legs then come back without my brother. That's what it meant to me. I had nightmares for fifty years after. He'd come back every night and he'd be all neatly dressed and smiling like he usually does and we'd have a communication and first thing I'd go to do something, he'd disappear.'

It was five weeks before Staff Sergeant Walter Ehlers found out what had happened to his older brother Staff Sergeant Rolland Ehlers. The two boys from Manhattan, Kansas had both fought in landings in North Africa and Sicily.

'I was in the north of Périers, just in the middle of the peninsula, the most westward part of Normandy, covering 'Utah' Beach. The funny thing was that the Germans were expecting a landing north of where the landing actually occurred, west of Ste-Mère-Église. On the first day I received no orders. I was my own boss. Most of the divisional commanders had been called to Rennes for an operational exercise. I tried to get through to the corps commander General Marcks.

'The only contact was by the normal French phone network. The Germans were forbidden to use this, officially, because of the spies. But I couldn't get through on our own network, because the French Resistance had prepared well for the invasion, sabotaging the phone lines.

'I first saw what was happening when I arrived in Ste-Côme-du-Mont. I had come across an old church tower, had got hold of the key and went up there to take a look out over the coast. An overwhelming picture presented itself. The horizon was strewn with hundreds of ships and countless landing boars and barges were moving back and forth between the ships and shore, landing troops and tanks. It was an almost peaceful picture. It reminded me of a beautiful summer day on the Wannsee. The noise of battle could not be heard and from the church tower there was no sign of German defence activities. Only a shot rang out here and there whenever the sentries of the German battalions came into contact with Allied paratroopers.

'I knew that I had to tell General Marcks what I had seen. I wanted to tell him that in my opinion the forces we had were not in a position to offer vigorous resistance to the invading forces. At every mile along the coastline was a German bunker and, of the three that I could see, only one was actually firing at the Americans. All the bunkers were manned, of course, but only one was firing. In my opinion, they feared for their lives, considering that they would be easily wiped out by the invading Americans. Only one bunker did its duty, forcing the Americans to spread out.

'I felt that my troops were very vulnerable with no artillery assistance. We had our heavy company with 12 cm mortars. I gave the order for them to get forward quickly and fire.

'When I saw the invading troops, I gave the order by radio to the regiment, but I didn't dare use the same route back to the Command Post. I made a detour and on this detour I came across a German battery which had been totally deserted. This was the second line of defence, the artillery line, about six guns in the battery, totally unmanned, but all ready to fire; the ammunition boxes open on the left side of each gun. I don't know what had happened to the gunners, but it was my opinion that they had deserted, though it is possible that they had received a new order. But all the Americans had to do was turn the guns round and fire them at our men. I had no artillery men with me, so I could do nothing with the guns.

'When I finally contacted Marcks I reported what I had seen. I told him I had to try to defend the line north of Côme-du-Mont and he agreed. But then I had to leave the place for two reasons. First, because someone, I don't know who, had given the order to the engineers to blow up all the bridges. So we had no way to fall back from Ste-Côme-du-Mont to Carentan. Then there was a funny thing. It was on the second or third day and all the forces who had been north of Carentan, including the Regimental Staff had been given the order to withdraw to the south, because we were afraid that we would be surrounded. The Americans attacked to the west and this attack would have led them to the south and behind me and so I said, no it's nonsense to stay in Ste-Côme-du-Mont, we should defend Carentan instead, because in my opinion Carentan was more important. But how the hell could we get to Carentan? All the bridges had been blown up. So, nearly all parts of my regiment, a reinforced battalion had to cross the water. It was up to our chests and we had all our heavy guns with us. But we had to do it. Thank goodness the Americans didn't spot this. They continued to attack Ste-Côme-du-Mont. Two of my soldiers drowned. One of them was a Jew who had signed up for the German Army using a false name. I had two Jews in my regiment. Both had used false names. One was the nephew of Albert Schweitzer, the famous German doctor and the other was the son of a German aristocrat whose mother was Jewish.

'At Carentan I had parts of the 2nd and parts of the 3rd Battalion with me and some regimental units, intelligence troops etc. Then I was given a reinforcement battalion of Russians, Georgians in fact. These were anti-Communist Russians fighting on the German side. They fought very well, but they couldn't stand the bombing from the air. The American bombers attacked my regiment near Carentan the whole day and after the attack the Russians deserted. The heaviest fighting was at the north-west part of the town. The Americans had managed to get over the flooded area by the railway bridge, which my 2nd Battalion had used. The only way of destroying this bridge would have been by bombing it from the air, but the Luftwaffe was held back by the superiority of the American air force. I did not see one German fighter plane. As we said then: 'We have the ground but the sky belongs to the

Americans'. So, in my opinion, the crucial factor was American air superiority - and second, the lack of unity among the German forces.'

37-year old Friedrich August Freiherr von der Heydte, commanding the 6th Parachute Regiment, part of the 2nd Parachute Division under Commanding General Ramcke, which fought at the French coast from 6 June onwards. In 1941 he secretly conspired against Hitler. On 12 June during his customary daily round of inspection of the invasion front General der Artillerie Erich Marcks died in his vehicle after a low flying attack by Allied fighters on a main road near Hébécrevon north-west of Ste Lô.

'Most of the bigger ships lie at anchor; through the haze they resemble an imaginary city with winking towers in the mist - 'The Golden City': as the troops call it.'

Helmut Berndt, a correspondent with the Kriegsmarine.

Carter Barber, an American newsreel cameraman on the attack transport APA 33 USS *Bayfield*, the HQ ship for Force 'U' which also was carrying 1,500 troops as part of Assault Group Red. He witnessed the landings on 'Omaha' Beach from a US Coast Guard wooden-hulled cutter (a small boat) just offshore.

'We slowed to a snail's pace and around 0445 the anchors rattled down into the water and I could hear some of the curses of men swinging their assault barges over the transport's side. At five, the barges were circling around in the water off their looming mother ship and the terrific barrages started from the battlewagons that had preceded us into the Bay of the Seine. One of the most beautiful sights ever was the quadruple balls of fire that streaked across the sky with their salvos. Blue-azured little Roman candle stuff, hard to realize tons of HE behind them.

'It was like a review, the way we took those barges into the beach. You couldn't see the heads of the troops over their sides…just the coxswain's helmet sticking up from the stern. For some reason I thought of Mitchell Jamieson's oil of the men going into Sicily in their landing boat. I saw that picture at Corcoran in Washington, which locale reminded me of flags. I looked aloft; saw our cutter's flag twisted around the mast and in a spurt of patriotism, climbed aloft, to free the banner. Just as I came down from the mast we saw our first bunch of men. It was light then and the scene was quickly changing from one of an even line of boats knifing in orderly rows behind their leaders towards the beach to a scene of carnage. One Higgins boat was completely disintegrated by a direct hit from shore. There were no survivors and I couldn't even see the dismembered parts of the troops aboard come down after they'd been blasted sky high.

'The noise was terrific as we neared the beach. For the first time I felt no need to kind of talk myself into 'This is IT! D-Day! What we've been waiting, working and worrying for, for months and years. This is going to be terrific.' I knew it WAS terrific when the noise started and the fact that the invasion had rushed upon me so swiftly in the past 24 hours didn't seem strange then.

'When we saw the LCF get hit and rushed to her aid, I noticed plenty of men already floating face down in the water. They might have just been stunned, sure. But I had to agree with the skipper that we couldn't stop for them just then but must keep on to get the other men floundering about. We passed one boy floating high and dry on a raft and nosed alongside the first big bunch of men and started to haul them aboard.

'The first bunch I took pictures of with my borrowed camera. Three minutes was enough and I put the camera down and went forward to throw heaving lines to other men in the water. Twos and threes of them were screaming 'Oh save me...I'm hurt bad...please, please, please' and I yelled back 'Hang on, Mac, we're coming' and looked astern at the guys on our boat hauling other wounded men aboard and wondered at the inadequacy of everything. We needed ten pairs of hands more.

'One big fellow who afterwards admitted he weighed 250lbs stripped had two legs broken and was in intense pain. We had a hell of a time getting him aboard because his clothing was waterlogged and he was weighted down with helmet, rifle, pack, ammunition, et al. The man screamed as we helped him aboard but we had to be a little callous so that we could get the man on deck and move to another group of survivors.

'I watched one man from the bow. He shouted 'I can't stay up, I can't stay up.' He didn't. I couldn't reach him with a heaving line and when we came towards him his head was in the water. We didn't stop and went onto seven or eight more men who were just about ready to sink too. When we got them aboard the first lad had completely disappeared apparently, slipping out of his lifejacket.

'Although it seemed like hours, we quickly got all the men aboard, including one old man who was so soaked in water that he was almost drowned. His face was always awash and his head was laid open almost to the brain. His eyes fluttered and his jaw moved, however, so we knew he was alive. It took five of us on our boat's fantail to hoist this man aboard, by placing boat hooks under his armpits. We got him on deck, got the water out of his chest and covered him with a tarpaulin. After we picked up the rest of them, including the boy who had drifted for an hour or so on his raft, we took the men to the *Bayfield,* which directed us to the [USS *Joseph T*]. *Dickman*, which was leaving immediately for England. We got all the men aboard, including the guy under the tarpaulin...still alive.

'This was when the transport surgeon looked at the boy in the lazarette and pronounced him dead. This kid had crawled into the lazarette by himself, although vomiting blood the whole while. He lay there for an hour while we picked up his mates and at the *Dickman* had apparently gone into a coma. Four hours later, the kid reappeared from the lazarette and went aboard the LST. 'You were supposed to be dead,' said one of our boys. 'Yeah', said the kid, onerously although spewing blood from his mouth.

'We were low on gas when we put the men on the *Dickman* and almost went back to Poole, but decided later not to. Good thing too, for we had another rescue coming up. First, however we disposed of the one man we hadn't put aboard the *Dickman* excepting the kid in the lazarette. This man was our only casualty.

'Apparently from shock, this man had died with his eyes open. Rigor mortis had already set in and we couldn't close his eyes. When we searched his pockets for identification, I thought it was the first time and last time anyone ever rolled this guy right under his eyes. He had a watertight wallet secured in a condom, with hundreds of pound notes and an American silver dollar around his neck. Been in the Navy five months, 39 years old. We stripped his clothes from him to his underwear, tied him to a rusty piece of steel the Dickman had given us and prepared to bury him. I tried to cross him arms over his chest, but they were too stiff. His flesh was green.

'McPhail, the skipper, reappeared on deck with his Bible, intoned the words and we stopped the cutter's engines. I took off my helmet and the rest of the boys followed suit. We slid the body into the sea.

'I've covered the story of the burning ammunition ship pretty well in my yarns. Only matter uncovered was gruesome sight of one man with broken ankles, swollen to the size of grapefruit and coloured like an avocado. This man shrieked, even after morphine. Then we saw his Z-shaped spine. He was the first man lifted yelling over the side of the LST.

'After we had these men on the LST and had no one else aboard and no other swimmers of survivors in sight, we called a wee time out.

'What time do you think it is, Barber?' asked McPhail.

'Way past noon, at least. Maybe four o'clock.'

'It's nine thirty this morning.'

We looked around at the heaps of clothing strewn on the deck, gear of the rescue, some abandoned and some cut off. I went below to look around and it was even worse. There were clothes in the smaller sink, on the stove, in the fo'c'sle, in the head, on the bunks. I stepped on a soggy bunch and blood oozed out. The whole boat below decks stank of blood, vomit and urine.

'We turned to, tossing all the clothes from below topside and swabbed out the decks as best we could. We brought some K-rations up from the lazarette and ate lunch. Then, with only the helmsman and motor machinist, we all sprawled on the deck, on the sodden heaps of clothing and went to sleep. The next I knew it was afternoon.

The sun had come out and there were no more boats in distress for the rest of that day. At night-time I sat in the pilot house and listened to the radio avidly for news of the landing. I think I was listening to Danny Kaye when we passed into D+1.'

The USS *Joseph T. Dickman*, APA 13 (attack transport), (formerly the United States Lines' *President Roosevelt*), Assault Group Green (Tare Green), embarked 2,050 troops at Tor Bay anchorage from landing craft from Torquay, arrived 'Utah' at 0240 on 6 June. The USS Bayfield, attack transport (APA 33) and HQ ship for Force 'U' embarked 1,545 troops at Plymouth, arriving at 'Utah' on 0229 hours on D-Day. LCF (Landing Craft, Flak), were British LCT's with 2-pounder (40mm) guns for anti-aircraft and E-boat defence.

The US Coast Guard was called upon only two months before the invasion to provide a 'rescue flotilla.' When the assault began, Lieutenant Commander Alexander V. Stewart USCG Reserve commanded three attack transports, 35 amphibious landing ships, sixty 83-foot vessels and nearly 1,000 men in position off shore. Within minutes of H-Hour a USCG cutter had picked up the first of 450 men to be saved on D-Day. By the close of Overlord, Coast Guard ships had manoeuvred through heavy traffic and Allied and enemy fire to rescue 1,437 Allied soldiers and sailors and one female nurse from English Channel waters.

'I remember the battleship *Texas* firing broadsides into the shore while we were close by. It was God awful, terrible explosions - muzzle blast in our ear - when they fired. The smoke ring passed by us and it looked like a funnel of a tornado, growing larger and larger and finally dissipating. Then they fired another one.'
Staff Sergeant William Lewis.

'They laid down a barrage and it was like the fourth of July. The battleship *Nevada* was firing over our head and also the *Texas* was nearby. The Germans, I don't think, would ever expect anyone to start an invasion in the weather conditions that we started out in.'
Maro P. Flagg, Chief Pharmacist's Mate US Navy.

'It was exactly 0630 and without warning the USS *Nevada* let off a broadside of its 14 inch guns in the direction of the coast. Following the belch of flame, huge clouds of brown cordite smoke veiled the ship. HMS *Black Prince* took up the challenge and it too fired a thunderous broadside. From the rear a barrage of fire from the USS *Tuscaloosa* flew over the shore bound armada. Shaken to the core, our adjectives seared the paintwork as our tiny barge and its crew trembled with the impact. Three fearful sailors startled by the roar of gunfire, shot up from the engine room and watched the display with astonishment. Mesmerised by the flames belching from the huge guns we stiffened ourselves for the next ear-splitting blast. The shells whistling overhead with terrifying potential and devastating results were at first nerve shattering. The creeping realisation that these weapons were after all on our side helped to allay these fears. At each broadside and scream of shells rushing overhead, three pairs of anxious eyes peered nervously towards the open hatch above. By the time we had reached the upper deck the shore batteries had begun to retaliate and shell bursts peppered the water nearby. Remembering our orders we continued sailing towards the beach, careful to keep between the two lines of bobbing Dan buoys, the line of markers placed in position the previous night to prevent ships straying into un-swept mine fields. I marvelled at the courage of the men who had so bravely ventured to plant the buoys under the noses of the German coastal defence forces the night before.

'The gunfire increased as landing craft mounted with rocket launchers, let off their devilish cargo. The sound of their release rendered the onlookers immobile, as a thousand rockets trailing fire and smoke screamed towards the shore. It was now fully light and the battle was at its height. Shells from the battleships behind the diminutive barges continued to scream overhead. The American 4th Infantry Division was dashing towards the beach in their assault craft, returning fire from those shore batteries not yet immobilised. While everyone around us appeared to be engaged in a task to ruthlessly destroy each other, we could only sit tight and forage slowly towards the beach.

'A sleek, grey patrol boat drew alongside. A British naval officer waved an arm in the direction he advised us to precede. 'Take station off shore, between the two petrol barges you see anchored yonder.' The tankers were easy to distinguish, as the hoarding above decks plainly spelt out 'HIGH OCTANE FUEL' for the benefit of those craft needing refuelling. It also spelt out to any

German gunner with an eagle eye, 'Why not aim at us?' The water barge had a similar sign 'WATER', in large letters painted over the tank. Turning the wheel, Irons made for the spot 200 yards from the beach. No sooner had Smithy and Manchester dropped the anchor, than a procession of assorted craft that had been on station for a few days began to arrive to replenish their meagre water reserves. Small patrol boats and American designed tugboats sidled alongside to fill their tanks. A stream of assault boats filled with GIs passed by and landed on the beach to spluttering bursts of small arms fire.

'While the frenzied activity below at sea level continued, a buzz of low flying Dakotas droned in from the sea towing camouflaged gliders, heavy with troops they swayed and disengaged their tow ropes to weave and turn and drop immediately behind the sand hills. Sounds of splintering wood and canvas filled the air as each vehicle landed clumsily in the small fields, some hitting and killing terrified cattle, others landing badly and ripping themselves in two pieces. Bodies were thrown like rag dolls across the grassy turf. Glider wings crumpled as the limited landing spaces became over crowded. We could only stare, no grief or shock, no emotion registered itself as the carnage ended as quickly as it started. It was just another episode in the battle.

'By early evening the sound of gunfire had receded into the distance. Activity to and from the shore was increasing as every conceivable type of transport was being thrown on to the beach. Tanks and trucks emerged from beached landing ships, wave after wave of troops ferried from transport ships anchored a mile or so off shore dodged huge motorised pontoons laboriously ploughing towards the beach loaded high with hundreds of tons of battle equipment, medical supplies and rations.

'A startling explosion nearby blew the stern from one of our companion barges as it was about to beach. We could only stare at the tragedy as the remnants of crew scrambled to safety. A pack of LCI's already beached, stood silently awaiting the next tide after disgorging their cargo of American troops. Once the smoke had subsided, it revealed the burnt out shells of military equipment on a disordered beach. The blackened skeleton of a troop carrier and a battle-scarred tank lay on its side, a sad reminder of the battle. The task began retrieving the mercifully few bodies of those that gave their lives. The personal mementoes of the same brave men littering the high water mark were being reverently collected. A posse of field grey uniformed prisoners rounded up by the efficient US guards were herded into a hastily erected barbed wire cage before being shipped to the UK for the duration.

'For those who had reached the coast in the early morning, after surviving a horrendous sea journey and experiencing the barrage of sound, an exhausting quietness emerged. The sea had ceased its furious battle with the invaders; the ground swell rocked the small craft in a kind of remorseful lullaby, perhaps regretting the savage beating it had enforced on us earlier. Content, for us the battle was over, though very aware that their war had just begun.

'...In a strange way it seemed as if the war was now passing us by. I scratched the growing stubble on my cheeks and mused. 'Was it only yesterday this sandy piece of land was the centre of confusion and noise?' I sat gazing at his companions resting on this grounded, unattractive, rusting piece of metal which had become our home. Twenty-four short hours ago, black smoke choked the poor devils that dared venture on to this shore. Red-hot chunks of steel seared and whizzed into its sandy core. I cast my eyes over the pockmarked sand hills, where a short time ago I had watched as American soldiers scorched a path through the German bunkers with terrifying flame-throwers. The smoke-blackened concrete bore witness that it had not been a horrible dream after all.

...A lull in the barge activity prompted some of us to take a walk along the beach. Manchester and Sammy Yates, anxious to see for them selves the scene of the previous day's battle, joined Bentley and me. Veering around beached landing craft and pieces of discarded military equipment, dodging fast moving jeeps and trucks pouring from beached landing ships, we plodded past the caged German prisoners, guarded by white helmeted GI's attentively nursing their loaded carbines. On past a deserted first aid post and up into the sand hills. On the other side the land was flat and scrubby. A farmhouse stood in isolation. The bloated bodies of black and white cattle lay in the fields, legs pointing skyward, either having been shot or died of fright. Wrecked gliders, displaying their white identifying wing chevrons lay abandoned by the airborne troops that had landed the previous day, eerily straddling the fields between the early summer flowering hedgerows. We walked in silence along the ridge of dunes towards the eastern end of the concrete fortifications. Pulling up sharply, we almost fell across the body of a young American soldier lying hidden in a dune. Silently staring at the efforts to revive him, the plasma tubes held in place by his rifle, stuck bayonet end in the sand then inserted in his ridged body proved useless. The boy's wounds were too severe. A fleeting, silent chill accompanying the terrible realisation of death passed through my mind. A lump came into my throat as I walked slowly away from the scene, chastened by the futility of war.

'Further along the sandy ridge a concrete German gun emplacement came to view, the huge muzzle pointed ominously out to sea...inside; we found remnants of meals and discarded wine bottles. After a brief inspection we escaped through a narrow exit tunnel. Straightening and blinking in the bright sunlight, the body of a soldier wearing the uniform of a German trooper confronted us. A pair of jackboots lay tidily beside the body, his steel helmet a few feet away. I murmured, 'He was someone's son I suppose.' Without malice, I picked up the helmet intending to keep it as a souvenir. Manchester's face contorted in rage as he lifted an iron bar, which lay discarded in the sand and took a vicious swipe at the dead man's head. Cursing and swearing vengeance for reasons he alone understood, we stood horrified by his actions.

'I'm 'avin' that ring on his finger,' he snarled, 'I'm going to cut his finger off to get it.' Not believing what we were hearing we stared inert as Manchester dropped his arm and retrieved the sheathed knife he carried on his belt. The man had flipped. The resentments of the last few months had surfaced. Some would call it traumatic shell shock. Maybe the poor sod had been through hell once too often. One thing for sure we were not going to let him carry out his threat. We stepped forward to restrain him. I saw the gaunt, tormented face beneath the untidy black beard relax. His dark ringed eyes turned moodily away from the scene, staring as if transfixed. For what seemed an eternity we stood silent and rigid. Ramming the knife back in its sheath, Manchester kicked into the sand and walked slowly down the dunes.'

Jack Culshaw, water barge LBW 1, 34th Flotilla, which landed at about 1000. 'The idea of using River Thames Lighters as Landing Barges came from Lord Louis Mountbatten, Chief of Combined Operations. Over 400 of these craft were converted as Supply and Maintenance Flotilla and for the transportation of vehicles, stores and ammunition in beach landings. Two Chrysler six cylinder engines where hastily bodged, with a primitive steering assembly, a tank to hold either water, petrol or diesel fuel was then installed; without prior deliberations as to whether the thing would float or sink when the contents where put aboard. Some were made into Kitchen barges to feed isolated troops or other seamen, others fitted out for Engineering Maintenance. The flotilla's where split between the invasion beaches. Most arrived safely at their destination, others did not. A basic seagoing crew of five men were on most of the barges, supplemented by extras prior to D-Day. Two engine men, two seamen and one Coxswain seaman. Supplemented, where appropriate by engineers, cooks etc.'

'We sailed from Dartmouth with US Army personnel and vehicles, but due to bad weather had to put into Portland. We set off again later and I remember that the majority of the troops were seasick and our mess deck was strewn with troops trying to sleep. We arrived at our rendezvous off 'Utah' Beach. When our turn came to go in, it felt like all the practice runs we had been through. We should have unloaded and backed off the beach, but due to the flatness the tide ran out leaving us high and dry. With all the troops ashore, the skipper opened up the rum and I, although being under age, had along with the others a large neat tot. This seemed to make the day much more pleasant until there was a loud bang close by and something whizzed past our heads. Four shrapnel holes had been made in the winch housing forward and suddenly the effect of the rum wore off. We decided that it would be safer ashore, so we left the craft and ran, dropping whenever a shell burst. We jumped into a trench with an American soldier chewing gum, who asked us if we were commandos. Our reply was that we were sailors waiting to get out as fast as we could!'

Michael Jennings, 18½-year-old Royal Navy seaman/wireman on LCT 795.

I took a last look at the greatest armada in history. It was too immense to describe. There were so many transports on the horizon that in the faint haze they looked like a shoreline. Destroyers were almost on the beach occasionally jolting out a salvo that was like a punch on the chin. Farther out, but still incredibly close to the beach, sat our huge battle-wagons and cruisers. Overhead, formations of fighters swept swiftly through the air with nothing to do. During this entire day I never saw a German plane or spoke to a man who had seen one.'

Thomas Treanor, NBC reporter, also broadcast on the BBC. A gifted war correspondent, he was also hired by the *Los Angeles Times.* **Treanor was killed a few weeks' later near Paris.**

Index